The Body

READERS IN CULTURAL CRITICISM
General Editor: *Catherine Belsey*

The Body	*Tiffany Atkinson*
Posthumanism	*Neil Badmington*
Theorizing Ireland	*Claire Connolly*
Postmodern Debates	*Simon Malpas*
Queer Theory	*Iain Morland and Annabelle Willox*
Reading the Past	*Tamsin Spargo*
Performance Studies	*Erin Striff*
Reading Images	*Julia Thomas*
Gender	*Anna Tripp*

Readers in Cultural Criticism
Series Standing Order
ISBN 0–333–78660–2 hardcover
ISBN 0–333–75236–8 paperback
(outside North America only)

You can receive future titles in this series as they are published by placing a standing order.
Please contact your bookseller or, in case of difficulty, write to us at the address below with your name and address, the title of the series and the ISBN quoted above.

Customer Services Department, Macmillan Distribution Ltd
Houndmills, Basingstoke, Hampshire RG21 6XS, England

The Body

Edited by Tiffany Atkinson

First published 2005 by
PALGRAVE MACMILLAN
Houndmills, Basingstoke, Hampshire RG21 6XS and
175 Fifth Avenue, New York, N.Y. 10010
Companies and representatives throughout the world.

PALGRAVE MACMILLAN is the global academic imprint of the Palgrave
Macmillan division of St. Martin's Press, LLC and of Palgrave Macmillan Ltd.
Macmillan® is a registered trademark in the United States, United Kingdom
and other countries. Palgrave is a registered trademark in the European
Union and other countries.

ISBN-13: 978 0333 765 333 hardback
ISBN-10: 0–333–76533–8 hardback
ISBN-13: 978 0333 765 340 paperback
ISBN-10: 0–333–76534–6 paperback

This book is printed on paper suitable for recycling and made from fully
managed and sustained forest sources.

A catalogue record for this book is available from the British Library.

Library of Congress Cataloging-in-Publication Data

The body / edited by Tiffany Atkinson.
   p. cm.—(Readers in cultural criticism)
Includes bibliographical references and index.
ISBN 0–333–76533–8 (cloth) – ISBN 0–333–76534–6 (pbk.)
   1. Body, Human – Social aspects I. Atkinson, Tiffany, 1972– II. Series.

HM636.B583 2005
306.4—dc22   2005047459

10 9 8 7 6 5 4 3 2 1
14 13 12 11 10 09 08 07 06 05

Printed in China

Contents

DECONSTRUCTIONS

General Editor's Preface

Culture is the element we inhabit as subjects.

Culture embraces the whole range of practices, customs and representations of a society. In their rituals, stories and images, societies identify what they perceive as good and evil, proper, sexually acceptable, racially other. Culture is the location of values, and the study of cultures shows how values vary from one society to another, or from one historical moment to the next.

But culture does not exist in the abstract. On the contrary, it is in the broadest sense of the term textual, inscribed in the paintings, operas, sculptures, furnishings, fashions, bus tickets and shopping lists which are the currency of both aesthetic and everyday exchange. Societies invest these artefacts with meanings, until in many cases the meanings are so 'obvious' that they pass for nature. Cultural criticism denaturalises and defamiliarises these meanings, isolating them for inspection and analysis.

The subject is what speaks, or, more precisely, what signifies, and subjects learn in culture to reproduce or to challenge the meanings and values inscribed in the signifying practices of the society that shapes them.

If culture is pervasive and constitutive for us, if it resides in the documents, objects and practices that surround us, if it circulates as the meanings and values we learn and reproduce as good citizens, how in these circumstances can we practise cultural *criticism*, where criticism implies a certain distance between the critic and the culture? The answer is that cultures are not homogeneous; they are not even necessarily coherent. There are always other perspectives, so that cultures offer alternative positions for the subjects they also recruit. Moreover, we have a degree of power over the messages we reproduce. A minor modification changes the script, and may alter the meaning; the introduction of a negative constructs a resistance.

The present moment in our own culture is one of intense debate. Sexual alignments, family values, racial politics, the implications of economic differences are all hotly contested. And positions are taken up not only in explicit discussions at political meetings, on television and in the pub. They are often reaffirmed or challenged implicitly in films and advertisements, horoscopes and lonely-hearts columns. Cultural criticism analyses all these forms in order to assess their hold on our consciousness.

There is no interpretative practice without theory, and the more sophisticated the theory, the more precise and perceptive the reading it makes possible. Cultural theory is as well defined now as it has ever been, and as strongly contested as our social values. There could not, in consequence, be a more exciting time to engage in the theory and practice of cultural criticism.

Catherine Belsey
Cardiff University

Acknowledgements

I should like to extend warmest thanks to all colleagues and friends who have been part of this project, but in particular to Margaret Bartley, Anna Sandeman and Sonya Barker at Palgrave for their patience and encouragement; to Peter Barry, Catherine Belsey, Andrew Hadfield, Claire Jowitt, Liz Oakley-Brown, Carl Plasa, Diane Watt and John Williams for inspiration, support and body-talk, and to Andrew Silvers for assistance with all things technical.

Tiffany Atkinson

The editor and publishers wish to thank the following for permission to use copyright material:

Maurizia Boscagli, for material from *Eye on the Flesh: Fashions of Masculinity in the Early Twentieth Century* (1998), pp. 77–91. Copyright © 1996 by Westview Press, by permission of Westview Press, a member of Perseus Books, LLC; Abigail Bray, for material from 'The Anorexic Body: Reading Disorders', *Cultural Studies*, 10:3 (1996), 413–29, by permission of Taylor & Francis Ltd; Judith Butler, for material from *Bodies That Matter: On the Discursive Limits of Sex* (1993), pp. 1–16, by permission of Routledge/Taylor & Francis Books, Inc; Catherine Clément, for material from 'Seduction and Guilt' in *The Newly Born Woman* by Hélène Cixous and Catherine Clément, trans. Betsy Wing (1986). Original French language edition copyright © 1975 by Union Générale d'Editions, Paris. English copyright © 1986 by the University of Minnesota, by permission of I.B. Tauris & Co Ltd and The University of Minnesota Press; René Descartes, for material from *Discourse on Method and the Meditations*, trans. F.E. Sutcliffe, Penguin Classics (1968), pp. 102–12. Copyright © F.E. Sutcliffe, 1968, by permission of Penguin Books Ltd; Frantz Fanon, for material from *Black Skin, White Masks*, trans. Charles Lam Markmann (1967), pp. 109–40. Copyright © 1967 by Grove Press, Inc, by permission of Grove/Atlantic, Inc; Michel Foucault, for material from *The History of Sexuality*, Vol. 1, trans. Robert Hurley, Allen Lane (1979), Random House, Inc (1978), pp. 40–57.

Copyright © Random House, Inc 1978, originally published in French as *La Volonté du Savoir*. Copyright © Editions Gallimard 1976, by permission of Penguin Books Ltd and Georges Borchardt, Inc on behalf of the Editions Gallimard; Sigmund Freud, for material from *The Pelican Freud Library, Vol. 2: Studies in Hysteria* (1980), pp. 205–35, by permission of Sigmund Freud Copyrights/Paterson Marsh Ltd; Sander L. Gilman, for material from ' "Who Kills Whores?" "I Do", says Jack: Race and Gender in Victorian London' from *Death and Representation*, ed. Sarah Webster Goodwin and Elizabeth Bronfen (1993), pp. 263–84, by permission of The Johns Hopkins University Press; Elizabeth Grosz, for material from *Volatile Bodies: Towards a Corporeal Feminism* (1994), pp. 160–80, by permission of Indiana University Press; Elspeth Probyn, for material from 'Beyond Food/Sex: Eating and an Ethics of Existence', *Theory, Culture and Society*, 16:2 (1999), 215–28. Copyright © ICPHS, International Council for Philosophy and Humanistic Studies, by permission of Sage Publications Ltd; Joan Riviere, for material from 'Womanliness as a Masquerade', *The International Journal of Psychoanalysis*, 10 (1929), by permission of Ruth Petrie, on behalf of the Melanie Klein Trust; Jonathan Sawday, for material from *The Body Emblazoned: Dissection and the Human Body in Renaissance Culture*, Routledge (1995), pp. 16–32, by permission of Taylor & Francis Ltd; Klaus Theweleit, for material from *Male Fantasies*, Vol. 2, *Male Bodies: Psychoanalyzing the White Terror*, trans. Stephen Conway (1987), pp. 143–64, originally published as *Männerphantasien: Vol 1, Frauen, Fluten, Körper, Geschichte*. Copyright © 1977 by Verlag Roter Stern. English translation copyright © 1987 by the University of Minnesota, by permission of Polity Press and the University of Minnesota Press; Marianna Torgovnick, for material from *Primitivism and the Quest for Ecstasy* (1993), Chap. 9. Copyright © 1993 by Marianna Torgovnick, by permission of Alfred A. Knopf, a division of Random House, Inc.

Every effort has been made to trace the copyright holders but if any have been inadvertently overlooked the publishers will be pleased to make the necessary arrangement at the first opportunity.

1

Introduction

Tiffany Atkinson

Step into the gallery where the exhibits are human corpses, immaculately preserved, then flayed, dissected, sliced and posed with an artist's precision and flair. Peer with impunity into the secret recesses of bellies, skulls, chest cavities, the wombs of pregnant women. Have your photograph taken with the skinned chess player whose brain rises like a loaf from his opened skull; gaze straight through a man laid out in thin transparent slices from the scalp to the hardened skin of the toes. In the gift shop afterwards, choose from a range of anatomical gadgets and desk toys, or post grisly cards to your friends. Before leaving you could even begin the legal procedure of bequeathing your own body to the project for subsequent exhibitions.

This is not futuristic fantasy, but the *Body Worlds* exhibition from German anatomist Gunther von Hagens, whose revolutionary technique of 'plastination' – removing the body's fluids and replacing them with liquid plastic – enables bodies to be presented and observed by the public as never before. The exhibition, which has been touring Japan and Europe for several years, has been both controversial and a huge commercial success. Yet one might wonder why, given that we don't need von Hagens to show us how bodies look on the inside: centuries of anatomical science already enable us to view them in infinitesimal depth and detail. The sensational appeal of *Body Worlds* has to do with the authenticity of the bodies on display: the viewer is not supposed to forget that they are *real*, a contemporary *momento mori*, asserting a democratising mortality in a culture which strives to keep disease and death as far as possible from everyday life. Here medicine, art and old-fashioned horror converge in a spectacle staged to challenge the taboos which dictate acceptable contexts for viewing the dead; or, in psychoanalytic terms, for containing the threat of the real.[1]

But these cadavers, glossy, exempt from decay, flamboyantly posed and, in von Hagens's own words, 'imbued with a new and characteristic identity',[2] have little to do with death's ineffable 'real'. Instead they reflect a sense of what it means to have a body in twenty-first century *life*; which is indeed to have a 'characteristic identity' above and beyond the blueprint of anatomy: a countenance which we likewise strive, by whatever means possible, to keep glossy, exempt from decay and appropriately (if not flamboyantly) posed.

If anything, the exhibition serves more as a *memento vivendi*, reminding the viewer less of the body's perishability than of its resilient plasticity in a technologised world. For how else is the body – living or dead – to be understood in a 'real' world informed by airbrushed images and special effects, cosmetic surgery and virtual reality, cybernetics and the genome? How do we recognise the real or natural in our own bodies? Even their most intimate processes own meanings which are not ours alone to determine, but always already inherited from culture, the medium in which we exist from earliest infancy. What we know of our bodies' 'nature' is available to us only through the ideologies which fashion our understanding of the world and our place in it. Even death itself offers no consensus in this field. Consider how the testaments in the *Body Worlds* guidebook, from people who have already donated their bodies to the project, engage widely differing world-views: 'I would like to make interested persons understand better what a "work of art" the human body is' stated one donor. 'I have always felt the need to provide my body for scientific purposes' declared another. 'Grave maintenance is obviously the last opportunity to fleece you' opined (ironically, in the event) a third, while a fourth maintained that 'when Jesus Christ rises from the dead, he will wake me up in a new body as it is written in the Bible'. What could the precise nature and meaning of the body possibly be in an era professing such divergent attitudes? How, for that matter, could any two people at the exhibition be seeing and understanding *the same thing*?

Contemporary culture loves body-gazing. Geri Halliwell's figure, David Beckham's tattoos, Michael Jackson's face, the *de rigeur* gore of horror films and medical dramas, the ravaged subjects of newsreel footage, the person in the magazine or changing-room who may or may not look better in those clothes than oneself: all take their place in the daily negotiation of what it means to be embodied. But this fascination, far from proving the essential naturalness of bodies, emphasises how they are produced and made meaningful *only* by the discursive frameworks which position them as objects of knowledge. Clearly, this makes the significance of bodies both radically unfixed and historically contingent. Chaucer, for instance, gave his Wife of Bath gap teeth to signal her implicit licentiousness, not to comment on the shortcomings of medieval orthodontics. For Chaucer's audience, physiognomy was a valid, common-sense way of discerning character through physique. Nor is this an entirely outmoded way of reading the body: the jutting jaw-line of the contemporary comic-book hero, for example, arguably functions in the same way.

Yet it is one thing to examine how the trappings of culture – fashion, body-language, permissible and taboo behaviours, sexual activity, even skin-colour – shape how the embodied subject is perceived. Only delve beneath the surface, however, and one will soon strike an inescapable material presence, the body as organism, whose status must be one of universal reality. Indeed, the biomedical rhetoric of *Body Worlds* suggests precisely that we are all, fundamentally, *the same on the inside*.

But even what we understand to be the 'inside' of the body has its own rich cultural history, and is intimately bound up with modern conceptions of the self. Notions of 'inner personhood' are a reflex which it seems counterintuitive to contest. As the ubiquitous TV talk-show verifies, expressing oneself, letting rip, coming clean, getting things off one's chest and out in the open, has become a cultural imperative. Keeping things 'bottled up' is almost akin to disease in the popular imagination:[3] thus we are daily enjoined by advertising, new age and therapy culture, pop lyrics and Hollywood cinema, to express our 'inner selves' as though our lives quite literally depended on it. The metaphors so often used to articulate this desire are an index of how closely expressive individuality is bound up with a profound sense of corporeal reality, privacy, depth and distinctness.

There is, however, an anecdote often invoked in critical discussions of embodiment which proves that the very *notion* of the body as a discrete social entity is neither universal, nor essential to human culture. Jonathan Sawday relates it thus:

A Melanesian, asked by [nineteenth-century anthropologist] Maurice Leenhardt what the west had contributed to the culture of the islands, did not reply by listing technological, scientific, or medical achievements, nor even (ironically) the disastrous disease history which was the product of western encounters with Pacific peoples ... Instead his response undermined the very categories which framed the question: 'What you have brought us is the body.'[4]

The western sense of 'bodiliness', apparently the most natural and self-evident ground of personhood, is thus revealed as a particular ideological understanding, and one which should by no means be taken for granted. On closer inspection, it is indeed hard to discern what exactly is denoted by 'the' body in an abstract, totalising sense, when even to visualise a body is to plunge immediately into the particulars of gender, race, age, posture and so forth. This in turn begs the question of why, and to what ends, a category of 'the body' exists for the west in ways so radically different from those of Pacific peoples. Michel Foucault's enquiry of a quarter-century ago, 'what mode of investment [in] the body is necessary and adequate for the functioning of a capitalist society like ours?' is still pertinent.[5] Or, to put it another way, we might ask how, to paraphrase Matthew Arnold, 'each culture gets the bodies it deserves'.

Of course, this is not to say that the physical body does not 'really' exist. Even as you read this, yours may be asserting its hunger, discomfort or restlessness in frank contradiction. It is, rather, to foreground that *how* it exists, or becomes meaningful for us as embodied subjects, is produced by culture in ways which are not always immediately apparent. As feminist theorist Judith Butler maintains, 'to call a presupposition into question is not the same as doing away with it; rather, it is to free it from its metaphysical lodgings in order to understand what political interests were secured in and by that metaphysical placing'.[6] The cultural critic therefore 'reads' bodies in much the same way as s/he might read a literary text: not in the hope of revealing an essential truth about embodiment, but precisely to expose how various 'truths' and norms are constructed and broadcast as bodies are discussed, represented and managed in everyday life. For the very instability of the body's significance offers leverage to the critic who is enlisted in processes of political change. The body's meanings (and they are always plural) can be contested and reconfigured, not simply through physical modifications, but by activating and putting into circulation alternative understandings of embodiment. One might consider how queer theory, for example, has enabled the articulation and validation of a range of subject positions beyond the heterosexual convention. This is not merely an instance of greater *discursive* freedom, but the claiming of a real political space within which the very 'norms' of sexual practice can be exposed and materially renegotiated. Indeed, the multiple ways in which sexuality, gender and race have been theorised in the interests of urgent social transformation have been crucial to the increasing sophistication of contemporary 'body theory' and its impact on mainstream culture.

The celebrated 'naturalness' of the body is a key point of debate in this kind of rethinking, for seldom is the 'natural' invoked where it cannot secure some kind of political or economic interest. A trivial example of this can be found in the 'bare-faced chic' so cherished by the cosmetics industry. Anyone who has tried to achieve the 'natural look' will probably agree that it requires more painstaking artifice and a vaster array of products than a more up-front maquillage; but the agenda is of course to *appear*, not actually to *be*, natural (and to bolster the industry in the process, without, what's more, even being *seen* to do so). 'Naturalness' is thus revealed as one among many masquerades available to the embodied subject, with the advantage, in an ageist culture, of suggesting youthfulness, innocence and purity. Yet, cosmetics aside, the positing of any kind of embodiment as 'natural' or 'normal' is freighted with political consequences, demanding as it must an opposing field of the *un*natural and deviant, often in ramified and subtle ways. Naturalising is a cultural process: as Derrida has remarked, 'there is no nature, only the effects of nature: denaturalisation or naturalisation'.[7] The normative body cannot exist without its 'other'. While it is relatively easy to observe this process with the advantage of cultural or historical distance, it takes a more astute and committed reader to examine current and familiar assumptions on the same critical terms. For bodies are not just objects of enquiry *out there*; they are the very location of the thinker's here and now, a site of ongoing negotiation between subject and object, inside and outside, thought and sensation, personal and political, self and world. Indeed, their complex materiality makes them both readily confirm and, at the same time, potentially disrupt almost any dichotomy which culture thinks to impose.

For all of these reasons, an intellectual fascination with bodies is not in itself new. Science, philosophy, art, and even literary criticism have long been preoccupied with the nature and representation of mortality, the relation of body to mind, and the status of flesh in the technological world. Histories of the human subject are inevitably histories of the body, or, more precisely, of the problems embodiment poses to human consciousness and categorisation. It has become conventional to describe western attitudes to embodiment, from at least as early as Plato, as dualistic and hierarchical to the extent that mind, spirit and rational processes are systematically valued over matter, flesh, and sensory experience. It is, moreover, a characteristic of symbolic oppositions like this to become overdetermined, as other, prevailing coupled terms, such as those of gender or race, are mapped onto the hierarchical structure. According to this logic, a common critical tactic is to scrutinise texts for traces of those equations whereby 'mind' = rationality = masculinity = culture = 'white', or 'body' = sensation = femininity = nature = 'black', and so on, in an infinitely extended articulation of antithesis. Such hierarchised codings operate at the very core of western culture and ideology.

When considering bodies, the cultural critic must be alert to this tendency to cement difference as opposition. Yet s/he should also be wary of supposing that symbolic patterns wholly determine the way we actually live, or of assuming that they never change. To medievalist scholar Caroline Bynum, this is especially pertinent when assessing the place of the physical in cultures far removed from our own. For example, while dualities can be found in medieval accounts of embodiment, the divisions did not work in the same way that they do in a world that, since Descartes, equates identity to consciousness and relegates the body to secondary status. The medieval opposition between body and soul, or *corpus* and *anima*, invests the body with a different value. After all, within a Christian Catholic culture, God is made flesh and consumed physically in the eucharist, so that flesh, both God's and the worshipper's, becomes the source of personal salvation and the immortality of the soul. This symbolic economy cannot be said to debase the body. On the contrary, as Bynum asserts, medieval corporeality was in fact a 'place for encounter with meaning, a locus of redemption'.[8] Indeed, following the thirteenth-century theology of Thomas Aquinas, matter was held to be activated and informed by the principle of soul to such an extent that '[the] body, restored at the resurrection, retained all the specific structures it had in earthly life (organs, height, even – in certain cases – scars)'.[9] Suffering and death thus owned radically different meanings from their present ones, when the body, as in the arch-narrative of Christ's crucifixion and resurrection, was seen as existing continuously between life and afterlife. Only within such a framework could holy relics acquire so potent a signifying charge: their latent power being their empirical connection to the resurrected body of the saint. The anatomised objectification of the human frame in the terms of *Body Worlds* would have been unthinkable in medieval culture, for the body was an integrated, immanently divine part of a theological cosmos. To unravel the material body would have been to pick at the very fabric of the world.

Bynum also stresses that gender difference does not map so neatly onto the medieval body/soul axis as the modern reader might expect, refuting the critical generalisation that 'vast binaries – reducible to a male/female binary – marched through the medieval past from Plato to Descartes'.[10] While gender oppositions can be traced in medieval practice, story and belief, they are rendered more complex than the essentialised relation of femininity to flesh that obtains in later culture. Christ's incarnation, the status of the Virgin, and the androgyny of God the creator and nurturer in Catholic theology all unsettle the grounds of a symbolically gendered hierarchy. Indeed, recent scholarship has tended to emphasise the fluidity of medieval gender positions, or at the very least, the radically different terms on which anything like an 'identity-position' was figured and experienced.[11] While this brief account of Bynum's work offers only the most simplistic preface to this collection's focus on modern embodiment, it may also be a reminder of the complexity of relations between present and past, and, where bodies are concerned, the perils of adopting an uncritical stance toward homology or difference.

It is, of course, impossible to point to an exact moment when pre-modern bodies ceded to those of modernity. But what can be discerned about the broad contexts in which the structuring relation of soul and body become one of antagonism between mind and body, and a source of anxiety to the divided 'self'? While medieval thought developed a richly nuanced concept of soul, it employed only rudimentary ideas of body, mind and person – all notions indispensable to modern individualist society. Clearly, at some point, the mind of the 'I' that thinks and reflects on itself, and the body that independently feels, desires, reproduces and sickens, emerged as objects of enquiry, thus founding the modern subject even as they threatened its coherence by pulling in opposite directions. Fields of knowledge which could establish body and mind as autonomous entities in this manner could not but have profound consequences for the ways in which human beings figured their own relation to the universe. The epistemological trails to this now familiar opposition were blazed most decisively in the early modern period by the strangely twinned discourses of anatomy and Cartesian philosophy.

With the opening of the cadaver to the scientific gaze, anatomists effectively became 'the first modern persons to distinguish man from his body'.[12] The first official public dissections, dated by the construction of the earliest anatomy theatres in Montpellier and Padua in the mid-sixteenth century, marked a decisive rupture of taboos around the 'divine' body which forbade dissection in the Middle Ages. Science was loosening the theological network which bound the natural universe to God. The dissected body, severed from its theological moorings, had become, like the rest of the material world, an object of human knowledge in its own right. As the corporeal mechanism was exposed, scrutinised, mapped and described as little more than the sum of its working parts, the modern biomedical body, 'the western sense of interiority' was born.[13] Jonathan Sawday's research into early modern anatomical discourse examines how the 'discovery' of the body interior not only shaped our now habitual sense of 'inner self', but was also entwined with the colonialist expansion and humanist moral philosophy of the early modern period, and became a central figurative concern of its art and literature.[14] Anatomy afforded a new sense of perspective in a yet more literal sense, for the development of perspectival drawing and chiaroscuro enabled the cubic body to be projected onto canvas with a newly convincing depth. As Sawday maintains:

> The study of anatomy *was* the study of the organisation of space. For, if it was nothing else, anatomy was concerned with volume, and it became the testing ground for that key experience, which was the transmission of three-dimensional space onto the flat surface of canvas, wood, fresco, or copper-plate.[15]

Perspectivalism was not, however, a neutral way of seeing, nor of grasping reality objectively. It was an organisation of reality, a formally codified view of the world through human eyes rather than God's, asserting the primacy of *people's* spatial co-ordinates and the ascendancy of the eye over the other bodily senses. It also naturalised a sense of authentic and private bodily depth which would remain largely unchallenged in western art until the early twentieth century.[16] The body henceforth owned a signifying interior, regardless of whether or not that interior was actually visible.

This would change the way that people thought about themselves. Against the backdrop of the early anatomy theatres (at which he was, significantly, a regular observer), René Descartes, in the *Meditations* of 1637, posed a series of questions crucial to the process of humanist individuation: 'What, then, am I? ... What is a thing that thinks?' when the consciousness of the thinker so palpably exceeds the 'assemblage of limbs', such as 'appears in a corpse ... designated by the name of body'.[17] When reality is grasped objectively only through mind's experience of itself, corporeal experience is by contrast reduced to the unreliable and mechanical – to the extent that Descartes can, in all seriousness, deny 'that I have any senses or body'. The absurdity of this claim is tempered only by acknowledging the magnitude of what had been constituted in the body (or body-as-world)'s place. For with Descartes, the sovereign subject, 'I', had appointed itself at the centre of discourse, and asserted the primacy of individual awareness (its own *perspective*), even as its knowledge would henceforth separate the subject from its objects – its own and others' bodies included.

So where does the body *go* in the face of this scepticism – in Francis Barker's words, 'banished from the scene of the state culture ... to a new – barely visible – place'?[18] Of course, it ceases neither to signify nor to function: after all, even the most ascetic populace needs to nourish, maintain and reproduce itself. Rather, its processes, passions and predilections, not unlike the organic systems studied in anatomy theatres, were gradually, infinitesimally, itemised and managed through a proliferation of discursive regimes; what would become the 'social sciences' such as criminology, sociology and psychology. Michel Foucault has explained how, once defined, the problematic person of the criminal or the lunatic could be confined, segregated and studied further with a view to ever more sophisticated diagnosis and management: thus the early modern spectacle of public torture and execution gave way to incarceration as the foundation of the modern penal system, and the assimilation of insanity by the community ceded to the asylum.[19] Foucault's extensive cultural history describes a new form of social control which was realised in multiple ways through the individual's body. Throughout the seventeenth century, the physical coercion of sovereignty over the collective body politic became a more diffuse, invisible circuitry of power based on ramified knowledges and observations of the embodied individual. But these disciplinary networks extended beyond state institutions such as law courts, prisons, church, school and army, and produced the autonomous subject in the very act of his or her private self-surveillance: an internalising of the disciplinary gaze which should be familiar to the modern reader in his or her own daily management of appearance and behaviour. To maintain one's own person within the bounds of the normative (and free) requires systematic scrutiny of both one's own and others' bodies for those signs of deviance which shore up a provisional sense of the 'proper' and 'normal'. The modern individual, in the deepening private enclosure of his or her body, became, through what Foucault describes as a 'micro-physics' of power, both subject and object of a 'compulsory visibility'.[20] The modern body is thus doubly 'occupied' by the subject, being both fleshly house of self *and* an unruly terrain whose mapping and control becomes, for the self-disciplining individual, a matter of almost military exactitude.

It is largely from this premise that work on the modern and contemporary body takes its many departures. This Reader does not attempt to provide an exhaustive historical survey. But it does aim to unravel the distinctive strands of modern discourse which contribute to a contemporary (common) sense of the body: a 'given' which the postmodern impulse is at the same time beginning to erode. The thinkers represented in this collection range historically from Descartes' meditation on the nature of body and mind to recent reflections on eating disorders and body-art, and the topics discussed in each of the book's three sections follow an approximate chronology. But the overall aim of the volume is not to offer a teleology of the body, or to produce a master-discourse of embodiment as, for example, a medical history might. Its concern is, rather, an epistemological one: to do with *how* these knowledges and definitions have been variously, often obliquely fashioned in modern culture, and to what ends. For this reason, the sections are organised primarily so that each represents a distinctive *mode* and *style* of thinking about bodies, for all that the essays within each employ different discursive frameworks and political agendas. In conclusion, a brief overview of the sections may help to situate the individual essays within the book's overall structure.

The first section, 'Depths', broadly historicises the ways in which modern embodiment has been figured as a fundamental relation between surface and depth, or 'superficial' and 'authentic' fields of knowledge. Central to these texts is a concern with how the body – or embodied individual – is to be *known* and described from without, whether in philosophy, anatomy, psychoanalysis, or the social institutions of Victorian bourgeois culture. All share a desire for the body to yield up its meanings, or 'contents', to the application of intellectual rigour, and thereby to be brought under a measure of discursive control. These are largely patriarchal discourses which map cultural terms onto an essentialised anatomical difference, ultimately coding the penetrable, knowable body as 'feminine', and the incisive, enquiring gaze as 'masculine'. Arguably, the very expressiveness of the volumetric body – its amenability to reading – is also the means of its potential subjection.

Seldom has this been accomplished more decisively than in the project of psychoanalysis. Freud and Breuer's seminal publication of 'the talking cure' in *Studies on Hysteria* (1895) marks the birth of the psychoanalytic subject, whose unconscious 'depths' break the surface of the body in the cryptic form of the physical symptom. In the classic Freudian schema, it is the task of the (male) analyst to prompt and interpret the (female) patient's verbal 'externalising' of her psychical conflict: a conflict invariably (and problematically) traced back to a sexual/anatomical difference which casts woman as 'lacking'. Freud memorably likens the process of uncovering the symptom's latent content to archaeology (see p. 36 below) – a trope which, coupled with his later description of femininity as a 'dark continent',[21] itself 'speaks volumes' about the colonial unconscious of his texts, and, indeed, of modernity itself. The evolutionary logic of imperialism is mapped by Freud onto the unconscious, which, as manifested by the hysteric, is the repository of all pre-civilised, polymorphously perverse desires. The ungovernable body of the primitive thus acquires a tantalising symbolic ubiquity in the late nineteenth and early twentieth century: it is simultaneously 'within' the subject as body and unconscious, and without, as the object of a burgeoning anthropological discourse. The neo-primitive art of the modernists sought precisely to recover this lost quality of supposed corporeal immediacy. As Lieve Spaas explains:

> The primitive is then a quality which mankind has lost, ignores, or has repressed, a quality which pre-literate societies may have preserved or which may lie hidden in the human consciousness … Whereas the anthropologist travels to exotic societies for an encounter with 'primitivism', the surrealist attempts to explore the 'primitive' within himself.[22]

Freud's analytic project, which seeks to externalise in language the 'truth' of the repressed carnal body, thus performs a powerful suturing of the Cartesian mind/body opposition, while at the same time mapping it more decisively onto the axes of gender and race.

The essays under the rubric of 'Difference' shift from a concern with plumbing the depths of the individual, to the definition and organising of communities and populations according to a distinctively western binary logic of identity and difference. These texts represent a range of both normalising and counter-discourses, and at stake in all of them is the tendency of 'normative' white male embodiment to appropriate, naturalise and codify cultural power at the expense of its others. Theorists as culturally different as Frantz Fanon and Catherine Clément, for example, both engage in a similar textual struggle to reverse the terms by which racial or sexual difference is solidified into opposition by those in power. Ultimately, however, the political efficacy of such reverse-discourses is doubtful, in so far as the framework of oppositions which underpins them rests fundamentally unchallenged.

With this in mind, the final section, 'Deconstructions', samples those theoretical approaches, broadly defined as poststructuralist, which challenge and destabilise depth-invested, dualistic or normative notions of the body, particularly in the field of sexual politics. Joan Riviere, for example, though chronologically a modern thinker, sets the scene for a more postmodern theoretical trajectory by outlining the paradox of femininity as *essentially superficial*, a masquerade or construct which takes effect without reference to an organic original: a contention which in some respects anticipates the complex theories of gender performativity as developed by Judith Butler. The remainder of the essays assume the post-Saussurean premise that meaning depends on difference, and that the impression of actuality is an *effect* of language, not its origin. They consider bodies as constituted in discourse and, at the same time, deferred or relegated by it. We know (or think we do) *in* language, and in the process language itself takes the place of the reality we seem to know. Though each of these texts recognises that the configuration of bodies and bodily identities is cultural and provisional, they mobilise this instability in different ways. None of them makes universal claims. On the contrary, they all foreground their partiality in both senses of the term: the knowledges they put forward are both committed to a position and incomplete. These essays tend to celebrate rather than limit the capacity of the body to signify in different ways, tracing a plurality of inscriptions and offering multiple readings. Discursive deconstruction, however, for all its textual complexity, need not imply disembodiment. Indeed, the final two essays in this section are concerned precisely not to lose sight of the contemporary body at 'gut level'.

This section reflects several potential futures for body-criticism, albeit in a an unstable climate where theories of the posthuman sit uneasily alongside the deepening political claims of the individual over his or her bodily destiny. Indeed, advances in medical technology seem to be pressing the point of individual corporeal rights to new levels of complexity, as evidenced by recent legal battles over issues such as euthanasia and reproductive autonomy.[23] Tensions like this make body criticism a complex, even contradictory business. It is precisely one such tension which characterises Marianna Torgovnick's troubled fascination with contemporary neo-primitive body-art in an essay which, usefully, raises more questions than it answers. How are tattoos and body-piercings to be understood in relation to their 'primitive' cultural antecedents, in a postmodern epoch, yet one which routinely invokes Freudian symptomatology to understand cultural 'deviance'? Of what, exactly, is body-art expressive? Torgovnick concludes, ironically, with the hope that through her reflections the reader will experience these superficial inscriptions as a *'gut issue'*: an explicitly visceral metaphor which invokes an instinctive, 'authentic' response, one which might be said to issue from the depths of the body itself. The challenge and reward for the cultural critic lies precisely in these vexed, instructive areas where body and theory collide. After all, it can be difficult to reconcile the finer points of academic analysis with everyday embodied experience. Discussion of 'the body' in the abstract becomes an altogether more unwieldy matter when it is 'your body' that is at stake.

2

The Renaissance Body: From Colonisation to Invention

Jonathan Sawday

BODY AND SOUL AT WAR

In the twentieth century it is virtually impossible to think about the body outside a prevailing medical-scientific discourse. But it was not always so. What we consider to be primarily the focus of medical attention – the accounts of physicians, surgeons, anatomists, physiologists, biologists – has, in other epochs, been entertained under quite different categories of description. Those categories, bounded by theology and cosmology – the polarities of ritual – did not admit the possibility of thinking about the body as a discrete entity. In the west, prior to the 'new science' of the late sixteenth and seventeenth centuries, the body's interior could not be understood without recourse to an analysis of that which gave its materiality significance – the essence contained within the body. A belief in the presence of that essence, a belief, that is, in the existence of an *anima*, a soul or a thinking entity, necessarily informed any possible perspective of the body. To consider the body in isolation was not merely difficult but, strictly speaking, impossible, since the body's primary function, it was held, was to act as a vessel of containment for the more significant feature of the soul.

Soul and body were not, however, easy participants in a greater unity. Instead, they existed under the constraints of struggle. The body was perpetually at war with that which it found residing in itself. The body was (depending on your point of view) either the unwilling host to a nagging and parasitical arbiter of right and wrong, or it was the close prison which perpetually sought to constrain the expansionary desire of the soul. Each participant in this combat had the power to ruin its opponent. The body's gross physicality could ensure the endless enslavement of the soul to corporeal existence, defined, in the soul's terms, as punishment. Equally, however, the soul's desire to escape the terrestrial existence of the body involved the destruction of its temporary and temporal residence. We may trace this conflict to Plato's *Phaedo*, where the soul is described as striving to achieve a disassociation from its bodily existence which will guarantee 'release from ... all other human evils'. Those

12

souls, on the other hand, which have cultivated too close an affinity with the body become 'tainted and impure'. Beguiled by the body, the impure soul is 'weighed down and dragged back into the visible world' so that at death, rather than a fleeing towards God, it is 'imprisoned once more in a body'.[1]

Plato's depiction of a perpetual dualistic struggle between body and soul, transmitted via Neoplatonism, patristic authority, and medieval theology, is the dominant model for understanding the relationship between body and soul within western culture prior to the fifteenth century. To consider the body as an isolated phenomenon – as a discrete entity in Platonic terms – was simply not possible, since the body was only one half of a bifurcated whole. Such a bisection is still fundamental to our perception of what might constitute individuality within western societies. For Augustine and the patristic writers, the reality of a dualistic struggle was equally essential for their definition of the relationship between God and humanity. 'The corruptible Body', says Augustine, 'is a burden to the Soul'.[2] Only through shaking off this burdensome body could the soul achieve union with God. Though the form of this struggle could, on occasion, shift, the protagonists remained constant. The body seemed to turn towards a visible and material world, whilst the soul sought to encounter an invisible and immaterial mode of being. Such dualistic habits of thought were, it is true, challenged at certain moments, but challenges were short-lived and seemed invariably to result in the reassertion of the struggle between interior and exterior.[3]

If anything, with the advent of the preliminary results of scientific investigation in the later sixteenth century, the interior war became even more fierce, since now fresh fuel was to be thrown onto the already blazing fire. Science gave an added impetus to the urge to peer into the recesses of the body. But Calvinistic theology, with its seemingly obsessive desire to chart the inner state of each individual's spiritual well-being, was to argue with a conviction equal to that of the scientist that the division between the realm of the body and the realm of the soul was now the concern of every thinking person. The internal human division, in other words, was now to be perceived as stretching into the sphere of all civil life.[4] The politics of the body – a politics which involve a form of self-reflexive violence – have begun to emerge.

What was at stake within this political sphere was mastery over the body and control of its internal processes. The uncovering of the body's interior by natural philosophy, the growing awareness that the body-interior was composed of a dynamic system in perpetual motion, seems to have posed a very real threat to those who, prompted by the impulse of science, turned inwards. Donne's famous lines on anatomical doubt in the second of his Anniversary poems of 1612 ('Of the Progresse of the Soule') trace the dimensions of this anatomical challenge. What Donne remarks upon in the poem is not merely ignorance of the body's operations (for all the discoveries of post-Vesalian science),[5] but instead the unknowable quality of the body's own motions. It is the fluid processes (literally the movement of fluids) which offer the clearest challenge to human certainty:

> Knowst thou but how the stone doth enter in
> The bladers cave, and never breake the skinne?
> Know'st thou how blood, which to the heart doth flow,
> Doth from one ventricle to th'other goe?
> And for the putrid stuffe, which thou dost spit,
> Know'st thou how thy lungs have attracted it?
> There are no passages, so that there is
> (For ought thou know'st) piercing of substances.
> And of those many opinions which men raise
> Of Nailes and Haires, dost thou know which to praise?
>   (Donne, *Poems*, pp. 234–5)[6]

These verses demonstrate much more than simply pre-Harveian ignorance of blood circulation.[7] Rather, Donne has opened the body only to discover that it seems to operate according to its own laws of hydraulic motion. The movement of gallstones, blood, and phlegm seems to challenge the laws of reason and the experience of observation. In a similar fashion the body's ability to excrete substances, or generate new substances from the interior casts a shadow over human perception. This sense of an inability to understand and hence control physical processes never left Donne. He was always alert to the potential defeat of reason, once the body had become the object of his gaze. The body's interior architecture concealed dizzying depths and capacities, reservoirs of fluid, in which the imagination could lose itself. In a sermon preached before the King at Whitehall in April 1620/1, for example, we find Donne meditating on a text from Proverbs (25.16): 'Has thou found honey? Eat so much as is sufficient for thee.' Honey, Donne interprets as worldly honour, or the things of the flesh. How much can we eat, he asks, before we are spiritually gagging? In searching for an answer, an anatomical expedition into the body-interior must be mounted:

> We know the receipt, the capacity of the Ventricle, the stomach of man, how much it can hold; and we know the receipt of all the receptacles of blood, how much blood the body can have; so do we of all the other conduits and cisterns of the body; but this infinite Hive of honey, this insatiable whirlpool of the covetous mind, no anatomy, no dissection, hath discovered to us.[8]

Gazing into the body with the eye of science, an eye skilled in measurement, the body appears at first to be finite in its capacity in comparison to the mind's insatiability.[9] But as Donne's gaze into the body becomes more intense, and as the authoritative tone of the passage (suggested by the collective 'We') gives way to a more personal note, doubt begins to intrude once more. Suddenly, under a more pressing analysis, the body is transformed. From being a safely measurable interior, it emerges as a reservoir of immense size and capacity:

> When I looke into the larders and cellars, and vaults, into the vessells of our body for drink, for blood, for urine, they are pottles and gallons; when I look into the furnaces of our spirits, the ventricles of the heart and of the braine, they are not thimbles. (*Sermons*, III. 236)

The eye has been deceived. A 'pottle' (according to the *OED*, approximately half a gallon) has been squeezed into a quart cup, the body's structure revealed as gloomy vaults, unsounded wells, panting furnaces, lakes of blood and urine.

'The concavities of my body are like another hell for their capacity.' So Sir Thomas Urquhart, in 1653, had observed in his translation of Rabelais's *Gargantua*.[10] Donne's evocation of an equally rapacious body-interior prompts us to understand this urge to master the body's processes within a directly political context. For the body's interior may be understood as 'grotesque' in that specialised sense associated with Bakhtin's analysis of the body.[11] Conflict between interior and exterior becomes, in this analysis, the new coordinate of a confrontation between the 'grotesque' and the 'classical'. As Peter Stallybrass and Allon White have observed, Bakhtin's 'classical body denotes the inherent form of the high official culture' whilst the 'grotesque ... designates the marginal, the low and the outside from the perspective of a classical body situated as high, inside and central by virtue of its very exclusions'.[12] In a fluid process of metamorphosis, the uncovering of a body-interior, as in the case of John Donne's peregrinations through the body's 'larders and cellars', announces the discovery that what is inside the body is associated with 'low' culture. In Donne's anatomical journey, we do not encounter staterooms, halls, or a privileged public space. Instead, we wander through service chambers, and gaze into barely understood industrial processes. [...] For Donne, writing on the brink of scientific transformation of the body, the features which demand our attention are those associated with the opposite of cool, reserved, classical forms. Gallstones, blood, phlegm, nails, hair, and urine – substances which have to be expelled from the body – are the touchstones of the experience of interiority.[13] It is as if the encounter with the body's interior has suddenly revealed a vista of an alternative (and dangerous) mode of existence in which the marginal, the low, the anti-rationalistic, reigns supreme. This, then, was the new battlefield in which the body-soul struggle was to take place.

We can glimpse the outlines of this struggle in poetic descriptions in the late sixteenth and early seventeenth centuries of the relationship between body and soul. If we remain with Donne for a moment, and turn to 'The Extasie' – that exercise in Platonic dualism – we observe the body depicted as a 'prison' in which is forced to reside the 'great Prince' which is the soul. In accordance with traditional ideas, the soul is envisaged in corporeal terms – a tripartite union of higher and lower faculties. This embodiment of an incorporeal entity, as Burton explained in *The Anatomy of Melancholy*, led to a welter of conflicting opinion. Were souls to be understood as single or multiple? Did the body contain within itself three distinct principles – the vegetal, sensible, and rational – or were these merely faculties of some higher union?[14] Already, the subject or individual can be seen to exist in a fundamentally fragmented state. But, at the same moment, a different kind of bodily union is explored in Donne's poem. The body, though it is the vehicle by which souls may encounter one another, is also the inferior partner, the medium of physical feeling, and crucially a source of dislocation and imbalance. Informing the poem's logic is the language of domination and ownership – the language of the soul itself, since the poem's narrator (of necessity) speaks for the soul which is the very reasoning power allowing the poem utterance. Bodies, Donne writes, 'are ours, though they are not wee' and he continues: 'Wee are The intelligences, they the Spheare' (Donne, *Poems*, p. 47). The relationship between body and soul is not only akin to the relationship between the celestial spheres and the divine intelligence which allows movement, but akin to the very structures of linguistic utterance: 'We' – souls – speak; 'they' – bodies – hear and obey.

Or should obey. The body's refusal to obey, its ability to fracture the supposed desire of the soul towards communion with God, and its recalcitrant and rebellious longing for physical and sensual existence, delineates the battle-lines between material and immaterial existence, as well as between subject and object in a grammatical sense. Under the promptings of a Calvinist theology, the battle for dominion became ever more ferocious. 'Mastery' over the body, the conquering of its desires, the endless war against the ravages of sin, or 'soul-sickness', is a feature of early-modern culture which provides the determining framework in which the body's internal dimensions were to be understood. [...] Within this framework, and amongst puritans, what has been termed the 'inner anxiety' of Calvinist doctrine became institutionalised, producing a seemingly obsessive desire to scrutinise the slightest 'perturbations' of the soul in its relationship to the exterior world in which the body was held to exist.[15] Hence, to peer into the body was to undertake a journey into a corrupt world of mortality and decay; it became a voyage into the very heart of the principle of spiritual dissolution. Within this mental universe, illness and sickness, the malfunction of the body, was a profoundly important spiritual state rather than a physiological problem to be encountered with the aid of medicine and technology. Written in the 1650s, Andrew Marvell's 'Dialogue Between the Soul and the Body' might stand as the definitive insider's account of the incessant internal war held to be taking place within each individual. The poem's opening is famous for its masterfully apposite display of a self-reflexive desire to escape the interior recesses of the body. But in demonstrating such desire, Marvell's poem also allows us access to a complex and contradictory fusion of puritan theology and new science in which the body appears as a sinister instrument of pain and torture. The soul opens the dialogue:

> *Soul*   O who shall from this Dungeon, raise
> A soul inslav'd so many wayes?
> With bolts of Bones, that fetter'd stands
> In feet; and manacled in hands.
> Here blinded with an Eye; and there
> Deaf with the drumming of an Ear.
> A Soul hung up, as t'were, in Chains
> Of Nerves, and Arteries, and Veins.
> Tortur'd, besides each other part,
> In a vain Head, and double Heart.[16]

To the poem's opening question – who shall raise me from this fleshly prison – there is, of course, only one answer: Christ. Christ, because of the willingness of the *Logos* to become flesh, can answer the soul's plea to escape the flesh.[17] Yet for the moment, imprisoned within the body, the soul transforms the delicate organs of sensory feeling into the instruments of its own torture. Ironically, in terms of seventeenth-century psychological theory, it is through just these organs – eyes, ears, hands – that the soul was allowed to experience, however imperfectly, the outward world. But in Marvell's evocation of the body as a prison-house, the 'higher' organs of feeling – the *viae mediae* between terrestrial and spiritual experience – are emblematic of the soul's barren inner existence.

Perhaps the most striking image of the poem's opening stanza is that of the body transformed into a self-reflexive instrument of torture, with network of veins, arteries, and nerves performing the office of the chains of a gibbet. It is in this image that we can sense a conjunction between the theologically informed understanding of the body–soul relationship and the searching gaze of pre-Cartesian science into the body's interior.[18] To be gibbeted, to be exposed after execution to public gaze, was a fate reserved for the worst male-factors, since it compounded the punishment with a denial of Christian burial. The soul's life in the body in Marvell's 'Dialogue' is, therefore, a very public form of death – a shaming and punishing ordeal of exposure. Yet, this image tallies not just with accounts of bodies gibbeted and exposed after execution, but with the records of contemporary anatomists, amongst whose skills was the preparation of demonstrations of 'arterial', 'venous', and 'nerval' figures. These preparations revealed to an admiring public a new image of the human figure, an image which traced the form of the body, whilst its material – flesh, tissue, organs, sinews – was, as it were, miraculously dissolved. The outline of the gibbet – a skeletal framework in which condemned bodies dissolved – and the spidery structure of the nerval figure appear congruent. The new internal topography, which soon came to replace the older schematic diagrams of the arterial, venous, and nervous systems, revealed the body as a delicate lattice-work of interconnecting vessels which traced in outline the new dispersed body. Eerily, it is just such a dispersal of the body which the gibbet, a technological aid to the exposure of the condemned corpse, was designed to achieve. [...]

Marvell's opening stanza of his 'Dialogue' gives us, then, the co-ordinates of a new version of the otherwise perpetual warfare taking place within the confines of the body. It shows us, too, the transformation of punishment into art. [...] The internal war has now encountered a new possibility – the body is to be no longer the preserve of the dogmatic controversialist. Its contours are now open to the colder eye of science.

CREATING THE MECHANICAL REPUBLIC

The colder eye of science – the new science of the body – is associated with the 'discovery' or, more properly, the rhetorical deployment during the seventeenth century, of a new language with which to describe the body's interior. This language is primarily associated with the post-Cartesian formulation of the body as a machine. But to the natural philosophers of the earlier seventeenth century, it was not a mechanistic structure that they first encountered as they embarked upon the project of unravelling the body's recesses. Rather, they found themselves wandering within a geographical entity. The body was a territory, an (as yet) undiscovered country, a location which demanded from its explorers skills which seemed analogous to those displayed by the heroic voyagers across the terrestrial globe.

The period between (roughly) 1540 and 1640, is, therefore, the period of the *discovery* of the Vesalian body as opposed to the later *invention* of the Harveian or Cartesian body. Guiding the followers of Vesalius was the belief that the human body expressed in miniature the divine workmanship of God, and that its form corresponded to the greater form of the macrocosm. Such ideas did not vanish overnight, to be replaced by the clear light of Cartesian rationality. Indeed William Harvey himself leaned on a system of beliefs inherited from Aristotle, which held that the universe and the human body – the interior and exterior worlds – were united in the common bond of correspondence. Within this system, features observed within the body were held to replicate features to be seen in the world at large. [...] Imitation, a central concept in Renaissance poetic theory, orders the body, the world, and the heavens into a pattern of replication, in which each component of the system finds its precise analogical equivalent in every other component. What Michel Foucault has termed the 'finitude of a world held firmly between the microcosm and the macrocosm' is thus rooted in an endlessly repetitive interplay of metaphor, similitude, and comparison.[19] It is probably not an overstatement to say that this vista of similarity lay at the very heart of every intellectual endeavour of early-modern culture, informing art, architecture, philosophy, theology, natural philosophy, and, in particular, poetry. Within this world the body lay entangled within a web of enclosing patterns of repetition.

During this phase, which opened with the publication of Vesalius' *De Humani Corporis Fabrica* in 1543, the interior of the body began to take on most of its modern features. Eustachius mapped the ear, Fallopius the female reproductive organs, Realdus Columbus and Fabricius of Aquapendente the venous system, and Michael Servetus the pulmonary transit of the blood. Like the Columbian explorers, these early discoverers dotted their names, like place-names on a map, over the terrain which they encountered. In their voyages, they expressed the intersection of the body and the world at every point, claiming for the body an affinity with the complex design of the universe. This congruence equated scientific endeavour with the triumphant discoveries of the explorers, cartographers, navigators, and early colonialists. And in the production of a new map of the body, a new figure was also to be glimpsed – the scientist as heroic voyager and intrepid discoverer.[20] The body was a remote and strange terrain into which the discoverer voyaged. Just how remote, and just how strange, is suggested in an observation of Sir Thomas Browne. When, in his *Religio Medici* of 1642, Browne came to consider the 'wals of flesh, wherein the soul doth seeme to be immured', the trope which ordered his experience of the body's physicality was one which, even by seventeenth-century standards of poetic conceit, must have appeared to have been verging on the grotesque. Browne wrote:

> *All flesh is grasse*, not onely metaphorically, but literally true, for all those creatures we behold, are but the herbs of the field, digested into flesh in them, or more remotely carnified in our selves. Nay further, we are what we all abhorre, *Anthropophagi* and Cannibals, devourers not onely of men, but of our selves; and that not in an allegory, but a positive truth; for all this masse of fleshe which we behold, came in at our mouths: this frame we looke upon, hath beene upon our trenchers; In briefe, we have devoured our selves.[21]

Browne's vision of the body, a vision which hovers on the edge of what was later to be termed scientific understanding, collapsed exterior and interior, the known and the unknown, into a carnificatory process in which the body was the devourer of itself. What we hate and fear, the cannibal, the Medusa, was held to be residing deep within us, rather than encountered in some distant and remote land. Browne's image of the body as cannibalistic may have been derived from Montaigne's essay 'On Cannibals' (published in 1580) where we read that, at the point of death, the cannibal who was himself about to be cannibalised asserted his own superiority over those about to eat him by reminding them that he had once eaten their ancestors. Flesh is united to flesh in an unbroken round of eating and being eaten:

> These muscles … this flesh, and these veins are yours, poor fools that you are! Can you not see that the substance of your ancestors' limbs is still in them? Taste them carefully, and you will find the flavour is that of your own flesh.[22]

It was into this cannibalistic universe that the scientist journeyed when the body was opened. [...]

The microcosmic explorer of the body laboured on a project the dimensions of which were held to be every bit as dark as the interior of the continent of the newly 'found' Americas. But the body's darkness, its strangeness, its alieneity did not preclude knowledge. The scientist who searched the cavities and recesses, the interior secrets, of the body was not faced with 'ne plus ultra' confronting earlier, theologically-bound, patterns of knowledge. Instead 'Plus Ultra' – 'yet further', the motto of the Emperor Charles V – became the watchword of the natural philosophers.[23] Though, on occasion, warning voices might be heard, this project was conducted with boundless optimism. No limit was to be placed on the possibility of gaining understanding. The task of the scientist was to voyage within the body in order to force it to reveal its secrets. Once uncovered, the body-landscape could be harnessed to the service of its owner. In thus establishing the body as 'useful' – a key term amongst the natural philosophers of the seventeenth century – we are able to perceive the language of colonialism and the language of science as meshing with one another. To say of the New World that it was like a body, as Donne observed in 1622 when he addressed the Virginia Company as 'not onely a *Spleene*, to drain the ill humours of the body, but a *Liver*, to breed good bloud', was to explore a metaphor, but it was also to appropriate the body in the service of colonial expansion.[24]

In this undertaking, part of that 'dominion over nature' which was the object of progressive western science throughout the seventeenth century, the body became subject to a new regime of language. First it had to be colonised. The process was truly colonial, in that it appeared to reproduce the stages of discovery and exploitation which were, at that moment, taking place within the context of the European encounter with the New World. First came the explorers, leaving their mark on the body in the form of features which were mapped and named and inhabitants who were encountered and observed. The second stage mirrored the narrative of conquest and exploitation insofar as these newly found features and peoples were understood as forming part of a complex economy – a system of production, distribution, and consumption – which was itself in perpetual movement. The project, then, was to harness this system to the use of the discoverer. Intrinsic to such a project was the creation of the body's interior as a form of property. Like property, the body's bounds needed to be fixed, its dimensions properly measured, its resources charted. Its 'new' owner – which would eventually become the thinking process of the Cartesian *cogito* – had to know what it was that was owned before use could be made of it.[25] In order to achieve such knowledge the owner had to see it, to view the landscape; but view it not as an abstract projection of semi-mythical traveller's tales, but rather as an objective reality. In exactly similar fashion, Christopher Columbus, describing the wealth of the Indies on returning from his first voyage of 1492–3, observed that 'although there was much talk and writing of these lands, all was conjectural, without ocular evidence. In fact, those who accepted the stories judged by hearsay rather than on any tangible information'. Such a statement was echoed in the writings of Vesalius and his contemporaries who, in their urge to overturn Galenic authority, stressed the primacy of 'ocular evidence' in their explorations of the body.[26] The important difference between their undertakings and those of classical authority, they continually claimed, was that, unlike Galen and those who followed Galen, they had *seen* the body with their own eyes. For Columbus, in the realm of exploration of the macrocosm, having seen what this new property might offer – gold, spices, cotton, mastic, aloes, slaves, rhubarb, cinnamon – the conclusion was that 'there will be countless other things in addition, which the people I have left there will discover'.[27] In similar measure, the human body was now understood to contain wealth, though of a kind peculiar to itself. So, in the 'Anniversary poems' that we have already glanced at, Donne writes of the body of Elizabeth Drury, the young woman who was the 'occasion' of the verses:

> The Westerne treasure, easterne Spicerie,
> Europe, and Afrique, and the unknown rest
> Were easily found, or what in them was best;
> And when w'have made this large discoverie
> Of all, in her some one part then will bee
> Twenty such parts, whose plenty and riches is
> Enough to make twenty such worlds as this;   (Donne, *Poems*, p. 233)

Poetic hyperbole? Of course. But the point is that Donne's language of praise and celebration was informed by the vocabulary of discovery and appropriation, so that colonialism and the discovery of the body appeared to complement one another. The rich resources of the new body/world would rejuvenate the old.

The language of property and appropriation came easily to Donne and his contemporaries whenever the body was considered. Reaching out to grasp this property, a rich land of promise, was not merely a right, but a duty which sanctioned the actions of the colonialist. This, the justification which informed Donne's 1622 sermon to the Virginia Company, was discernible at other, perhaps less obviously appropriate moments. Donne's erotic hymn to the female body (Elegie XIX) deployed the language of discovery in order to evoke a sinister combination of sensuality and physical exploitation:

> Licence my roaving hands, and let them go,
> Before, behind, between, above, below.
> O my America! My new-found-land,
> My kingdome, safeliest when with one man man'd.
> My Myne of precious stones, My Emperie,
> How blest am I in this discovering thee!
> To enter in these bonds, is to be free;
> Then where my hand is set, my seal shall be.   (Donne, *Poems*, p. 107)

'How blest am I in this discovering thee!' Donne's exclamation carried the full weight of a colonising dynamic which might almost have stood as the credo of the enquiring seventeenth-century scientist. It was with just such a proprietal gesture that Vesalius, on the great title-page of the *Fabrica*, had himself pictured placing his right hand on the dissected female body, in a gesture of ownership – a gesture which may bring to mind Donne's hand reaching out in Elegie XIX: 'Then where my hand is set, my seal shall be'. Just as the woman's body in Elegie XIX was transformed into an America, and hence was ready for subjection via discovery, first, and then the bonds of property and ownership, so the 'scientific' body was transformed into an object of discovery and a regime of ownership in which 'health' existed as a goal to be imposed on bodies which, operating according to their own perverse designs, too often seemed to find refuge in sickness.[28] But the Vesalian gesture of ownership is also a gesture of revelation. The right hand opens the woman's body to the gaze of all who care to see. Like Donne's roving hands, the roving hands of the anatomist have opened the body's cavities and claimed the body, if not for sex, then for knowledge. But then, what was the difference? As a licensed colonialist, or as a roving pirate of the bedchamber, or as an enquiring anatomist, the discourses of knowledge seemed to flow into one another.[29]

But the knowledge of the body, despite Donne's portrayal of an easy erotic triumph, was in reality hard to come by. No matter how diligently the search for this new continent was conducted, its expanses were so (microcosmically) vast, its recesses so hidden, that understanding followed only after the greatest exertion. The term that endlessly seems to structure the voyage into the body's interior in the seventeenth century was the 'America' which Donne's roving hands sought to clutch. The exultant yell of discovery in Donne's elegy on the female body – 'O my America!' – a cry of possession and feverish sexual excitement, echoes with just as much force when we hear it in the exclamations of the natural philosophers of the later seventeenth century. 'America' became synonymous with the triumph of the human imagination as it strove to unravel passages which seemed to become ever more tortuous, ever more complex. For Joseph Glanvill, a founder member of the Royal Society, the body's 'inward frame' was indeed 'an *America*', but it was also, therefore, 'a yet undiscovered Region' in which the scientist could win enduring fame and honour.[30] Glanvill's immediate contemporary, the poet and savant Abraham Cowley, expressed the case in similar fashion. Cowley, like Glanvill an enthusiastic proponent of the new science, saw the body as a *terra incognita* within which would be uncovered 'work enough for our posterity'.[31] Cowley was to claim that the whole scientific impulse of his own age was akin to the discovery of America. But others seemed less secure when faced with this vast prospect. The English anatomist, Walter Charleton, writing in 1680 seemed to balk at the huge labour which the colonisation of this internal America would, of necessity, involve:

> There are yet, alas! Terrae incognitae in the lesser world, as well as the greater, the Island of the Brain, the Isthmus of the Spleen, the streights of the Renes and ... some other Glanduls, the North-East passage of the drink from the Stomach to the Kidnies, and many other things, remain to be further enquir'd into by us, and perhaps by posterity also.[32]

The riot of geographical metaphors betrays a profound level of insecurity. No one individual could hope to encompass such knowledge. Despite the optimism of the internal voyagers, some were beginning to sense that the body's interior had become too vast, too complex; it demanded a pattern of investigation which would examine not its coasts, rivers, and tributaries, but something different. It was at this point that the machine-body, an automaton of movement whose existence had been postulated some fifty years earlier, emerged to stride, once and for all, within the body's interior.

The reduction of the body 'to a mere mechanical contrivance' may not have begun with Descartes, but the Cartesian formulation of 1637, which suggested that the operations of the body have to be analysed in terms of the 'many different automata or moving machines the industry of man can devise' represented the summation of half a century of voyages into the interior to which Descartes was the heir.[33] After Descartes, the image of the body as America was to be gradually (and one needs to stress the slow process of paradigmatic change) replaced by one of the body as a machine.[34] Mechanism offered the prospect of a radically reconstituted body. Forged into a working machine, the mechanical body appeared fundamentally

different from the geographic body whose contours expressed a static landscape without dynamic interconnection. More than this, however, the body as
machine, as a clock, as an automaton, was understood as having no intellect
of its own. Instead, it silently operated according to the laws of mechanics.
We move, then, from an interior in which the body seems (as in Marvell's
dialogue) to speak its own part, to the modern conception of a physiological
system no more capable of speech than is an hydraulic pump – the machine
with which Harvey himself had sought to explain the operation of cardiac
valves.[35] As a machine, the body became objectified; a focus of intense curiosity, but entirely divorced from the world of the speaking and thinking subject.
The division between Cartesian subject, and corporeal object, between an
'I' that thinks, and an 'it' in which 'we' reside, had become absolute.

The political implications of this process of thought were immense.
Hitherto, the body had always been available as a rich source of metaphors
with which to describe systems of government which were held to be both
organic (and hence natural) and hierarchical. No longer was this the case. The
easy familiarity with which early-modern political commentators could point
to the body (mediated, it is true, by St. Paul's more communitarian model) as
a demonstration of monarchical authority was now open to question.
Menenius' fable of the belly in Shakespeare's *Coriolanus* had become simply
irrelevant in any literal sense. The soul's power within the body was no longer
analogous to the king's power within the state, or even God's power within the
universe: the triple bond of authority had been broken down into a world of
mechanical process. If God still existed, then he was certainly no architect,
perhaps not even a creator in the older sense of a fashioning and forming
deity. Rather he was a mechanic, an engineer, a watchmaker even, whose
presence was no longer required for the continuing operation of the orderly
movement of the machine.

Of course, the argument did not rest there. To many of the followers of
Descartes and Harvey, the fact that the body could be thought of as a
machine suggested that, like all machines, a maker was required. But the
machine, others pointed out, could (and did) run without need of supervision. Once set in motion, the engineer's will or desire could have no effect on
the whirling processes which now seemed to be in operation. We can trace the
implications, within a political sphere, of these new conceptions of the body
in Harvey's own work. In 1628, when *De Motu Cordis* first appeared (in
Latin) Harvey dedicated his discovery of circulatory processes to the
monarch, Charles I. To the king, knowledge of the heart's operation within
the body, Harvey wrote 'cannot be unprofitable ... as being a divine example
of his own actions (so have ever men been wont to compare small things with
great)'.[36] When, in 1653, an English translation of the text appeared (based on
the Latin edition of 1648) this language of similarity had undergone a subtle
but nevertheless crucial shift. In 1653, the king, had he still existed, might

have looked inside the body to discover 'a divine resemblance of his actions (so us'd they small things with great to compare)'.[37] A divine 'example' has metamorphosed into a divine 'resemblance', an observation of similarity which is placed firmly within the historical past. In 1628, when the king was still on the throne of England, the heart was offered as an example of kingly rule. By 1653, in the turmoil of the new experiment in government which was the nascent English Republic, the sovereign heart had become no more than an example, one amongst many, by which the body was once known.

Was the transformation of the body into a machine responsible for this dethronement of a hierarchically organised body? Was it even possible that the turmoil of the revolutionary years in England in the 1640s and 1650s encouraged the creation of a radically different conceptual organisation of the body?[38] We can see, for example, the organic language of the body still deployed within a political sphere in the lyrics of Richard Lovelace, whose posthumous collection of poems *Lucasta* (1659) abounded in images of bodily dissolution. But rather than the body being illustrative of the integrity of form, it was witness, now, to a collapse in hierarchies and order. Bodily form was dispersed into liquefaction, or jelly-like viscosity, or (as here in 'A Mock Song') an anatomical tumble of distributed structure which stretches over the cosmos:

> Now the *Sun* is unarm'd
> And the *Moon* by us charm'd
> All the *Stars* dissolv'd to a Jelly:
> Now the *Thighs* of the Crown,
> And the *Arms* are lopp'd down,
> And the *Body* is all but a Belly:[39]

Lovelace's lyric is an epitaph to the decapitated king. But in that act of violation of the sovereign body, Lovelace perceives a wider morphological dissolution. It is not just that the republican 'belly' has superseded the heart or sovereign power, but that the body as a whole (together with the universe of which it was once an emblem) has become translated into a carnivalesque and grotesque single organ.

Whatever precise political structure ruled within the body, the natural philosophers who now entered the body were sure of encountering processes susceptible to logical analysis, rather than mystical affinity. The development of the machine image dramatically transformed the attitude of investigators towards the body's interior, and towards their own tasks of investigation. They no longer stood before the body as though it was a mysterious continent. It had become, instead, a system, a design, a mechanically organised structure, whose rules of operation, though still complex, could, with the aid of reason, be comprehended in the most minute detail. At least, that was the theory. As early as 1620, in the *Novum Organum*, Francis Bacon had claimed that investigation should proceed by principles which would concentrate on 'number, weight, and measure ... a combination of physics and mathematics that generates practice'.[40] Bacon's stress on 'number, weight, and measure' was, it is true, an echo of scriptural injunction.[41] But it was also understood as a call to a mechanics which opened the door to a vision of the body in which human ingenuity would unravel the mechanism as surely as it was known that the mechanism had been constructed according to clearly defined mechanical theory in the first place. 'In mechanical things', Thomas Willis wrote in the 1660s:

> when any one would observe the motions of a clock or Engine, he takes the machine itself to pieces to consider the singular artifice, and doth not doubt that he will learn the causes and properties of the Phaenomenon.[42]

The mechanical body dispelled doubt, uncertainty and indecision. A technology of the body had become apparent; a technology, moreover, which could itself be investigated, reflexively, with the aid of technology. For Henry Power, an exponent of the mechanical philosophy, the body's technological processes, no matter that they resided in the smallest parts and the most subtle motions, were to be discerned through the ingenious application of what he termed 'modern industry', which had produced the 'artificial Eys' (microscopes) with which to peer into the body.[43] The body as a mechanism was now itself subject to mechanism, a technique, a field of productive labour which relied on ingenious invention and instrumentation. Measurement took over from description, the 'power' of the soul gave way to a sequence of mechanical movements.[44] Hierarchy was overthrown, and the mystery of continental interiors replaced by the silent forces of springs, wheels, and cogs, operating as a contrived whole. The modern body had emerged: a body which worked rather than existed.

3

Second Meditation: Of the Nature of the Human Mind; and that it is Easier to Know than the Body

René Descartes

The Meditation of yesterday has filled my mind with so many doubts that it is no longer in my power to forget them.[1] And yet I do not see how I shall be able to resolve them; and, as though I had suddenly fallen into very deep water, I am so taken unawares that I can neither put my feet firmly down on the bottom nor swim to keep myself on the surface. I make an effort, nevertheless, and follow afresh the same path upon which I entered yesterday, in keeping away from everything of which I can conceive the slightest doubt, just as if I knew that it was absolutely false; and I shall continue always in this path until I have encountered something which is certain, or at least, if I can do nothing else, until I have learned with certainty that there is nothing certain in the world.

Archimedes, in order to take the terrestrial globe from its place and move it to another, asked only for a point which was fixed and assured.[2] So also, I shall have the right to entertain high hopes, if I am fortunate enough to find only one thing which is certain and indubitable.

I suppose therefore that all the things I see are false; I persuade myself that none of those things ever existed that my deceptive memory represents to me; I suppose I have no senses; I believe that body, figure, extension, movement and place are only fictions of my mind. What, then, shall be considered true? Perhaps only this, that there is nothing certain in the world.

But how do I know there is not some other thing, different from those I have just judged to be uncertain, about which one could not have the slightest doubt? Is there not a God, or some other power, which puts these thoughts into my mind? But that is unnecessary, for perhaps I am capable of producing them myself. Myself, then, at least am I not something? But I have already denied that I have any senses or any body. I hesitate, however, for what follows from that? Am I so dependent on body and senses that I cannot exist without them? But I had persuaded myself that there was nothing at all in the world: no sky, no earth, no minds or bodies; was I not, therefore, also persuaded that I did not exist? No indeed; I existed without doubt, by the fact that I was persuaded, or indeed by the mere fact that I thought at all. But there is some deceiver both very powerful and very cunning, who constantly uses all his wiles to deceive me. There is therefore no doubt that I exist, if he deceives me; and let him deceive me as much as he likes, he can never cause me to be nothing, so long as I think I am something. So that, after having thought carefully about it, and having scrupulously examined everything, one must then, in conclusion, take as assured that the proposition: *I am, I exist*, is necessarily true, every time I express it or conceive of it in my mind.

But I, who am certain that I am, do not yet know clearly enough what I am; so that henceforth I must take great care not imprudently to take some other object for myself, and thus avoid going astray in the knowledge which I maintain to be more certain and evident than all I have had hitherto.

For this reason, I shall now consider afresh what I thought I was before I entered into these last thoughts; and I shall retrench from my former opinions everything that can be invalidated by the reasons I have already put forward, so that absolutely nothing remains except that which is entirely indubitable. What, then, did I formerly think I was? I thought I was a man. But what is a man? Shall I say rational animal? No indeed: for it would be necessary next to inquire what is meant by animal, and what by rational, and, in this way, from one single question, we would fall unwittingly into an infinite number of others, more difficult and awkward than the first, and I would not wish to waste the little time and leisure remaining to me by using it to unravel subtleties of this kind. But I shall rather stop to consider here the thoughts which sprang up hitherto spontaneously in my mind, and which were inspired by my own nature alone, when I applied myself to the consideration of my being. I considered myself, firstly, as having a face, hands, arms, and the whole machine made up of flesh and bones, such as it appears in a corpse and which I designated by the name of body. I thought, furthermore, that I ate, walked, had feelings and thought, and I referred all these actions to the soul; but I did not stop to consider what this soul was, or at least, if I did, I imagined it was something extremely rare and subtle, like a wind, flame or vapour, which permeated and spread through my most substantial parts. As far as the body was concerned, I was in no doubt as to its nature, for I thought I knew it quite distinctly, and, if I had wished to explain it according to the notions I had of it, I would have described it in this way: by body, I understand all that can be terminated by some figure; that can be contained in some place and fill a space in such a way that any other body is excluded from it; that can be perceived, either by touch, sight, hearing, taste or smell; that can be moved in many ways, not of itself, but by something foreign to it by which it is touched and from which it receives the impulse. For as to having in itself the power to move, to feel and to think, I did not believe in any way that these advantages might be attributed to corporeal nature; on the contrary, I was somewhat astonished to see that such faculties were to be found in certain bodies.

But as to myself, who am I, now that I suppose there is someone who is extremely powerful and, if I may so say, malicious and cunning, who employs all his efforts and industry to deceive me? Can I be sure of having the least of all the characteristics that I have attributed above to the nature of bodies? I pause to think about it carefully, I turn over all these things in my mind, and I cannot find one of which I can say that it is in me. There is no need for me to stop and enumerate them. Let us pass, then, to the attributes of the soul, and see if there are any of these in me. The first are eating and walking; but if it is true that I have no body, it is true also that I cannot walk or eat. Sensing is another attribute, but again this is impossible without the body; besides, I have frequently believed that I perceived in my sleep many things which I observed, on awakening, I had not in reality perceived. Another attribute is thinking, and I here discover an attribute which does belong to me; this alone cannot be detached from me. *I am, I exist*: this is certain; but for how long? For as long as I think, for it might perhaps happen, if I ceased to think, that I would at the same time cease to be or to exist. I now admit nothing which is not necessarily true: I am therefore, precisely speaking, only a thing which thinks, that is to say, a mind, understanding, or reason, terms whose significance was hitherto unknown to me. I am, however, a real thing, and really existing; but what thing? I have already said it: a thing which thinks. And what else? I will stir up my imagination in order to discover if I am not something more. I am not this assemblage of limbs called the human body; I am not a thin and penetrating air spread through all these members; I am not a wind, a breath of air, a vapour, or anything at all that I can invent or imagine, since I have supposed that all those things were nothing, and yet, without changing this supposition, I find I am nevertheless certain that I am something.

But also, it may be that these same things that I suppose do not exist, because they are unknown to me, are not in truth different from me whom I know. I do not know; I am not debating this point now. I can judge only of things which are known to me: I have recognised that I exist, and I, who recognise I exist, seek to discover what I am. It is most certain, however, that this notion and knowledge of myself, thus precisely taken, do not depend on things the existence of which is not yet known to me; neither, consequently, and *a fortiori*, do they depend on any of those which are feigned and invented by the imagination.[3] And even these terms feigning and imagining, warn me of my error; for I should be feigning, in truth, if I were to imagine that I am anything, since imagining is nothing other than contemplating the figure or image of a corporeal object. Now I know already for certain that I exist, and at the same time that it is possible that all those images, and, in general, all the things one relates to the nature of body, are nothing but dreams or chimera.

From this I see clearly that it is as unreasonable for me to say: I shall stir up my imagination in order to know more distinctly what I am, as to say: I am now awake, and I perceive something real and true; but, because I do not perceive it clearly enough, I shall go to sleep expressly so that my dreams may show this object to me with greater truth and clearness. And in this way, I recognise certainly that nothing of all that I can understand by means of imagination belongs to this knowledge that I have of myself, and that it is necessary to call one's mind back and turn it away from this mode of thinking, so that it can itself recognise its own nature very distinctly.

But what, then, am I? A thing that thinks. What is a thing that thinks? That is to say, a thing that doubts, perceives, affirms, denies, wills, does not will, that imagines also, and which feels. Indeed this is not a little, if all these properties belong to my nature. But why should they not so belong? Am I not still this same being who doubts of almost everything; who nevertheless understands and conceives certain things; who affirms those alone to be true; who denies all the rest; who wishes and desires to know more of them and does not wish to be deceived; who imagines many things, even sometimes in spite of himself; and who also perceives many, as if through the intermediary of the organs of the body? Is there nothing in all this which is as true as it is certain that I am, and that I exist, even though I were always to be sleeping, and though he who has given me my being should use all his power to deceive me? Is there also any one of these attributes which may be distinguished from my thought, or that one could say was separate from me? For it is so self-evident that it is I who doubt, who understand and who wish, that there is no need here to add anything to explain it. And I have equally certainly the power to imagine, for even though it may be (as I have supposed above) that the things I imagine are not true, nevertheless, this capacity for imagining does not cease to be really in me, and forms part of my thinking. Finally, I am the same being who senses, that is to say who apprehends and knows things, as by the sense-organs, since, in truth, I see light, hear noise and feel heat. But it will be said that these appearances are false and that I am dreaming. Let it be so; all the same, at least, it is very certain that it seems to me that I see light, hear a noise and feel heat; and this is properly what in me is called perceiving and this, taken in this precise sense, is nothing other than thinking. From this I begin to know what I am, a little more clearly and distinctly than hitherto.

But I cannot help believing that corporeal objects, whose images are formed by my thoughts, and which come under the senses, are more distinctly known to me than that, I know not what, part of me which does not fall within the grasp of the imagination; although in truth it may seem very strange that things I find doubtful and distant, are more dearly and easily known to me than those which are true and certain, and which belong to my own nature. But I see very well how it is: my mind likes to wander, and cannot yet contain itself within the precise limits of truth. Let us therefore give it its head once more, so that, later on, tightening the rein gently and opportunely, we shall the more easily be able to govern and control it.

Let us begin by considering the most common things, those which we believe we understand the most distinctly, namely, the bodies we touch and see. I am not speaking of bodies in general, for these general notions are usually more confused, but of one body in particular. Let us take, for example, this piece of wax which has just been taken from the hive; it has not yet lost the sweetness of the honey it contained; it still retains something of the smell of the flowers from which it was gathered; its colour, shape and size, are apparent; it is hard, cold, it is tangible; and if you tap it, it will emit a sound. So, all the things by which a body can be known distinctly are to be found together in this one.

But, as I am speaking, it is placed near a flame: what remained of its taste is dispelled, the smell disappears, its colour changes, it loses its shape, it grows bigger, becomes liquid, warms up, one can hardly touch it, and although one taps it, it will no longer make any sound. Does the wax remain after this change? One must admit that it does remain, and no one can deny it. What, then, was it that I knew in this piece of wax with such distinctness? Certainly it could be nothing of all the things which I perceived by means of the senses, for everything which fell under taste, smell, sight, touch or hearing, is changed, and yet the same wax remains. Perhaps it was what I now think, namely, that the wax was not the sweetness of honey, or the pleasant smell of flowers, the whiteness, or the shape, nor the sound, but only a body which a little earlier appeared to me in these forms, and which is now to be perceived in other forms. But to speak precisely, what is it that I imagine when I conceive it in this way? Let us consider it attentively, and setting aside everything that does not belong to the wax, let us see what remains. Indeed nothing remains, except something extended, flexible and malleable. Now, what does that mean: flexible and malleable? Is it not that I imagine that this wax, being round, is capable of becoming square, and of passing from a square to a triangular figure? No indeed, it is not that, for I conceive of it as capable of undergoing an infinity of similar changes, and as I could not embrace infinity by my imagination, consequently this conception I have of the wax is not the product of the faculty of imagination.

What, now, is this extension? Is it not also unknown, since it increases as the wax melts, is greater when the wax is completely melted, and very much greater still when the heat is intensified; and I should not conceive clearly and to truth what the wax is, if I did not remember that it is capable of taking on more variations in extension than I have ever imagined. I must therefore agree that I could not even conceive by means of the imagination what this wax is, and that it is my understanding alone which conceives it. I say this piece of wax in particular, for, as to wax in general, this is still more evident. Now, what is this wax, which cannot be conceived except by the understanding or mind? Indeed it is the same which I see, touch, imagine, and which I knew from the start. But, and this is to be noted, the perception of it, or the action by which one perceives it, is not an act of sight, or touch, or of imagination, and has never been, although it seemed so hitherto, but only an intuition of the mind, which may be imperfect and confused, as it was formerly, or else clear and distinct, as it is at present according as my attention directs itself more or less to the elements which it contains and of which it is composed.

However, I am greatly astonished when I consider the weakness of my mind, and its proneness to error. For although, without speaking, I consider all this in my own mind, yet words stop me, and I am almost led into error by the terms of ordinary language. For we say we see the same wax if it is put before us, and not that we judge it to be the same, because it has the same colour and shape: whence I would almost conclude that one knows the wax by the eyesight, and not by the intuition of the mind alone. If I chance to look out of a window on to men passing in the street, I do not fail to say, on seeing them, that I see men, just as I say that I see the wax; and yet, what do I see from this window, other than hats and cloaks, which can cover ghosts or dummies who move only by means of springs? But I judge them to be really men, and thus I understand, by the sole power of judgement which resides in my mind, what I believed I saw with my eyes.

A man who wishes to lift his knowledge above the common, must feel ashamed to seek occasions for doubting from the forms and terms of common speech. I prefer to avoid this and to go on to consider whether I conceived more evidently and perfectly what the wax is when I first saw it, and believed I knew it by means of my external senses, or at the very least by the common sense, as it is called, that is to say by the imaginative faculty, than I conceive it at present, after having more carefully examined what it is and by what means it can be known. Indeed, it would be ridiculous to have any doubt on this point. For what was there in that first perception that was distinct and evident, and which could not be perceived in the same way by the senses of the least of animals? But when I distinguish the wax from its external forms, and, just as if I had removed its garments, I consider it quite naked, it is certain that, although some error in my judgement may be encountered, I cannot conceive of it in this way without possessing a human mind.

But finally, what shall I say of this mind, that is to say of myself? For so far I admit in myself nothing other than a mind. What shall I say of myself, I ask, I who seem to conceive so clearly and distinctly this piece of wax? Do I not know myself, not only with much more truth and certainty, but also more distinctly and clearly? For if I judge that the wax is, or exists, because I see it, certainly it follows much more evidently from the same fact that I myself am, or exist. For it may well be that what I see is not in effect wax; it may also be that I do not even have eyes with which to see anything; but it cannot be that, when I see or (which I no longer distinguish) think I see, I, who think, am nothing. Similarly, if I judge that the wax exists because I touch it, the same conclusion follows, namely, that I am. And if I judge thus because my imagination persuades me that it is so, or on account of any other cause whatever, I shall still draw the same conclusion. And what I have said here about the wax can apply to all the other things external to me.

Now, if my notion and knowledge of the wax seems to be more precise and distinct after it has become known to me not only by sight or touch, but also in many other ways, with how much greater distinctness, clarity and precision must I know myself, since all the means which help me to know and perceive the nature of wax, or of any other body, prove much more easily and evidently the nature of my mind? And so many other things besides are to be found in the mind itself, which can contribute to the clarification of nature, that those which depend on the body, such as these mentioned here, scarcely deserve to be taken into account.

But now I have come back imperceptibly to the point I sought; for, since it is now known to me that, properly speaking, we perceive bodies only by the understanding which is in us, and not by the imagination, or the senses, and that we do not perceive them through seeing them or touching them, but only because we conceive them in thought, I know clearly that there is nothing more easy for to me know than my own mind. But, because it is almost impossible to rid oneself so quickly of a long-held opinion, I should do well to pause at this point, so that, by long meditation, I may imprint this new knowledge more deeply in my memory.

4

A Case of Hysteria: Fräulein Elisabeth von R.

Sigmund Freud

In the autumn of 1892 I was asked by a doctor I knew to examine a young lady who had been suffering for more than two years from pains in her legs and who had difficulties in walking. When making this request he added that he thought the case was one of hysteria. [...] He told me that he knew the family slightly and that during the last few years it had met with many misfortunes and not much happiness. First the patient's father had died, then her mother had had to undergo a serious eye-operation and soon afterwards a married sister succumbed to a heart-affection of long standing after a confinement. In all these troubles and in all the sick-nursing involved, the largest share had fallen to our patient.

My first interview with this young woman of twenty-four years of age did not help me to make much further progress in understanding the case. She seemed intelligent and mentally normal and bore her troubles, which interfered with her social life and pleasures, with a cheerful air – the *belle indifférence* of a hysteric,[1] I could not help thinking. She walked with the upper part of her body bent forward, but without making use of any support. Her gait was not of any recognised pathological type, and moreover was by no means strikingly bad. All that was apparent was that she complained of great pain both in walking and in standing, and that after a short time she had to rest. The pain was of an indefinite character; I gathered that it was something in the nature of a painful fatigue. A fairly large, ill-defined area of the anterior surface of the right thigh was indicated as the focus of the pains, from which they most often radiated and where they reached their greatest intensity. In this area the skin and muscles were also particularly sensitive to pressure and pinching (though the prick of a needle was, if anything, met with a certain amount of unconcern). This hyperalgesia of the skin and muscles was not restricted to this area but could be observed more or less over the whole of both legs.[2] There were no other symptoms, so there was no ground for suspecting the presence of any serious organic affection. The disorder had developed gradually during the previous two years and varied greatly in intensity.

I did not find it easy to arrive at a diagnosis, but I decided for two reasons to assent to the one proposed by my colleague [viz. that it was a case of hysteria]. In the first place I was struck by the indefiniteness of all the descriptions of the character of her pains given to me by the patient, who was nevertheless a highly intelligent person. A patient suffering from organic pains will, unless he is neurotic in addition, describe them definitely and calmly. He will say, for instance, that they are shooting pains, that they occur at certain intervals, that they extend from this place to that and that they seem to him to be brought on by one thing or another. Again, when a neurasthenic[3] describes his pains, he gives an impression of being engaged on a difficult intellectual task to which his strength is quite unequal. His features are strained and distorted as though under the influence of a distressing affect.[4] His voice grows more shrill and he struggles to find a means of expression. He rejects any description of his pains proposed by the physician, even though it may turn out afterwards to have been unquestionably apt. He is clearly of opinion that language is too poor to find words for his sensations and that those sensations are something unique and previously unknown, of which it would be quite impossible to give an exhaustive description. All this is because his pains have attracted his whole attention to themselves. Fräulein von R. behaved in quite an opposite way; and we are driven to conclude that, since she nevertheless attached sufficient importance to her symptoms, her attention must be dwelling on something else, of which the pains were only an accessory phenomenon – probably on thoughts and feelings, therefore, which were connected with them.

But there is a second factor which is even more decisively in favour of this view of the pains. If one stimulates an area sensitive to pain in someone with an organic illness or in a neurasthenic, the patient's face takes on an expression of discomfort or physical pain. Moreover he flinches and draws back from the examination and resists it. In the case of Fräulein von R., however, if one pressed or pinched the hyperalgesic skin and muscles of her legs, her face assumed a peculiar expression, which was one of pleasure rather than pain. She cried out – and I could not help thinking that it was as though she was having a voluptuous tickling sensation – her face flushed, she threw back her head and shut her eyes and her body bent backwards. None of this was very exaggerated but it was distinctly noticeable, and it could only be reconciled with the view that her disorder was hysterical, and that the stimulation had touched upon a hysterogenic zone.[5]

Her expression of face did not fit in with the pain which was ostensibly set up by the pinching of her muscles and skin; it was probably more in harmony with the subject-matter of the thoughts which lay concealed behind the pain and which had been aroused in her by the stimulation of the parts of the body associated with those thoughts. I had repeatedly observed expressions of similar significance in undoubted cases of hysteria, when a stimulus was applied to their hyperalgesic zones. Her other gestures were evidently very slight hints of a hysterical attack.

[...]

When one starts upon a cathartic treatment of this kind, the first question one asks oneself is whether the patient herself is aware of the origin and the precipitating cause of her illness. If so, no special technique is required to enable her to reproduce the story of her illness. The interest shown in her by the physician, the understanding of her which he allows her to feel and the hopes of recovery he holds out to her – all these will decide the patient to yield up her secret. From the beginning it seemed to me probable that Fräulein Elisabeth was conscious of the basis of her illness, that what she had in her consciousness was only a secret and not a foreign body. Looking at her, one could not help thinking of the poet's words:

Das Mäskchen da weissagt verborgnen Sinn.[6]

In the first instance, therefore, I was able to do without hypnosis, with the reservation, however, that I could make use of it later if in the course of her confession material arose to the elucidation of which her memory was unequal. Thus it came about that in this, the first full-length analysis of a hysteria undertaken by me, I arrived at a procedure which I later developed into a regular method and employed deliberately. This procedure was one of clearing away the pathogenic psychical material layer by layer, and we liked to compare it with the technique of excavating a buried city. I would begin by getting the patient to tell me what was known to her and I would carefully note the points at which some train of thought remained obscure or some link in the causal chain seemed to be missing. And afterwards I would penetrate into deeper layers of her memories at these points by carrying out an investigation under hypnosis or by the use of some similar technique. The whole work was, of course, based on the expectation that it would be possible to establish a completely adequate set of determinants for the events concerned. I shall discuss presently the methods used for the deep investigation.

The story which Fräulein Elisabeth told of her illness was a wearisome one, made up of many different painful experiences. [...] The first mention of a young man opened up a new vein of ideas the contents of which I now gradually extracted. It was a question here of a secret, for she had initiated no one, apart from a common friend, into her relations with the young man and the hopes attached to them.[7]

After her father had fallen seriously ill and she had been so much taken up with looking after him, Fräulein Elisabeth's meetings with her friend became more and more rare. The evening which she had first remembered represented what had actually been the climax of her feeling; but even then there had been no *éclaircissement* between them. On that occasion she had allowed herself to be persuaded, by the insistence of her family and of her father himself; to go to a party at which she was likely to meet him. She had wanted to hurry home early but had been pressed to stay and had given way when he promised to see her home. She had never had such warm feelings towards him as while he was accompanying her that evening. But when she arrived home late in this blissful frame of mind, she found her father was worse and reproached herself most bitterly for having sacrificed so much time to her own enjoyment. This was the last time she left her sick father for a whole evening. She seldom met her friend after this. But this disappointment in her first love still hurt her whenever she thought of him.

It was therefore in this relationship and in the scene described above in which it culminated that I could look for the causes of her first hysterical pains. The contrast between the blissful feelings she had allowed herself to enjoy on that occasion and the worsening of her father's state which had met her on her return home constituted a conflict, a situation of incompatibility. The outcome of this conflict was that the erotic idea was repressed from association and the affect attaching to that idea was used to intensify or revive a physical pain which was present simultaneously or shortly before. Thus it was an instance of the mechanism of conversion for the purpose of defence.

I therefore questioned her about the causes and circumstances of the first appearance of the pains. By way of answer her thoughts turned towards her summer visit to the health resort before her journey to Gastein, and a number of scenes turned up once more which had not been treated very completely. She recalled her state of feeling at the time, her exhaustion after her anxieties about her mother's eyesight and after having nursed her at the time of her operation, and her final despair of a lonely girl like her being able to get any enjoyment out of life or achieve anything in it. Till then she had thought herself strong enough to be able to do without the help of a man; but she was now overcome by a sense of her weakness as a woman and by a longing for love in which, to quote her own words, her frozen nature began to melt. In this mood she was deeply affected by her second sister's happy marriage. It was no doubt to be regretted that the second pregnancy followed so soon after the first, and Elisabeth knew that this was the reason of her sister's illness; but how willingly she bore it because he was its cause. On the occasion of the walk which was so intimately connected with Elisabeth's pains, her brother-in-law had at first been unwilling to join in it and had wanted to stay by his sick wife. She, however, persuaded him with a look to go with them, because she thought it would give Elisabeth pleasure. Elisabeth remained in his company all through the walk. They discussed every kind of subject, among them the most intimate ones. She found herself in complete agreement with everything he said, and a desire to have a husband like him became very strong in her. Then, a few days later, came the scene on the morning after the departure of her sister and brother-in-law when she made her way to the place with a view, which had been a favourite object of their walks. There she sat down and dreamt once again of enjoying such happiness as her sister's and of finding a husband who would know how to capture her heart like this brother-in-law of hers. She was in pain when she stood up, but it passed off once more. It was not until the afternoon, when she had had the warm bath, that the pains broke out, and she was never again free from them.

It had inevitably become clear to me long since what all this was about; but the patient, deep in her bitter-sweet memories, seemed not to notice the end to which she was steering, and continued to reproduce her recollections. She went on to her visit to Gastein, the anxiety with which she looked forward to every letter, finally the bad news about her sister. [...] Her memories now went on to their arrival in Vienna [...] the short journey from Vienna to the summer resort in its neighbourhood where her sister lived, their reaching there in the evening [...], how her brother-in-law was not there to receive them, and how they stood before the bed and looked at her sister as she lay there dead. At that moment of dreadful certainty that her beloved sister was dead without bidding them farewell and without her having eased her last days with her care – at that very moment another thought had shot through Elisabeth's mind, and now forced itself irresistibly upon her once more, like a flash of lightning in the dark: 'Now he is free again and I can be his wife'.

Everything was now clear. The analyst's labours were richly rewarded. The concepts of the 'fending off' of an incompatible idea, of the genesis of hysterical symptoms through the conversion of psychical excitations into something physical and the formation of a separate psychical group through the act of will which led to the fending-off – all these things were, in that moment, brought before my eyes in concrete form. Thus and in no other way had things come about in the present case. This girl felt towards her brother-in-law a tenderness whose acceptance into consciousness was resisted by her whole moral being. She succeeded in sparing herself the painful conviction that she loved her sister's husband, by inducing physical pains in herself instead; and it was in the moments when this conviction sought to force itself upon her (on her walk with him, during her morning reverie, in the bath, by her sister's bedside) that her pains had come on, thanks to successful conversion. At the time when I started her treatment the group of ideas relating to her love had already been separated from her knowledge. Otherwise she would never, I think, have agreed to embarking on the treatment. The resistance with which she had repeatedly met the reproduction of scenes which operated traumatically corresponded in fact to the energy with which the incompatible idea had been forced out of her associations.

The period that followed, however, was a hard one for the physician. The recovery of this repressed idea had a shattering effect on the poor girl. She cried aloud when I put the situation drily before her with the words: 'So for a long time you had been in love with your brother-in-law'. She complained at this moment of the most frightful pains, and made one last desperate effort to reject the explanation: it was not true, I had talked her into it, it *could* not be true, she was incapable of such wickedness, she could never forgive herself for it. It was easy to prove to her that what she herself had told me admitted of no other interpretation. But it was a long time before my two pieces of consolation – that we are not responsible for our feelings, and that her behaviour, the fact that she had fallen ill in these circumstances, was sufficient evidence of her moral character – it was a long time before these consolations of mine made any impression on her.

[...]

While Fräulein Elisabeth von R. was nursing her father, as we have seen, she for the first time developed a hysterical symptom – a pain in a particular area of her right thigh. It was possible by means of analysis to find an adequate elucidation of the mechanism of the symptom. It happened at a moment when the circle of ideas embracing her duties to her sick father came into conflict with the content of the erotic desire she was feeling at the time. Under the pressure of lively self-reproaches she decided in favour of the former, and in doing so brought about her hysterical pain. According to the view suggested by the conversion theory of hysteria what happened may be described as follows. She repressed her erotic idea from consciousness and transformed the amount of its affect into physical sensations of pain. It did not become clear whether she was presented with this first conflict on one occasion only or on several; the latter alternative is the more likely. An exactly similar conflict – though of higher ethical significance and even more clearly established by the analysis – developed once more some years later and led to an intensification of the same pains and to an extension beyond their original limits. Once again it was a circle of ideas of an erotic kind that came into conflict with all her moral ideas; for her inclinations centred upon her brother-in-law, and, both during her sister's lifetime and after her death, the thought of being attracted by precisely this man was totally unacceptable to her. The analysis provided detailed information about this conflict, which constituted the central point in the history of the illness. The germs of the patient's feeling for her brother-in-law may have been present for a long time; its development was favoured by physical exhaustion owing to more sick-nursing and by moral exhaustion owing to disappointments extending over many years. The coldness of her nature began to yield and she admitted to herself her need for a man's love. During the several weeks which she passed in his company at the health resort her erotic feelings as well as her pains reached their full height.

The analysis, moreover, gave evidence that during the same period the patient was in a special psychical state. The connection of this state with her erotic feelings and her pains seems to make it possible to understand what happened on the lines of the conversion theory. It is, I think, safe to say that at that time the patient did not become clearly conscious of her feelings for her brother-in-law, powerful though they were, except on a few occasions, and then only momentarily. If it had been otherwise, she would also inevitably have become conscious of the contradiction between those feelings and her moral ideas and would have experienced mental torments like those I saw her go through after our analysis. She had no recollection of any such sufferings; she had avoided them. It followed that her feelings themselves did not become clear to her. At that time, as well as during the analysis, her love for her brother-in-law, was present in her consciousness like a foreign body, without having entered into relationship with the rest of her ideational life. With regard to these feelings she was in the peculiar situation of knowing and at the same time not knowing.

5

The Incitement to Discourse

Michel Foucault

The seventeenth century was the beginning of an age of repression emblematic of what we call the bourgeois societies, an age which perhaps we still have not completely left behind. Calling sex by its name thereafter became more difficult and more costly. As if in order to gain mastery over it in reality, it had first been necessary to subjugate it at the level of language, control its free circulation in speech, expunge it from the things that were said, and extinguish the words that rendered it too visibly present. And even these prohibitions, it seems, were afraid to name it. Without even having to pronounce the word, modern prudishness was able to ensure that one did not speak of sex, merely through the interplay of prohibitions that referred back to one another: instances of muteness which, by dint of saying nothing, imposed silence. Censorship.

Yet when one looks back over these last three centuries with their continual transformations, things appear in a very different light: around and apropos of sex, one sees a veritable discursive explosion. We must be clear on this point, however. It is quite possible that there was an expurgation – and a very rigorous one – of the authorised vocabulary. It may indeed be true that a whole rhetoric of allusion and metaphor was codified. Without question, new rules of propriety screened out some words: there was a policing of statements. A control over enunciations as well: where and when it was not possible to talk about such things became much more strictly defined; in which circumstances, among which speakers, and within which social relationships. Areas were thus established, if not of utter silence, at least of tact and discretion: between parents and children, for instance, or teachers and pupils, or masters and domestic servants. This almost certainly constituted a whole restrictive economy, one that was incorporated into that politics of language and speech – spontaneous on the one hand, concerted on the other – which accompanied the social redistributions of the classical period.

At the level of discourses and their domains, however, practically the opposite phenomenon occurred.[1] There was a steady proliferation of discourses concerned with sex – specific discourses, different from one another both by their form and by their object: a discursive ferment that gathered momentum from the eighteenth century onward. Here I am thinking not so much of the

41

probable increase in 'illicit' discourses, that is, discourses of infraction that crudely named sex by way of insult or mockery of the new code of decency; the tightening up of the rules of decorum likely did produce, as a counter-effect, a valorisation and intensification of indecent speech. But more important was the multiplication of discourses concerning sex in the field of exercise of power itself: an institutional incitement to speak about it, and to do so more and more; a determination on the part of the agencies of power to hear it spoken about, and to cause it to speak through explicit articulation and endlessly accumulated detail.

Consider the evolution of the Catholic pastoral and the sacrament of penance after the Council of Trent.[2] Little by little, the nakedness of the questions formulated by the confession manuals of the Middle Ages, and a good number of those still in use in the seventeenth century, was veiled. One avoided entering into that degree of detail [...] believed indispensable for the confession to be complete: description of the respective positions of the partners, the postures assumed, gestures, places touched, caresses, the precise moment of pleasure – an entire painstaking review of the sexual act in its very unfolding. Discretion was advised, with increasing emphasis. The greatest reserve was counselled when dealing with sins against purity: 'This matter is similar to pitch, for, however one might handle it, even to cast it far from oneself, it sticks nonetheless, and always soils'.[3] And later, Alfonso de' Liguori prescribed starting – and possibly going no further, especially when dealing with children – with questions that were 'roundabout and vague'.[4]

But while the language may have been refined, the scope of the confession – the confession of the flesh – continually increased. This was partly because the Counter Reformation busied itself with stepping up the rhythm of the yearly confession in the Catholic countries, and because it tried to impose meticulous rules of self-examination; but above all, because it attributed more and more importance in penance – and perhaps at the expense of some other sins – to all the insinuations of the flesh: thoughts, desires, voluptuous imaginings, delectations, combined movements of the body and the soul; henceforth all this had to enter, in detail, into the process of confession and guidance. According to the new pastoral, sex must not be named imprudently, but its aspects, its correlations, and its effects must be pursued down to their slenderest ramifications: a shadow in a daydream, an image too slowly dispelled, a badly exorcised complicity between the body's mechanics and the mind's complacency: everything had to be told. A twofold evolution tended to make the flesh into the root of all evil, shifting the most important moment of transgression from the act itself to the stirrings – so difficult to perceive and formulate – of desire. For this was an evil that afflicted the whole man, and in the most secret of forms: 'Examine diligently, therefore, all the faculties of your soul: memory, understanding, and will. Examine with precision all your senses as well. ... Examine, moreover, all your thoughts, every word you speak, and all your actions. Examine even unto your dreams, to know if, once awakened, you did not give them your consent. And finally, do not think that in so sensitive and perilous a matter as this, there is anything trivial or insignificant.'[5] Discourse, therefore, had to trace the meeting line of the body and the soul, following all its meanderings: beneath the surface of the sins, it would lay bare the unbroken nervure of the flesh. Under the authority of a language that had been carefully expurgated so that it was no longer directly named, sex was taken charge of, tracked down as it were, by a discourse that aimed to allow it no obscurity, no respite.

It was here, perhaps, that the injunction, so peculiar to the West, was laid down for the first time, in the form of a general constraint. I am not talking about the obligation to admit to violations of the laws of sex, as required by traditional penance; but of the nearly infinite task of telling – telling oneself and another, as often as possible, everything that might concern the interplay of innumerable pleasures, sensations, and thoughts which, through the body and the soul, had some affinity with sex. This scheme for transforming sex into discourse had been devised long before in an ascetic and monastic setting. The seventeenth century made it into a rule for everyone. It would seem in actual fact that it could scarcely have applied to any but a tiny elite; the great majority of the faithful who only went to confession on rare occasions in the course of the year escaped such complex prescriptions. But the important point no doubt is that this obligation was decreed, as an ideal at least, for every good Christian. An imperative was established: Not only will you confess to acts contravening the law, but you will seek to transform your desire, your every desire, into discourse. Insofar as possible, nothing was meant to elude this dictum, even if the words it employed had to be carefully neutralised. The Christian pastoral prescribed as a fundamental duty the task of passing everything having to do with sex through the endless mill of speech.[6] The forbidding of certain words, the decency of expressions, all the censorings of vocabulary, might well have been only secondary devices compared to that great subjugation: ways of rendering it morally acceptable and technically useful.

One could plot a line going straight from seventeenth-century pastoral to what became its projection in literature, 'scandalous' literature at that. 'Tell everything', the directors would say time and again: 'not only consummated acts, but sensual touchings, all impure gazes, all obscene remarks … all consenting thoughts'.[7] Sade takes up the injunction in words that seem to have been retranscribed from the treatises of spiritual direction: 'Your narrations must be decorated with the most numerous and searching details; the precise way and extent to which we may judge how the passion you describe relates to human manners and man's character is determined by your willingness to disguise no circumstance; and what is more, the least circumstance is apt to have an immense influence upon the procuring of that kind of sensory irritation we expect from your stories.'[8] And again at the end of the nineteenth century, the anonymous author of *My Secret Life* submitted to the same prescription; outwardly, at least, this man was doubtless a kind of traditional libertine; but he conceived the idea of complementing his life – which he had almost totally dedicated to sexual activity – with a scrupulous account of every one of its episodes. He sometimes excuses himself by stressing his concern to educate young people, this man who had eleven volumes published, in a printing of only a few copies, which were devoted to the least adventures, pleasures, and sensations of his sex. It is best to take him at his word when he lets into his text the voice of a pure imperative: 'I recount the facts, just as they happened, insofar as I am able to recollect them; this is all that I can do'; 'a secret life must not leave out anything; there is nothing to be ashamed of ... one can never know too much concerning human nature.'[9] The solitary author of *My Secret Life* often says, in order to justify his describing them, that his strangest practices undoubtedly were shared by thousands of men on the surface of the earth. But the guiding principle for the strangest of these practices, which was the fact of recounting them all, and in detail, from day to day, had been lodged in the heart of modern man for over two centuries. Rather than seeing in this singular man a courageous fugitive from a 'Victorianism' that would have compelled him to silence, I am inclined to think that, in an epoch dominated by (highly prolix) directives enjoining discretion and modesty, he was the most direct and in a way the most naïve representative of a plurisecular injunction to talk about sex. The historical accident would consist rather of the reticences of 'Victorian puritanism'; at any rate, they were a digression, a refinement, a tactical diversion in the great process of transforming sex into discourse.

This nameless Englishman will serve better than his queen as the central figure for a sexuality whose main features were already taking shape with the Christian pastoral. Doubtless, in contrast to the latter, for him it was a matter of augmenting the sensations he experienced with the details of what he said about them; like Sade, he wrote 'for his pleasure alone', in the strongest sense of the expression; he carefully mixed the editing and rereading of his text with erotic scenes which those writers' activities repeated, prolonged, and stimulated. But after all, the Christian pastoral also sought to produce specific effects on desire, by the mere fact of transforming it – fully and deliberately – into discourse: effects of mastery and detachment, to be sure, but also an effect of spiritual reconversion, of turning back to God, a physical effect of blissful suffering from feeling in one's body the pangs of temptation and the love that resists it. This is the essential thing: that Western man has been drawn for three centuries to the task of telling everything concerning his sex; that since the classical age there has been a constant optimisation and an increasing valorisation of the discourse on sex; and that this carefully analytical discourse was meant to yield multiple effects of displacement, intensification, reorientation, and modification of desire itself. Not only were the boundaries of what one could say about sex enlarged, and men compelled to hear it said; but more important, discourse was connected to sex by a complex organisation with varying effects, by a deployment that cannot be adequately explained merely by referring it to a law of prohibition. A censorship of sex? There was installed rather an apparatus for producing an ever greater quantity of discourse about sex, capable of functioning and taking effect in its very economy.

This technique might have remained tied to the destiny of Christian spirituality if it had not been supported and relayed by other mechanisms. In the first place, by a 'public interest'. Not a collective curiosity or sensibility; not a new mentality; but power mechanisms that functioned in such a way that discourse on sex – for reasons that will have to be examined – became essential. Toward the beginning of the eighteenth century, there emerged a political, economic, and technical incitement to talk about sex. And not so much in the form of a general theory of sexuality as in the form of analysis, stocktaking, classification, and specification, of quantitative or causal studies. This need to take sex 'into account', to pronounce a discourse on sex that would not derive from morality alone but from rationality as well, was sufficiently new that at first it wondered at itself and sought apologies for its own existence. How could a discourse based on reason speak of *that*? 'Rarely have philosophers directed a steady gaze to these objects situated between disgust and ridicule, where one must avoid both hypocrisy and scandal.'[10] And nearly a century later, the medical establishment, which one might have expected to be less surprised by what it was about to formulate, still stumbled at the moment of speaking: 'The darkness that envelops these facts, the shame and disgust they inspire, have always repelled the observer's gaze. ... For a long time I hesitated to introduce the loathsome picture into this study.'[11] What is essential is not in all these scruples, in the 'moralism' they betray, or in the hypocrisy one can suspect them of, but in the recognised necessity of overcoming this hesitation. One had to speak of sex; one had to speak publicly and in a manner that was not determined by the division between licit and illicit, even if the speaker maintained the distinction for himself (which is what these solemn and preliminary declarations were intended to show): one had to speak of it as of a thing to be not simply condemned or tolerated but managed, inserted into systems of utility, regulated for the greater good of all, made to function according to an optimum. Sex was not something one simply judged; it was a thing one administered. It was in the nature of a public potential; it called for management procedures; it had to be taken charge of by analytical discourses. In the eighteenth century, sex became a 'police' matter – in the full and strict sense given the term at the time: not the repression of disorder, but an ordered maximisation of collective and individual forces: 'We must consolidate and augment, through the wisdom of its regulations, the internal power of the state; and since this power consists not only in the Republic in

general, and in each of the members who constitute it, but also in the faculties
and talents of those belonging to it, it follows that the police must concern
themselves with these means and make them serve the public welfare. And
they can only obtain this result through the knowledge they have of those different assets.'[12] A policing of sex: that is, not the rigour of a taboo, but the
necessity of regulating sex through useful and public discourses.

A few examples will suffice. One of the great innovations in the techniques
of power in the eighteenth century was the emergence of 'population' as an
economic and political problem: population as wealth, population as man-
power or labour capacity, population balanced between its own growth and
the resources it commanded. Governments perceived that they were not dealing simply with subjects, or even with a 'people', but with a 'population', with
its specific phenomena and its peculiar variables: birth and death rates, life
expectancy, fertility, state of health, frequency of illnesses, patterns of diet
and habitation. All these variables were situated at the point where the characteristic movements of life and the specific effects of institutions intersected.
At the heart of this economic and political problem of population was sex: it
was necessary to analyse the birth-rate, the age of marriage, the legitimate and
illegitimate births, the precocity and frequency of sexual relations, the ways of
making them fertile or sterile, the effects of unmarried life or of the prohibitions, the impact of contraceptive practices – of those notorious 'deadly
secrets' which demographers on the eve of the Revolution knew were already
familiar to the inhabitants of the countryside.[13]

Of course, it had long been asserted that a country had to be populated if
it hoped to be rich and powerful; but this was the first time that a society had
affirmed, in a constant way, that its future and its fortune were tied not only
to the number and the uprightness of its citizens, to their marriage rules and
family organisation, but to the manner in which each individual made use of
his sex. Things went from ritual lamenting over the unfruitful debauchery of
the rich, bachelors, and libertines to a discourse in which the sexual conduct
of the population was taken both as an object of analysis and as a target of
intervention; there was a progression from the crudely populationist arguments of the mercantilist epoch to the much more subtle and calculated
attempts at regulation that tended to favour or discourage – according to the
objectives and exigencies of the moment – an increasing birthrate.

Through the political economy of population there was formed a whole
grid of observations regarding sex. There emerged the analysis of the modes
of sexual conduct, their determinations and their effects, at the boundary line
of the biological and the economic domains. There also appeared those systematic campaigns which, going beyond the traditional means – moral and
religious exhortations, fiscal measures – tried to transform the sexual conduct
of couples into a concerted economic and political behaviour. In time these
new measures would become anchorage points for the different varieties of

racism of the nineteenth and twentieth centuries. It was essential that the state know what was happening with its citizens' sex, and the use they made of it, but also that each individual be capable of controlling the use he made of it. Between the state and the individual, sex became an issue, and a public issue no less; a whole web of discourses, special knowledges, analyses, and injunctions settled upon it.

The situation was similar in the case of children's sex. It is often said that the classical period consigned it to an obscurity from which it scarcely emerged before the *Three Essays* or the beneficent anxieties of Little Hans.[14] It is true that a longstanding 'freedom' of language between children and adults, or pupils and teachers, may have disappeared. No seventeenth-century pedagogue would have publicly advised his disciple, as did Erasmus in his *Dialogues*, on the choice of a good prostitute. And the boisterous laughter that had accompanied the precocious sexuality of children for so long – and in all social classes, it seems – was gradually stifled. But this was not a plain and simple imposition of silence. Rather, it was a new regime of discourses. Not any less was said about it; on the contrary. But things were said in a different way; it was different people who said them, from different points of view, and in order to obtain different results. Silence itself – the things one declines to say, or is forbidden to name, the discretion that is required between different speakers is less the absolute limit of discourse, the other side from which it is separated by a strict boundary, than an element that functions alongside the things said, with them and in relation to them within over-all strategies. There is no binary division to be made between what one says and what one does not say; we must try to determine the different ways of not saying such things, how those who can and those who cannot speak of them are distributed, which type of discourse is authorised, or which form of discretion is required in either case. There is not one but many silences, and they are an integral part of the strategies that underlie and permeate discourses.

Take the secondary schools of the eighteenth century, for example. On the whole, one can have the impression that sex was hardly spoken of at all in these institutions. But one only has to glance over the architectural layout, the rules of discipline, and their whole internal organisation: the question of sex was a constant preoccupation. The builders considered it explicitly. The organisers took it permanently into account. All who held a measure of authority were placed in a state of perpetual alert, which the fixtures, the precautions taken, the interplay of punishments and responsibilities, never ceased to reiterate. The space for classes, the shape of the tables, the planning of the recreation lessons, the distribution of the dormitories (with or without partitions, with or without curtains), the rules for monitoring bedtime and sleep periods – all this referred, in the most prolix manner, to the sexuality of children.[15] What one might call the internal discourse of the institution – the one it employed to address itself, and which circulated among those who made it function – was largely based on the assumption that this sexuality existed, that it was precocious, active, and ever present. But this was not all: the sex of the schoolboy became in the course of the eighteenth century – and quite apart from that of adolescents in general – a public problem. Doctors counselled the directors and professors of educational establishments, but they also gave their opinions to families; educators designed projects which they submitted to the authorities; schoolmasters turned to students, made recommendations to them, and drafted for their benefit books of exhortation, full of moral and medical examples. Around the schoolboy and his sex there proliferated a whole literature of precepts, opinions, observations, medical advice, clinical cases, outlines for reform, and plans for ideal institutions.

It would be inexact to say that the pedagogical institution has imposed a ponderous silence on the sex of children and adolescents. On the contrary, since the eighteenth century it has multiplied the forms of discourse on the subject; it has established various points of implantation for sex; it has coded contents and qualified speakers. Speaking about children's, sex, inducing educators, physicians, administrators, and parents to speak of it, or speaking to them about it, causing children themselves to talk about it, and enclosing them in a web of discourses which sometimes address them, sometimes speak about them, or impose canonical bits of knowledge on them, or use them as a basis for constructing a science that is beyond their grasp – all this together enables us to link an intensification of the interventions of power to a multiplication of discourse. The sex of children and adolescents has become, since the eighteenth century, an important area of contention around which innumerable institutional devices and discursive strategies have been deployed. It may well be true that adults and children themselves were deprived of a certain way of speaking about sex, a mode that was disallowed as being too direct, crude, or coarse. But this was only the counterpart of other discourses, and perhaps the condition necessary in order for them to function, discourses that were interlocking, hierarchised, and all highly articulated around a cluster of power relations.

One could mention many other centres which in the eighteenth or nineteenth century began to produce discourses on sex. First there was medicine, via the 'nervous disorders'; next psychiatry, when it set out to discover the aetiology of mental illnesses, focusing its gaze first on 'excess', then onanism, then frustration, then 'frauds against procreation', but especially when it annexed the whole of the sexual perversions as its own province; criminal justice, too, which had long been concerned with sexuality, particularly in the form of 'heinous' crimes and crimes against nature, but which, toward the middle of the nineteenth century, broadened its jurisdiction to include petty offences, minor indecencies, insignificant perversions; and lastly, all those social controls, cropping up at the end of the last century, which screened the sexuality of couples, parents and children, dangerous and

endangered adolescents – undertaking to protect, separate, and forewarn, signalling perils everywhere, awakening people's attention, calling for diagnoses,
piling up reports, organising therapies. These sites radiated discourses aimed
at sex, intensifying people's awareness of it as a constant danger, and this in
turn created a further incentive to talk about it.

One day in 1867, a farm hand from the village of Lapcourt, who was
somewhat simple-minded, employed here then there, depending on the
season, living hand-to-mouth from a little charity or in exchange for the worst
sort of labour, sleeping in barns and stables, was turned in to the authorities.
At the border of a field, he had obtained a few caresses from a little girl, just
as he had done before and seen done by the village urchins round about him;
for, at the edge of the wood, or in the ditch by the road leading to Saint-
Nicolas, they would play the familiar game called 'curdled milk'. So he was
pointed out by the girl's parents to the mayor of the village, reported by the
mayor to the gendarmes, led by the gendarmes to the judge, who indicted him
and turned him over first to a doctor, then to two other experts who not only
wrote their report but also had it published.[16] What is the significant thing
about this story? The pettiness of it all; the fact that this everyday occurrence
in the life of village sexuality, these inconsequential bucolic pleasures, could
become, from a certain time, the object not only of a collective intolerance but
of a judicial action, a medical intervention, a careful clinical examination,
and an entire theoretical elaboration. The thing to note is that they went so
far as to measure the brainpan, study the facial bone structure, and inspect for
possible signs of degenerescence the anatomy of this personage who up to
that moment had been an integral part of village life; that they made him talk;
that they questioned him concerning his thoughts, inclinations, habits, sensations, and opinions. And then, acquitting him of any crime, they decided
finally to make him into a pure object of medicine and knowledge – an object
to be shut away till the end of his life in the hospital at Marieville, but also one
to be made known to the world of learning through a detailed analysis. One
can be fairly certain that during this same period the Lapcourt schoolmaster
was instructing the little villagers to mind their language and not talk about
all these things aloud. But this was undoubtedly one of the conditions
enabling the institutions of knowledge and power to overlay this everyday bit
of theatre with their solemn discourse. So it was that our society – and it was
doubtless the first in history to take such measures – assembled around
these timeless gestures, these barely furtive pleasures between simple-minded
adults and alert children, a whole machinery for speechifying, analysing, and
investigating.

Between the licentious Englishman, who earnestly recorded for his own
purposes the singular episodes of his secret life, and his contemporary, this
village halfwit who would give a few pennies to the little girls for favours the
older ones refused him, there was without doubt a profound connection: in

any case, from one extreme to the other, sex became something to say, and to say exhaustively in accordance with deployments that were varied, but all, in their own way, compelling. Whether in the form of a subtle confession in confidence or an authoritarian interrogation, sex – be it refined or rustic – had to be put into words. A great polymorphous injunction bound the Englishman and the poor Lorrainese peasant alike. As history would have it, the latter was named Jouy.[17]

Since the eighteenth century, sex has not ceased to provoke a kind of generalised discursive erethism.[18] And these discourses on sex did not multiply apart from or against power, but in the very space and as the means of its exercise. Incitements to speak were orchestrated from all quarters, apparatuses everywhere for listening and recording, procedures for observing, questioning, and formulating. Sex was driven out of hiding and constrained to lead a discursive existence. [...] It may well be that we talk about sex more than anything else; we set our minds to the task; we convince ourselves that we have never said enough on the subject, that, through inertia or submissiveness, we conceal from ourselves the blinding evidence, and that what is essential always eludes us, so that we must always start out once again in search of it. It is possible that where sex is concerned, the most long-winded, the most impatient of societies is our own.

But as this first overview shows, we are dealing less with a discourse on sex than with a multiplicity of discourses produced by a whole series of mechanisms operating in different institutions. The Middle Ages had organised around the theme of the flesh and the practice of penance a discourse that was markedly unitary. In the course of recent centuries, this relative uniformity was broken apart, scattered, and multiplied in an explosion of distinct discursivities which took form in demography, biology, medicine, psychiatry, psychology, ethics, pedagogy, and political criticism. More precisely, the secure bond that held together the moral theology of concupiscence and the obligation of confession (equivalent to the theoretical discourse on sex and its first-person formulation) was, if not broken, at least loosened and diversified: between the objectification of sex in rational discourses, and the movement by which each individual was set to the task of recounting his own sex, there has occurred, since the eighteenth century, a whole series of tensions, conflicts, efforts at adjustment, and attempts at retranscription. So it is not simply in terms of a continual extension that we must speak of this discursive growth; it should be seen rather as a dispersion of centres from which discourses emanated in a diversification of their forms, and the complex deployment of the network connecting them. Rather than a massive censorship, beginning with the verbal proprieties imposed by the Age of Reason, what was involved was a regulated and polymorphous incitement to discourse.

The objection will doubtless be raised that if so many stimulations and constraining mechanisms were necessary in order to speak of sex, this was because there reigned over everyone a certain fundamental prohibition; only definite necessities – economic pressures, political requirements – were able to lift this prohibition and open a few approaches to the discourse on sex, but these were limited and carefully coded; so much talk about sex, so many insistent devices contrived for causing it to be talked about – but under strict conditions: does this not prove that it was an object of secrecy, and more important, that there is still an attempt to keep it that way? But this often-stated theme, that sex is outside of discourse and that only the removing of an obstacle, the breaking of a secret, can clear the way leading to it, is precisely what needs to be examined. Does it not partake of the injunction by which discourse is provoked? Is it not with the aim of inciting people to speak of sex that it is made to mirror, at the outer limit of every actual discourse, something akin to a secret whose discovery is imperative, a thing abusively reduced to silence, and at the same time difficult and necessary, dangerous and precious to divulge? We must not forget that by making sex into that which, above all else, had to be confessed, the Christian pastoral always presented it as the disquieting enigma: not a thing which stubbornly shows itself, but one which always hides, the insidious presence that speaks in a voice so muted and often disguised that one risks remaining deaf to it. Doubtless the secret does not reside in that basic reality in relation to which all the incitements to speak of sex are situated – whether they try to force the secret; or whether in some obscure way they reinforce it by the manner in which they speak of it. It is a question rather of a theme that forms part of the very mechanics of these incitements: a way of giving shape to the requirement to speak about the matter, a fable that is indispensable to the endlessly proliferating economy of the discourse on sex. What is peculiar to modern societies, in fact, is not that they consigned sex to a shadow existence, but that they dedicated themselves to speaking of it *ad infinitum*, while exploiting it as *the* secret.

6

From 'Seduction and Guilt'

Catherine Clément

The disrupting event acts as moral suffering would; instead of remorse, the hysteric's physical suffering is produced, and it affects the body at the very spot implicated in the occurrence. 'What *is* it that turns into physical pain here? A cautious reply would be: something that might have and should have become *mental* pain' (Freud's *Studies on Hysteria*). The tremendous stakes in the distinction between physical unconscious pain and mental conscious pain begin to be apparent. There is scarcely a doubt that Freud privileges the moral categories of consciousness – remorse, regret, the whole package of guilty feelings. The therapy of hysteria, and consequently of all analytical therapy, consists of locating the pain in the register of conscious morality and getting rid of all the organic substitutions that the psyche is capable of making. It is a huge displacement whose consequences are still in part unknown: suffering is still suffering in every case, but this time it is for guilt rather than for no known reason. A tragic morality, the morality of psychoanalysis according to Freud [...]

FIRST SCENE, 'THE PERVERSE FATHERS'

In Freudian theory, the seduction scene is the point around which he pivots the Real, grasping the fantasy in the very structure of the scene, and thereby introducing the Symbolic and the Imaginary into the position of the subject. Psychoanalysis begins by running into an 'obstacle': the hysteric's implausible tale of seduction. For this implausibility Freud substitutes progressively and not without distress an idea that is still more implausible – that of infantile sexuality. It is a history that goes by stages, in which Freud does his best to find someone who is guilty: there is misery, therefore there is fault. Who is going to be in the wrong? It fluctuates widely. From 1892 on, Freud recognises that the aetiological factors of neuroses are 'sexual traumas experienced before the age of understanding'. But this hypothesis includes perversion, the corruption of the norm. The other aetiological factors are: '(1) Exhaustion by means of abnormal gratifications (2) Sexual inhibition (3) Affects which accompany these practices' (*Origins of Psychoanalysis*, manuscript A).

These factors will be transformed and extended to include all humans and will later be applied to childhood in general. Perversion then disperses itself and spills onto all the children; this is polymorphous and universal perversion, cancelling, by its extent, its immorality and anomaly. But first Freud will have had time to cover every point of family structure. Everyone will be a target while he takes a bead on them with guilt; finally there will be yet another accusation stronger than all the others. Here we see it.

The story of the seduction scene unfolds according to a double process. Freud begins by discovering, in the analysis of cases which he or Breuer is treating, that the patients have been victims of early seductions; the narratives accumulate, the patients are telling – more and more; there is an avalanche of seduction. Simultaneously, the gap between the patient's degree of consciousness at the moment of traumatic shock and the aftereffects (*nachträglichkeiten*) experienced as physical suffering is accentuated. The traumas go further and further back into childhood. A vertiginous regression that Freud will only escape by braking sharply – at fantasy. Freud discovers what he calls 'the great clinical secret: hysteria is the result of a presexual *sexual shock*, obsessional neurosis is the result of presexual sexual pleasure which is later transformed into a feeling of guilt.' What is wrong is stripped bare; it comes from pleasure. From pleasure that has been experienced, obtained before puberty, the physiological age of normal sexuality inscribed in culture's apportionment through initiations. 'Presexual' means *before puberty*, before the appearance of sexual secretions that are tied to reproduction. The incidents in question then act as memories; therefore, it is necessary to detect in the patient's biography the triggering incident, the traumatic memory, and its affect – initially one of pleasure but later transformed into suffering. There is, hence, a divorce between the event and the effect produced: the latter is inadequate to the memory, it is disproportionate, inordinate, and this excessiveness – is it tragic? – is at the origin of somatic distress. It is a 'defect of translation'. [...] The scene of seduction, hence, occurs in an age in which translation into verbal images is impossible, which is to say, in very early childhood. The memory by itself has no effect; the effect comes from overabundant sexual energy, which is unusable and held in reserve, a surplus; a zero sexuality, as Lévi-Strauss describes 'mana' – having a zero symbolic value, which makes the series of signifiers possible.

Then a decisive factor intervenes that comes from listening to the patients. 'A person' is part of this trauma of earliest childhood. Therefore, one must seek out whoever is responsible: 'the troublemakers in general must be sought among the patient's closest relations ... an indispensable condition proven by the existence of infantile sexual incidents' (*Origins of Psychoanalysis*, manuscript A). Thus the hysterics are accusing; they are pointing – with their paralyses, their dyspneas, their knotted limbs. And they point to either the father, a dreadful figure, or to some other male kin. The *Studies on Hysteria* present a parade of young (or less young) persons who provocatively – but with provocation addressed to whom? – hide their story of love with an exploiting relative.

Katharina, 'a tall, heavy girl with an unhappy face', questions Freud and routs him from his daydreams: 'Aren't you a doctor, sir?' She is suffering from breathlessness, dizziness, like all the others she is subjected to some intolerable pressure: 'At first I feel something pressing against my eyes. ... I feel a weight on my chest and I can't get my breath.' She imagines 'that someone is behind me and is going to grab me suddenly'. Freud is quick, he is not going to beat around the bush, he is especially interested 'to learn that neuroses could thrive so well at an altitude of more than 6000 feet'. (Katharina is the daughter of an innkeeper at a refuge in the Tauern Mountains.) Does she see anything as he approaches? 'A dreadful face, who looks at her frighteningly'. Does she recognise this face? No. Freud insists: 'Two years ago you must have seen or heard something that greatly embarrassed you.' Illumination! Now she remembers. She breaks in emotionally: 'Jesus! that's true. I saw my uncle with this girl ...' through a window, because the room was locked, it was dark, her uncle was lying on top of her cousin. She can't get her breath ... she vomits. Then several incidents return to her: it seems her uncle had surprised her several times at night. She woke up feeling his body next to hers: 'What are you doing, Uncle? Why don't you stay in your bed?' Another night she awoke and saw a tall, white shape next to the door, lifting the latch. 'Oh! Jesus! Uncle, it's you, what are you doing at the door?' etcetera. A fairy tale litany, a story built on repetition, which points to the uncle as guilty, perverse, lustful. A note from 1924 is specific: 'Many years having gone by since this time, I feel authorised to break the self-imposed rule of discretion and to add that Katharina was not the niece but the daughter of the innkeeper. The girl's illness was caused, therefore, by her own father's approaches.' But in 1924, it no longer mattered at all that the father be pointed out as the guilty party by the girl. It had been a long time since Freud believed that.

Rosalie is a singer. She studies singing until the day she loses her voice: choking, a constricted throat, the sound no longer comes out. An unhappy childhood had forced her to live with an aunt who was abused by her husband. A new symptom appears, a certain prickling in her fingertips forces her to twitch her hands rapidly. The scene is reconstructed: 'The bad man, who suffered from rheumatism, had demanded that she rub his back and she dared not refuse. He was in bed, and, suddenly, throwing off the covers, he stood up and tried to grab her and throw her down.'

Elisabeth suffers leg pains that prevent her from walking and that she calmly endures.[1] One of her thighs is affected by hyperalgesia; at this one spot she feels too much. So much that, when she is pinched at this painful spot, 'she cried out as if she were being tickled voluptuously [Freud says to himself], she flushed, threw back her head and torso and shut her eyes.' One day

Freud discovers a basic point: the girl's thigh was where her father put his swollen foot every morning while she changed his bandages. There are other traumas appearing as well, focusing the conversion onto the legs: she is 'nailed to the spot' when her father is brought home stricken with a heart attack; she is immobilised next to her sister's deathbed when she suddenly realises that the brother-in-law she is fond of will be free. Elisabeth is caught in the erotic network of nursing the sick. Freud underlines the extent to which nurses are in a difficult position: lack of sleep, obsessive worrying, 'their own bodily neglect', but especially the habit of forced indifference. 'Thus any nurse accumulates many affectively charged impressions, which are barely perceived and which abreaction has not been able to attenuate.' The nurse, constantly solicited by the other's body, is constantly forced to repress. Paternal seduction, seduction by a brother-in-law: two guilty parties are named. In one of the first sessions, Elisabeth remembers having had to get out of bed, barefoot, when her father called her. [...]

Emmy breaks off every two minutes with exclamations of fear and disgust; she jumps when someone comes into the room; she stutters and clucks when she talks. Bit by bit her story becomes clear. The entreaty 'don't touch me' is related to the following incidents: at nineteen, her brother, who had been made very ill by the great amount of morphine he was taking, used to suddenly grab her during his dreadful attacks. Later, a gentleman whom she knew suddenly went crazy at her house and grabbed her arm. Lastly, when she was twenty-eight, she had almost been choked by her younger daughter, who was delirious and held onto her fiercely. 'And then a friend also', who liked to sneak into the room and suddenly appear before her; a madman gets into her room by mistake and stands right next to her bed.

The hysteric suffers from Symbolic transgression as much as she suffers from memories. In her kinship relations, she suffers because her father, her brother, and her brother-in-law come to act as sexual aggressors, arousing feelings that will convert to sufferings, to hangups, to aesthetic points – anaesthetic or hyperaesthetic. So the guilty one is unmasked. This observation leads Freud to set up a schema of the relations between fathers and hysterical daughters: 'hysteria seems to me always to result more from the seducer's perversion: heredity follows a seduction by the father. Thus an exchange is established between the generations: "first generation: perversion, second generation: hysteria, and consequently, sterility. ..." In fact, in hysteria it is a question more of a rejection of a perversion than of a refusal of sexuality.' Thus the perverse generation, accursed as in Greek tragedy or in Judeo-Christian myth, dies out by itself, stricken with sterility. The fathers sin, the daughters are punished in reproduction itself. The figure of the father takes on an importance that it will later have again in Freudian theory, doubtlessly less in the oedipal structure, which is divided between the father and the mother, than in the scientific myth of the primitive horde. The paternal

figure, in this first scene of the story of seduction, is described as 'prehistoric':
'Everything is blamed on someone else but particularly it is blamed on this
other person, who is prehistoric, unforgettable, whom later no one will be able
to equal.' That is why Freud's young hysterics are looking everywhere for an
ideal man, are unsuccessful at reconstituting the family, are failures in exoga-
mous exchange. 'In the demands formulated by amorous hysterics, in their
submission to the beloved object or in their incapacity to marry, as a result of
longing after inaccessible ideals, I discern the influence of the paternal figure.
Obviously, the cause is located in the stature of the father who condescends to
lower himself to the child's level' (*Origins of Psychoanalysis*, letters 52
and 57). Such is the father: at the root of a timeless, ahistorical origin.
Correlatively, individual history, like the collective history whose design
Freud later will trace, is the infinite repetition of the relations of the original
child to the unforgettable, perverse, seductive figure. The 'important other
person' is the model for all others; he is the foundation for otherness, no
longer as an important person but as a *place* in the structure of the subject,
the place in relation to which the subject establishes itself in a *dependent position*. The father is the Law; the austerity of the Symbolic, the privileged force
of the order, come from the looming, immemorial figure of the prehistoric
father. This father is overpossessive: the perverse Law. Thou shalt love none
other than me. The hysterics' narratives put into question the social structure
in its family roots, in the thread of generations each succeeding the other. [...]

HISTORY OF SEDUCTION: SECOND SCENE, 'THE LYING DAUGHTERS'

At the same time that he puts the seduction scene in place, Freud begins to
work on the gap between the reality of this traumatic scene and the fiction of
the recollection that is inscribed from it. Indeed, to account for the affective
persistence of the traumatic shock, an inscription must take place in the
unconscious of the individual involved without his or her knowing it, for 'the
memory acts as a present event' on the one hand, and, on the other, 'the consciousness and the memory are mutually exclusive'. Then must there be an
unconscious recollection? Reminiscence? Known or unknown? An impasse
similar to the aporias of original sin: Adam–Eve – did they or didn't they
know, and can one be guilty of an *unknown* sin? 'With respect to God we are
always wrong', Søren Kierkegaard proposes at the end of *Either ... Or*. That
is the easiest solution: keeping oneself in a state of permanent guilt is to
constitute oneself as a subject. For the time being the guilty one is not the
hysteric, but the hysteric is also not entirely a subject. Caught up in themes
which are not hers, repeating her cues, always somewhere between sleep and
wakefulness, between a hypnotic and an excited state, she is not she, but

through the play of identifications, she is successively each one of the others. They are going to help her become a subject: they are going to make her guilty. But to do it, it will be necessary, through a process of decomposing hysterical narratives, to introduce doubt, sow the seeds of suspicion onto the reality of what they all are telling. So it begins:

I have obtained an exact notion of the structure of hysteria. Everything demonstrates that it is a question of the reproduction of certain scenes which sometimes one may reach directly and sometimes only in passing through intervening fantasies. The latter come from things that have been heard but only much later comprehended. Naturally all the materials are real. They represent protective constructions, sublimations, the embellishment of facts that serve at the same time as justification. (*Origins of Psychoanalysis*, letter 61)

The gap between the real and the fictive, an unconscious construction, is deepening; sometimes one can get to the real (later one will no longer be able to), sometimes one only finds fantasy. Doubt begins to weigh heavily over this story of seduction by the father.

The 'L' manuscript of 1897 further complicates the combinative:

Structure of hysteria: the aim seems to be to return to the primal scenes. Sometimes one can get there directly, but in certain cases, it is necessary to take roundabout ways, passing through fantasies. These actually erect psychic defences against the return of those recollections which they must also purge and sublimate. Elaborated with the help of things that have been *heard* and only *later* (*nachträglich*) utilised, they combine lived events, narratives of past occurrences (concerning their parents' and ancestors' history) and things that the subject himself has seen.

What is left of reality, the dreadful faces framed in a doorway, the shadowy white figures looming at a bedside? Very little: bits of family legend passed from mouth to mouth, ear to ear; fragments of scenes, of understanding, and very little of anything actually seen. So little. From the moment the fantasy is based on what is heard, the spectacular element, which is so powerful in hysterical emotion, moves in the direction of fiction. The mechanism becomes clear. Reality is framed by language, spoken and heard. Somewhat later, in the 'M' manuscript, Freud formulates the fantasy as *distortion* and *fusion*, but he particularly attributes an objective to distortion. 'These tendencies aim at making recollections, which could or might cause symptoms, inaccessible. ... This process makes discovery of the original connection impossible.' There you have it: one will never know, hence it all risks – how would we know? – being distorted. Falsified? False? The reality of the seduction disappears. From then on two elements make access to the real impossible: on the one hand, the gap between the seen and the heard and, on the other, the fragmentation relating to fantasy.

A few months later, Freud writes again to Fliess, 'a great secret'. 'I must confide in you the great secret which during these past months has slowly been revealed. I no longer believe in my *neurotica*' (the hypothesis of a pre-sexual shock in hysterical structure). He then lays out the reasons that persuaded him to change his tack. 'First of all there were the repeated disappointments I experienced during my attempts to push my analyses to their true culmination, the flight of the people whose cases seemed to me to lend themselves best to this treatment.' Several times, in fact, the patients ran away, were no longer heard from, disappeared at the very moment when they were going to reveal the secret of the primal scene to him. 'One of my proud ships has sunk', says this captain of the expedition, commanding a discoverer's fleet to the Americas of hysteria. ... They were on the verge of ... They were just about to ... The moment of revelation is suspended. Then, since the great secret doesn't want to come out, Freud pursues the questioning of his hypotheses further. Second, 'the surprise in observing that in each case it was necessary to accuse the father of perversion, the notion of the unexpected frequency of hysteria in which the same determining cause is met up with again, whereas that perverse acts committed against children be so widespread seems very unlikely.' Now the corner's turned, retreat completed. Faced with including paternity in perversion, the spirit recoils. Once again blame will fall on the daughter, then on the child, in the form of the Oedipus complex and of infantile sexuality. Third, 'the conviction that no "reality-index" exists in the unconscious so that it is impossible to distinguish truth from fiction that is affectively invested (which is why a solution remains possible, it is provided by the fact that sexual fantasy always plays itself out around the parents).' The trick is played: the perverse father exonerated; guilt disseminated and, at this historical moment, preferably attributed to the one who knew how to fantasise a reality that, it seems, is to remain undecipherable. Throughout the period in which he listened to hysteria, Freud was like a prisoner of the mythology of origins. Pursuing a real cause, he sought to discover a true story. When this discovery became impossible – the patients ran away, were liars, one just didn't know ... a definitive corner was turned. Once the real had become inaccessible, it passed into the realm of reconstruction, of what was recorded, but also of what was impossible, hence the anxiety as one approached it, always on the borderline. It is the frequency of the seduction scene that remains to be read: its repetition will engender Oedipus, the structure belonging to a childhood caught up in parental sexuality. And then the therapeutic possibilities diminish. 'Fourth, I have come to notice that in the most advanced psychoses, the unconscious memory does not burst forth, so that the youthful incident, even in the most frenzied cases, is not revealed.

When one remarks that the unconscious never succeeds in conquering conscious resistance, one ceases to hope that, during analysis, the reverse process might take place and result in a complete domination of the unconscious by the conscious.' The secret is still inviolate.

The cure's termination becomes more distant, infinitely deferred. If there is no buttress showing the disorder's real foundation, is there no longer anything able to signify the end of the analysis? 'Considering this', Freud ends in saying, 'I was ready to give up on two things – the total elimination of a neurosis and the exact knowledge of its aetiology in childhood.'

But from this point on, the hysteric will be accused of lying. In *Project for a Scientific Psychology*, an entire section of the study is devoted to the 'first hysterical lie'. The story of Emma comes from another reading. Emma is no longer able to go into a shop by herself. This problem stems from when she was thirteen: she went in and two salesmen, seeing her, began to laugh. She interprets it herself: the men laughed at the way she was dressed, and she desired one of them. A second memory makes its appearance: when she was eight she went into a shop to buy some candy, and the shopkeeper pawed her. But she went back several times after this incident, as if she hoped to provoke him. Freud's reading consists of linking the first and second scenes together. The shopkeeper laughed when he touched her: laughter, therefore, and her being alone will be the symbol, the link. The two salesmen actualised once again the first scene, arousing anxiety in the presence of desire. Still, we are no more certain that this was the first scene, was there another one before it?

Finally, there is the circuit of lies where that pearl of hysterics, Dora, is imprisoned. Dora, whose symptoms are the symptoms of emerging desire, at the same time is keeping herself for some obscure circuit: she coughs, she is mute, she writes, she feels pressure. As soon as the couple, referred to as the K.'s, come into Freud's narrative, accusation begins: Dora's accusation against Mr. K.; it seems he declared his love to her beside the lake. 'The one accused forcefully denied having done the least thing which might merit such an interpretation.' The accusation is turned back against Dora, through the intermediary of Mrs. K., who claims that Dora is only interested in sexual things and that she reads pornographic books. Because he passed this information on, Freud will see Dora leave half-way through analysis. The circuit is complete: in the first scene – Dora the victim, Dora seduced; Dora, licentious and perverse in the second. Next, Dora accuses her father: he is having an affair with Mrs. K. Immediately afterward, Freud notes: 'This way in which patients defend themselves against self-reproach by reproaching someone else for the same thing, is something which is unquestionably automatic. The model for it is found in the replies of children who immediately respond "Liar! You're one yourself!" when someone has accused them of lying.' Freud begins to accuse Dora; Dora would accuse herself. She makes accusations against her father: he gave Dora's mother a venereal disease caught from

Mrs. K. – Dora's self-accusation. Freud concludes: She masturbates. Now she's trapped. She turns against Freud, accuses him in turn, since he is the object of the transference.

She runs away; Freud sees it as revenge. In Freud's note added in 1923, in which he recognises that the flaw in this analysis lies in not recognising Dora's homosexuality, it seems the only one who emerges intact from the circuit of accusation is Mrs. K. Dora is 'protecting' her, even though it was Mrs. K. who encouraged her interest in the bookish erotic secrets. The Nambikwara call homosexuality 'the love-lie': let's borrow their expression, just for fun. In the circuit made up of one person or another's lies, it is Dora, nevertheless, who is compromised. Girls are liars. This is a return to moralistic theories on the subject of therapy for hysteria. The celebrated Jules Falret, in *Folie raisonnable ou folie morale (Reasonable Madness or Moral Madness)*, very calmly writes: 'These patients are real actresses; they have no greater pleasure than in deceiving the people with whom they have some relationship. ... In a word, the hysterics' life is nothing but a perpetual lie; they act pious and devoted and succeed in passing themselves off as saints, while in secret they abandon themselves to the most shameful acts, and within themselves make the most violent scenes with their husbands and children, scenes in which they say disgusting and sometimes obscene things and abandon themselves to the most reckless deeds.'

Freud will not take these positions, of course, and I am not going to hold it against him merely for having *done as the others* did regarding femininity. Freud faithfully reflects the ideological bedrock that makes the hysteric 'the family invalid', as he refers to Elisabeth. Like everyone, he is a captive in the family circus that attempts to charge each member in turn with pathogenic guilt. The circuit of seduction only echoes family structure, which Freud obviously could not change by himself. It is good enough that, even if unwittingly, he has given us the instruments for thinking of these changes, of their limits, and of something else that may break open these limits.

HISTORY OF SEDUCTION: THIRD SCENE, 'THE GUILTY MOTHER'

The circuit has not ended. For, if the primal scene concerns the parents' sexual relationship – the problem of generation, the question put to the father must have a homologue in a question put to the mother, who until now has been strangely absent. Having first believed in and then disproved seduction by the father, Freud constructs the Oedipus complex; then keeping on the tortuous track of the first seduction, always with his sights on the first genital pleasure, he begins to talk (he had to), about seduction by the mother. Let's examine the text where Freud doggedly retraces the path.

During the period in which one was especially preoccupied with discovering the sexual traumas of childhood, almost all my patients told me they had been seduced by their father. I finally concluded from this that these allegations were false and I thus learned that hysterical symptoms did not ensue from real facts, but from fantasies. It was only later that I realised that this fantasy of seduction by the father, was the expression of the typical Oedipus complex in women. In the little girl's pre-oedipal history one also finds this seduction fantasy, but then it is the mother who is the seducer. Here the fantasy borders on reality, for perhaps the mother was really the one who caused, even perhaps aroused the first pleasurable genital sensations, and did so while caring for the child's bodily needs. (*New Introductory Lectures*)

This goes several degrees beyond the period in which the *Studies* were produced: all women, and not just those who 'it's obvious' are struggling with the fantasy of seduction by the father, a normal sign of family structure. What is more, the little girl is seduced by the mother. And if it is the mother, this other possible combination necessarily goes back to an earlier stage, since bodily care is mentioned. The distribution of work within the family, which one must certainly refer to as bourgeois, takes shape here. According to Freud, maids, governesses, and coachmen surround the hysterics, and Freud is careful to mention apropos Katharina that her clothes clearly reveal that she is not a servant at the inn but the daughter of the innkeeper, despite her serving him his dinner. Mothers take care of the bodies, Fathers intervene as law. Dirtiness and cleanliness are women's prerogative, even daughters' prerogative, in their function as nurses for their old and sick fathers. The only mention made of Dora's mother depicts her as 'uneducated' and suffering from 'housewife's psychosis'. Dora doesn't get along with her anymore because she refuses to integrate herself into the household tasks that her mother demands of her. Cleanliness of the (propertied) body, a crud hunt that turns back on the family: beneficial, well done. So, in caring for the youngest children, the mother handles bodies, sexual organs, fools around in the folds of the body, fondles: that, according to Freud, is her seduction. But the trap is even fuller than that; for if one looks at the analysis of little Hans, what does one see? There it is the child himself who is the seducer. 'Hans is four years three months old. This morning his mother gives him his daily bath and, after his bath she dries and powders him. While she is powdering around his penis, carefully not touching it, Hans asks: "Why don't you put your finger on it?" '

Mother: Because it's nasty.
Hans: What's that? Nasty? Why?
Mother: Because it's not proper, not nice.
Hans (laughing): But lots of fun!

In a note, a little girl, about Hans's age, plays the same game, closing her thighs on her mother's hand. Whether she steers clear of it or not, whether she goes around the penis, the genitals, or handles them, whether she follows the law or transgresses it, she is caught: seductress. A seductress in the apprenticeship of proper cleanliness: dirty despite herself, right down to the physical techniques which she is made culturally responsible for transmitting. Proper. *What a fine mess.*

Indeed, Michelet had noted the *child*'s seduction: neither girl nor boy, androgynous rather, sexual every which way. The serf's wife loved sprites and goblins, who came into the house with the children and made the cradle rock gently. The fireside goblin hides – in a butter jar, in a rose, in the sparkling embers. 'He is nimble and daring, and if one didn't hold onto him, perhaps he would get away. He watches and hears too much. ... And, with all that, there is something of the lover about him. More intrusive than anyone else, and so small, he slips around everywhere.' He invades her, possesses her, then grows up to be a demon. She is the very devil with him in her body. 'Something makes her skin crawl strangely, making her toss and turn, unable to sleep. She sees weird figures. The Spirit who was so little and so sweet seems to have become imperious. He is presumptuous. She is worried and indignant, wants to get up. She stays but she moans, feels she is becoming dependent, says to herself: "So now I don't belong to myself anymore!" ' The Devil emerges through the seductive child, but at least the poor serf-woman is cleared of any seduction.

On the other hand, there is the terrifying mother figure described by Melanie Klein.[2] Here the guilt for seduction and the resulting anxiety, whether one is object or subject of this seduction, are pushed to extremes. All because the breast is taken away. 'I consider the loss of the breast as the most fundamental cause of conversion toward the father. Identification with the father is less charged with anxiety than identification with the mother.' In the earlier stages of oedipal conflict, the figure of a castrating mother is found, one who is powerful and devouring and at the same time seductive.

> Fear of the mother is so crushing because it is combined with an intense fear of castration by the father. The destructive tendencies whose object is the belly-womb are aimed equally, with their full intensity of oral and anal sadism, at the father's penis which must – according to the child's idea – be there. During this period the fear of castration by the father is concentrated on the penis. The feminine phase is therefore characterised by an anxiety linked to the mother's belly and the father's penis, and this anxiety subjects the boy to the tyranny of a superego which devours, dismembers and castrates, and which is formed of maternal and paternal images at the same time.   (Klein, *Essais de Psychanalyse*)

Now she is a *penis thief*: the father's penis must certainly be in her belly. Let's return to *The Witches' Hammer*: 'What [asks the Inquisitor] is to be thought of these witches who collect this way [by taking away the male organ], sometimes collecting a great number of them [20 or 30] and who then go around putting them in birds' nests or shutting them up in boxes, where they keep on moving like living organs, eating oats or other things as some have seen and as they are generally believed to do?' ('How witches can take the male organ from a man.') The sorceress takes men's penes, as, from the child's point of view, the mother takes the father's penis. We find ourselves in a kind of primal scene, which is internalised to the space within the body. The centre of that space is opaque and organic: there the father-penis encounters the mother-belly. One can't see any more. But one well imagines the dreadful encounter from which these excrement-children will again emerge. The fact remains that in this phantasmic mythology the scorceress and mother come together again – are one and the same. Guilty. The hysteric is indeed the witch's daughter.

7

'Who Kills Whores?' 'I Do', Says Jack: Race and Gender in Victorian London

Sander L. Gilman

'I am down on whores and I shan't quit ripping them till I do get buckled', wrote Jack the Ripper to the Central News Agency on 18 September 1888.[1] The question I raise in this essay reflects not only on the reality of Jack the Ripper – real he was, and he never did get buckled – but on the contemporary fantasy of what a Jack the Ripper could have been. To understand the image of Jack, however, it is necessary to understand the image of the prostitute in Victoria's London. It is also necessary to comprehend the anxiety that attended her image in 1888, an anxiety that, like our anxieties a hundred years later, focused on diseases labelled sexual and attempted to locate their boundaries within the body of the Other.[2]

Who could truly kill the prostitute but the prostitute herself? Who else could expiate her sins against the male? For the prostitute's life must end in suicide. In Alfred Elmore's image *On The Brink*, exhibited at the Royal Academy in 1865, we see the initial step before the seduction of the female, the beginning of the slide toward prostitution and eventual self-destruction. Alone, outside the gambling salon in Bad Homburg, having lost her money, the potential object of seduction (Everywoman) is tempted by the man to whom she is indebted.[3] Women, all women, were seen as potentially able to be seduced, as having a 'warm fond heart' in which 'a strange and sublime unselfishness, which men too commonly discover only to profit by' exists – or so writes W. R. Greg in the *Westminster Review* of 1850.[4]

The well-dressed woman has come to the spa, has exposed herself to exploitation by the male, and is caught between the light and darkness of her future, a future mirrored in the representation of her face, half lighted by the moon, half cast in shadow. She is at the moment of choice, caught between the lily and the passionflower. According to *The Language of Flowers*, a standard handbook of Victorian culture, the lily signifies purity and sweetness, and the passionflower, strong feelings and susceptibility.[5] The gambling salon was the wrong locus for the female. As early as Hogarth's *The Lady's Last*

Stake (1758–59), the female's seduction might be seen as the result of being in the wrong place. Males can gamble; females cannot. Males can indulge their passions; females cannot. Sexuality is a game for the male; it is not for the female. But gambling here is also a metaphor, though a socially embedded one, for the process by which the seduction of the female takes place. Playing upon the innate biological nature of the female makes the seduction possible, but the metaphor of losing at gambling also points to the model of infection and disease.

Alfred Elmore's picture shared this vocabulary. Gambling is a 'fever' (*Times* [London]), the gambler is 'infected by the fever of gambling' (*Illustrated London News*), the gambler is thus 'feverish' (*Athenaeum*).[6] Gambling is a disease that infects and makes ill, infiltrating the purity of the female. Seduction thus has a course of illness: it begins with the signs and symptoms of disease, the fever of gambling, the result of the individual's being out of place – much like the colonial explorer expecting to get malaria – and leads inexorably to the next stages of the disease: prostitution and death. The image of the gambler who stands at the moment of choosing between vice and virtue, who is gambling with life itself, is appropriate. Gambling is the sign of the moment before seduction, the male stands in proximity to the female, but not touching her. The sexualised touch is prepared but has not been consummated. Once it is (if it is, and that is the ambiguity of this image), the course is inevitable – at least for the female – for 'seduction must, almost as a matter of course, lead to prostitution', as W. M. Sanger observed in 1859.[7]

The appropriate end of the prostitute is suicide, 'deserted to a life of misery, wretchedness, and poverty ... terminated by self-destruction'.[8] This is her penalty for permitting herself to be seduced by immoral men, to be infected, and thus to spread infection to – innocent men? This is the chain of argument that places the seducer and the prostitute beyond the boundary that defines polite sexuality: a sexuality that led Victoria's prime minister William Gladstone, who was fascinated with prostitutes, to attempt their conversion at his own hearthside and to simultaneously solicit sexual contact with them. The seducer and the prostitute are the defining borders of diseased sexuality. The seducer is parallel to the image of Bram Stoker's *Dracula* (1897), for in the act of seduction he transforms the innocent female into a copy of himself, just as Dracula's victims become vampires. She becomes the prostitute as seductress, infecting other males as he has infected her with the disease of licentiousness (and not incidentally, syphilis). Sexuality, disease, and death are linked in the act of seduction. As a contemporary reformist source noted, in this image 'the Deceiver recognizes the Deceived ... he, the tempter, the devil's agent ... Men, seducers, should learn from this picture and fallen women, look at this, and remember "the wages of sin is death" '.[9] The sign of transmission of the disease of polluted (and polluting) sexuality, the sexualised touch, is as of this moment missing in Elmore's icon of seduction. In Thomas Hood's widely cited poem on the death of the prostitute, 'The Bridge of Sighs' (1844), the sexualised touch, the source of disease, becomes the forgiving touch of the dead prostitute:

> Take her up instantly,
> Loving not loathing,
> Touch her not scornfully;
> Think of her mournfully,
> Gently and humanly:
> Not of the stains of her,
> All that remains of her
> Now is pure womanly ...[10]

Death seems to purge the dead prostitute of her pollution in a series of images of dead prostitutes in the nineteenth century, from Georges Frederic Watt's *Found Drowned* (1845–50) through to the ubiquitous death mask of the *Beautiful Dead Woman from the Seine* that decorated so many bourgeois parlours in France and Germany during the *fin de siècle*.[11] The touching of the dead body is not merely a piteous gesture toward the 'fallen', it is a permitted touching of the female, a not contagious, not infecting touch, a control over the dead woman's body.

Once the prostitute was dead by her own hand, it was the physician who could touch her. His role was to examine and dissect the body condemned to death by its fall from grace. And that body becomes the object of study, the corpse to be opened. For one of the favourite images of late nineteenth-century medical art is the unequal couple transmogrified into the image of the aged pathologist contemplating the exquisite body of the dead prostitute before he opens it. In the striking image by Enriquet Simonet (1890) we are present at the moment when the body has been opened and the pathologist stares at the heart of the whore. What will be found in the body of these drowned women? Will it be the hidden truths of the nature of the woman, what women want, the answer to Freud's question to Marie Bonaparte? Will it be the biological basis of difference, the cell with its degenerate, potentially infectious nature that parallels the image of the female and her potential for destroying the male? Will it be the face of the Medusa, with all its castrating power? Remember that in that age of 'syphiliphobia' the 'Medusa' masks the infection hidden within the female. In Louis Raemaker's 1916 Belgian poster representing the temptation of the female as the source of the disease, much of the traditional imagery of the seductress can be found. Standing among rows of graves, wearing a black cloak and holding a skull that represents her genitalia, she is the essential femme fatale. But there is a striking *fin-de-siècle* addition to the image – for here 'La Syphilis' is the Medusa. Her tendrils of hair, her staring eyes, present the viewer with the reason for the male's seduction – not his sexuality, but her vampire-like power to control his rationality. The Medusa is the genitalia of the female, threatening, as Sigmund Freud has so well demonstrated, the virility of the male, but also beckoning him to 'penetrate' (to use Freud's word) into her mysteries.[12]

What will be found in the body of these drowned women? If we turn to the German expressionist Gottfried Benn's 1912 description of the autopsy of a beautiful drowned girl, we get an ironic, twentieth-century answer to this question:

The mouth of a girl, who had long lain in the reeds
looked so gnawed upon.
When they finally broke open her chest, the esophagus was so full of holes.
Finally in a bower below the diaphragm they found a nest of young rats.
One of the little sisters was dead.
The others were living off liver and kidneys,
drinking the cold blood, and had
here spent a beautiful youth.
And death came to them too beautiful and quick
We threw them all into the water.
Oh, how their little snouts squeaked![13]

The physician-poet Benn ironically transfers the quality of the aesthetic ascribed to the beautiful dead prostitute to the dead and dying rats. What is found within the woman is the replication of herself: the source of disease, of plague, the harbour rats, nestled within the gut. The birthing of the rats is the act of opening the body, exposing the corruption hidden within. The physician's eye is always cast to examine and find the source of pathology, in the role assigned by society. Here again it is the male physician opening the body of the woman to discover the source of disease, here the plague, hidden within the woman's body.

But in the fantasy of the nineteenth century the physician could not remove the prostitute from the street. Only the whore could kill the whore. Only the whore, and Jack. Killing and dismembering, searching after the cause of corruption and disease, Jack could kill the source of infection because he too was diseased. The paradigm for the relationship between Jack and the prostitutes can be taken from the popular medical discourse of the period: *Similia similibus curantur*, 'like cures like', the motto of C. F. S. Hahnemann, the founder of homeopathic medicine. The scourge of the streets, the carrier of disease, can be eliminated only by one who is equally corrupt and diseased. And that was Jack.

Jack, as he called himself, was evidently responsible for a series of murders that raised the anxiety level throughout London to fever pitch in the cold, damp fall of 1888. The images of the murders in the London *Illustrated Police News* provide an insight into how the murderer was seen and also how the 'real' prostitute, not the icon of prostitution or of seduction, was portrayed in mass art. The murders ascribed to Jack the Ripper all took place in the East End of London, an area that had been the scene of heavy Eastern European Jewish immigration. Who, within the fantasy of the thought collective, can open the body? Who besides the physician? No one but Jack, the emblem of human sexual perversion out of all control, out of all bounds. Jack becomes the sign of deviant human sexuality destroying life, the male parallel to the destructive prostitute. He is the representative of that inner force, hardly held under control, that has taken form – the form of Mr. Hyde. Indeed, an extraordinarily popular dramatic version of Robert Louis Stevenson's *Dr. Jekyll and Mr. Hyde* was playing in the West End while Jack (that not-so-hidden Mr. Hyde) terrorised the East End.

The images of the victims of 'Jack' – ranging in number from four to twenty depending on which tabulation one follows – were portrayed as young women who had been slashed and mutilated. The Whitechapel murders most probably included Emma Smith (2 April 1888), Martha Tabram (7 August 1888), Mary Ann Nichols (31 August 1888), and Annie Chapman (8 September 1888). Elizabeth Stride and Catherine Eddowes were both murdered on 30 September 1888. But because of the sensibilities of even the readers of the *Illustrated Police News*, the mutilation presented is the mutilation of the face (as in the image of Annie Chapman). The reality, at least the reality that terrified the London of 1888, was that the victims were butchered. Baxter Philips, who undertook the postmortem description of Mary Ann Nichols, described the process: 'The body had been completely disembowelled and the entrails flung carelessly in a heap on the table. The breasts had been cut off, hacked for no apparent purpose, and then hung on nails affixed to the walls of the room. Lumps of flesh, cut from the thighs and elsewhere, lay strewn about the room, so that the bones were exposed. As in some of the other cases, certain organs had been extracted, and, as they were missing, had doubtless been carried away'.[14]

[...] Such sexual disfigurement, along with the amputation of the breasts of some of the victims, made it clear to both the police and the general public that Jack's actions were sexually motivated. And indeed, most of the theories concerning Jack's identity assumed that he (or a close family member) had been infected with syphilis by a prostitute and was simply (if insanely) taking his revenge. But the vague contours of Jack the 'victim' soon gave a very specific visual image of Jack.

'Jack' is the caricature of the Eastern Jew. Indeed, the official description was of a man 'age 37, rather dark beard and moustache, dark jacket and trousers, black felt hat, spoke with a foreign accent'.[15] There appeared scrawled on the wall in Goulston Street, near the place where a blood-covered apron was discovered, the cryptic message: 'The Juwes are The men That not be Blamed for nothing'.[16] The image of the Jews as sexually different, the Other even in the killing of the Other, led to the arrest of John Pizer, 'Leather Apron', a Polish shoemaker. Pizer was eventually cleared and released, but a high proportion of the 130 men questioned in the Ripper case were Jews.

Sir Robert Anderson, the police official in charge of the case, noted in his memoir:

One did not need to be a Sherlock Holmes to discover that the criminal was a sexual maniac of a virulent type; that he was living in the immediate vicinity of the scenes of the murders; and that, if he was not living absolutely alone, his people knew of his guilt, and refused to give him up to justice. During my absence abroad the Police had made a house-to-house search for him, investigating the case of every man whose circumstances were such that he could go and come and get rid of his blood-stains in secret. And the conclusion we came to was that he and his people were low-class Jews, for it is a remarkable fact that people of that class in the East End will not give up one of their number to Gentile justice. ... I will only add that when the individual whom we suspected was caged in an asylum, the only person who had ever had a good view of the murderer at once identified him, but when he learned the suspect was a fellow-Jew he declined to swear to him.[17]

[...] The powerful association between the working class, revolutionaries, and the Jews combines to create the visualisation of Jack the Ripper as a Jewish worker, marked by his stigmata of degeneration as a killer of prostitutes. Here Jack had to intervene. In one of his rhyming missives sent in 1889 to Sir Melville MacNaghten, chief of the Criminal Investigation Division at Scotland Yard, he wrote:

I'm not a butcher, I'm not a Yid
Nor yet a foreign skipper,
But I'm your own light-hearted friend,
Yours truly, Jack the Ripper.[18]

When during the 1890s the German playwright Frank Wedekind visualised his Jack the Ripper killing the archwhore Lulu, he represented him as a degenerate working-class figure: 'He is a square-built man, elastic in his movements, with a pale face, inflamed eyes, thick arched eyebrows, drooping moustache, sparse beard, matted side whiskers and fiery red hands with gnawed finger nails. His eyes are fixed on the ground. He is wearing a dark overcoat and a small round hat'.[19] This primitive figure was quite in line with the views shared by the Italian forensic psychiatrist Cesare Lombroso[20] and his French rival, Alexandre Lacassagne,[21] as to the representative image (if not origin) of the criminal, but specifically the sadist. For the Germans, at least for liberals such as Wedekind, Jack was also seen as member of the lumpenproletariat in reaction to the charge, made in 1894 in the anti-Semitic newspapers in Germany, that Jack was an Eastern European Jew functioning as part of the 'international Jewish conspiracy'.[22] But in Britain this image evoked a very specific aspect of the proletariat, that of London's East End, the Eastern Jew.

[...] The search for Jack the Ripper was the search for an appropriate murderer for the Whitechapel prostitutes. The murderer had to be representative of an image of sexuality that was equally distanced and frightening. Thus the image of Jack the Ripper as the shochet, the ritual butcher, arose at a moment when there was a public campaign by the antivivisectionists in England and Germany against the 'brutality' of the ritual slaughter of kosher meat.

This image of the Jewish Jack rested on a long association of the image of the Jew in the West with the image of the mutilated, diseased, different appearance of the genitalia. This mark of sexual difference was closely associated with the initial image of the syphilitic Jack. The Jew remains the representation of the male as outsider, the act of circumcision marking the Jewish male as sexually apart, as anatomically different. (It is important to remember that there is a constant and purposeful confusion throughout the late nineteenth and early twentieth centuries of circumcision with castration.) The prostitute is, as has been shown, the embodiment of the degenerate and diseased female genitalia in the nineteenth century. From the normative perspective of the European middle class, it is natural that the Jew and prostitute must be in conflict and that the one 'opens up' the other, since both are seen as 'dangers' to the economy of the state, both fiscal and sexual. This notion of the association of the Jew and the prostitute is also present in the image of 'spending' semen (in an illicit manner) that dominates literature on masturbation in the eighteenth and early nineteenth centuries. For the Jew and the prostitute are seen as negating factors, outsiders whose sexual images represent all the dangers felt to be inherent in human sexuality. And to consciously destroy, indeed touch, the polluting force of the Other, one must oneself be beyond the boundaries of acceptability.

The linkage between Jew and prostitute is much older than the 1880s. This association is related to the image of the black and the monkey (two icons of 'deviant' sexuality) in the second plate of Hogarth's *A Harlot's Progress*. Here Moll Hackabout, the harlot, has become the mistress of a wealthy London Jew. The Jew has been cheated by the harlot; her lover is about to leave the scene. But her punishment is forthcoming. She will be dismissed by him and begin her slow slide downward. Tom Brown, Hogarth's contemporary and the author of 'A Letter to Madam—, Kept by a Jew in Covent Garden', which may well have inspired the plate, concludes his letter on the sexuality of the Jew by asking the young woman 'to be informed whether Aaron's bells make better music than ours'.[23] It is this fascination with the sexual difference of the Jew, parallel to the sexual difference of the prostitute, that relates them even in death. Each possesses a sexuality different from the norm, a sexuality that is represented in the unique form of their genitalia.

The relationship between the Jew and the prostitute also has a social dimension. For both Jew and prostitute have but one interest, converting sex into money or money into sex. 'So then', Brown writes to the lady, ''tis neither circumcision nor uncircumcision that avails any thing with you, but money, which belongs to all religions'.[24] The major relationship, Tom Brown and Hogarth outline, is a financial one; Jews buy specific types of Christian women, using their financial ability as a means of sexual control. 'I would never have imagined you … would have ever chosen a gallant out of that religion which clips and diminishes the current coin of love, or could ever be brought to like those people that lived two thousand years on types and figures.'[25]

By the end of the nineteenth century this linkage had become a commonplace in all of Christian Europe […] The association of the venality of the Jew with capital is retained even into the latter half of the twentieth century. In a series of British comic books from the 1980s in which an anthropomorphised phallus plays the central role, the Jew is depicted as masturbating, committing an 'unnatural' act (whereas the other phalluses are depicted as having a potential female partner) while reading a financial journal. What is striking in these comics is that all the phalluses are circumcised.[26] This is a problem of contemporary culture. In the post-World War II decades circumcision became a commonplace – even among non-Jews – in the United States and … Great Britain. How then to differentiate between the Jew and the non-Jew, between the 'deviant' and the 'normal'? We are faced with a problem analagous to why George Eliot's eponymous character Daniel Deronda did not know he was a Jew. Did he ever look at his penis? Here the hidden is not marked upon the skin, for the skin hides rather than reveals. It is the Jew within that surfaces. Here, in seeing a financial journal as the source of power and therefore of sexual stimulation; in Eliot's novel, with the 'natural' sexual attraction between the crypto-Jew Deronda and the beautiful Jewess Mirah Cohen. (Deronda never defines himself as sexually different, for his own body is the baseline that defines for him the sexually 'normal'. His circumcised penis is not a sign of difference until he understands himself to be a Jew.)

The image of the Jew revealed in his sexuality seems to be an accepted manner of labelling the image of the deviant. Even his phallus does not know for sure until he performs a 'perverse' act. Here the icon is a reversal of the traditional image of the phallus as the beast out of control. In this image it is the man, not his phallus, who is bestial (read Jewish). The perversion of the

Jew (and thus the 'humour' of this depiction of the phallus) lies in his sexualised relationship with capital. This of course echoes the oldest and most basic calumny against the Jew, his avarice, an avarice for the possession of 'things', of 'money', which signals his inability to understand (and produce) anything of transcendent aesthetic value. The historical background to this is clear. Canon law forbade charging interest, which according to Thomas Aquinas was impossible, since money, not being alive, could not reproduce. Jews, in charging interest, treated money as a sexualised object. The Jew takes money, as does the prostitute, as a substitute for higher values, for love and beauty. And thus the Jew becomes the representative of the deviant genitalia, the genitalia not under the control of the moral, rational conscience.

But the image of the Jew as prostitute is not merely a reflection of the economic parallel between the sexuality of the Jew and that of the prostitute. That relationship also reveals the nature of the sexuality of both Jew and prostitute as diseased, as polluting. Just as the first image of Jack the Ripper was that of the victim of the prostitute, the syphilitic male, so too were the Jews closely identified with sexually transmitted diseases. For the Jew was also closely related to the spread and incidence of syphilis. This charge appeared in various forms, as in the anti-Semitic tractate *England under the Jews* (1901) by Joseph Banister, in which there is a fixation on the spread of 'blood and skin diseases'.[27] Such views had two readings. Banister's was the more typical. The Jews were the carriers of sexually transmitted diseases and spread them to the rest of the world. This view is to be found in Hitler's discussion of syphilis in *Mein Kampf*, and there he links it to the Jew, the prostitute, and the power of money: 'Particularly with regard to syphilis, the attitude of the nation and the state can only be designated as total capitulation ... The cause lies, primarily, in our prostitution of love. ... The Jewification of our spiritual life and mammonisation of our mating instinct will sooner or later destroy our entire offspring.'[28]

Hitler's views, like those of Banister and the earlier British anti-Semite, also linked Jews with prostitutes. Jews were the archpimps; Jews ran the brothels; Jews infected their prostitutes and caused the weakening of the national fibre. Indeed, according to Hitler, it was the realisation of this very 'fact' during the first few days of his stay in Vienna in 1907 that converted him to anti-Semitism. The hidden source of the disease of the body politic is the Jew, and his tool is the whore: 'If you cut even cautiously into such a tumour, you found, like a maggot in a rotting body, often dazzled by the sudden light – a kike!'.[29]

Such a view of the Jew as the syphilitic was not limited to the anti-Semitic fringe of the turn of the century. It was a view that possessed such power that even 'Jewish' writers (writers who felt themselves stigmatised by the label of being 'Jewish') subscribed to it. One such was Marcel Proust, whose uncomfortable relationship with his mother's Jewish identity haunted his life almost

as much as did his gay identity. In Proust's *Remembrance of Things Past*, the
series of novels written to recapture the world of the 1880s and 1890s, one of
the central characters, Charles Swann, is a Jew who marries a courtesan. This
link between Jew and prostitute is mirrored in Proust's manner of representing the sexuality of the Jew. For Proust, being Jewish is analogous to being
gay – it is 'an incurable disease'.[30] But what marks this disease for all to see?
For in the *mentalité* of the turn of the century, syphilis in the male must be
written on the skin, just as it is hidden within the sexuality of the female.
Proust, who in the same volume discusses the signs and symptoms of syphilis
with a detailed clinical knowledge, knows precisely what marks the sexuality
of the Jew upon his physiognomy.[31] It is seen upon his face as 'ethnic
eczema'.[32] It is a sign of sexual and racial corruption as surely as the composite photographs of the Jew that Francis Galton made at the time reveal the
true face of the Jew.[33]

This mark upon the face is Hitler's and Banister's sign of the Jew's sexual
perversion. It is the infectious nature of that 'incurable disease', the sexuality
of the Jew, Proust's Jew fixated upon his courtesan. [...] The Jew's sexuality,
the sexuality of the polluter, is written on his face in the skin disease that
announces the difference of the Jew. For Proust, all his Jewish figures (including Swann and Bloch), are in some way diseased, and in every case this image
of disease links the racial with the sexual, much as Proust's image of the
homosexual links class (or at least the nobility) with homosexuality.
('Homosexuality' is a 'scientific' label for a new 'disease' coined by Karoly
Benkert in 1869 at the very same moment in history when the new 'scientific'
term for Jew hating, 'anti-Semitism', was created by Wilhelm Marr.) [...]

Joseph Banister saw the Jews as bearing the stigmata of skin disease (as a
model for discussing sexually transmitted disease): 'If the reader desires to
know what kind of blood it is that flows in the Chosen People's veins, he cannot do better than take a gentle stroll through Hatton Garden, Maida Vale,
Petticoat Lane, or any other London "nosery". I do not hesitate to say that in
the course of an hour's peregrinations he will see more cases of lupus,
trachoma, favus, eczema, and scurvy than he would come across in a week's
wanderings in any quarter of the Metropolis'.[34] Banister is fixated on the nose
of the Jew, a not so subtle anti-Semitic reference to the circumcised and, thus,
diseased, phallus. For the 'nose' is the iconic representation of the Jew's phallus throughout the nineteenth century. Indeed, Jewish social scientists, such as
the British savant Joseph Jacobs, spend a good deal of their time denying the
salience of 'nostrility' as a sign of the racial cohesion of the Jews.[35] It is clear
that for Jacobs (as for Wilhelm Fliess in Germany) the nose is the displaced
locus of anxiety associated with the marking of the male Jew's body through
circumcision, given the debate about the 'primitive' nature of circumcision
and its reflection on the acculturation of the Western Jew during the late
nineteenth century.[36]

Jews bear their diseased sexuality on their skin. Indeed, they bear the salient stigma of the black skin of the syphilitic. For at least in the Latin tradition, syphilis (like leprosy, another disease understood to be sexually transmitted) was understood to turn one black, the syphilitic rupia. Francisco Lopez de Villalobos, court physician to Charles V, in his long poem on syphilis of 1498, observes that the 'color of the skin becomes black' when one has the 'Egyptian disease', the plague of boils recounted in the account of the Jews' escape from slavery.[37] Blackness marks the sufferer from disease, sets him outside the world of purity and cleanliness.

The Jews are black, according to nineteenth-century racial science, because they are 'a mongrel race which always retains this mongrel character'. So says Houston Stewart Chamberlain, arguing against the 'pure' nature of the Jewish race.[38] Jews had 'hybridised' with blacks in Alexandrian exile, and they were exposed to the syphilis that becomes part of their nature. They are, in an ironic review of Chamberlain's work by the father of modern Yiddish scholarship, Nathan Birnbaum, a 'bastard' race whose origin was caused by their incestuousness. But the Jews were also seen as black.[39] Adam Gurowski, a Polish noble, 'took every light-colored mulatoo for a Jew' when he first arrived in the United States in the 1850s.[40] Jews are black because they are different, because their sexuality is different, because their sexual pathology is written upon their skin.

Gurowski's contemporary Karl Marx associates leprosy, Jews, and syphilis in his description of his archrival Ferdinand Lassalle (in 1861): 'Lazarus the leper, is the prototype of the Jews and of Lazarus-Lassalle. But in our Lazarus, the leprosy lies in the brain. His illness was originally a badly cured case of syphilis'.[41] Jews = lepers = syphilitics = prostitutes = blacks. This chain of association presents the ultimate rationale for the Jewish Jack the Ripper, for the diseased destroy the diseased, the corrupt the corrupt. They corrupt in their act of touching, of seducing, the pure and innocent, creating new polluters. But they are also able in their sexual frenzy to touch and kill the sexual pariahs, the prostitutes, who like Lulu at the close of Frank Wedekind's play (and Alban Berg's opera) go out to meet them, seeking their own death. Being unclean, being a version of the female genitalia (with his amputated genitalia), the male Jew is read (as Jack's Viennese contemporary Otto Weininger[42] had read him) as really nothing but a type of female. The parish can thus touch and kill the pariah, the same destroy the same. Wedekind's Lulu dies not as a suicide but as the victim of the confrontation between two libidinal forces – the unbridled, degenerate sexuality of the male and the sexual chaos of the sexually emancipated female. But die she does, and Jack leaves the stage, having washed his hands like Pontius Pilate, ready to kill again.

8

Nietzscheanism and the Novelty of the Superman

Maurizia Boscagli

The most outstanding trope of [the post-World War I] culture of the body as the site of spontaneous naturalness and authenticity for the individual was the image of the Nietzschean superman.[1] Nietzsche's ideas had become extremely popular among young educated Europeans from the 1890s onward, when his critique of German Wilhelmine society and of Judeo-Christian morality gave impetus to and fused with a wide range of political positions from anarchism, sexual libertarianism, and feminism to right-wing nationalism and socialism.[2] (By 1918 Thomas Man could write that one did not merely read Nietzsche, 'one experienced him'.) Nietzsche's work was itself the product of a late nineteenth century shift in intellectual and cultural attitudes; it was influenced by, even as it influenced, the *fin de siècle* disaffection with liberal pieties and the kind of polemics that read the social body through tropes of the strength of the physical body. As such, Nietzscheanism contributed to a series of antirationalist movements of social and cultural protest of the time. These included the generational rebellion of groups (like that around Rupert Brooke) that helped fuel a new 'youth culture' and the anticapitalist and neoromantic desire to return to the land, which in turn informed both the *Volkisch* ideology of the Ramblers in Germany and the versions of vitalism developed by modernists such as Forster and D. H. Lawrence.

Nietzsche's superman, the *Übermensch*, provided the petty bourgeois with a larger-than-life identity on which to model his own self. Yet as Forster's own ultimately romanticised view of the peasants in *Howard's End* shows, the animality of the superman was already encoded in the body of the lower class labourer, either the peasant or the proletarian. Before turning to the early twentieth century readings of Nietzsche and to the Nietzschean text itself, one needs to remember that the immediate precedent for the superman's physical power and instinctuality was the body of the proletarian. Given these antecedents, to claim that the new class of clerks found in the image of the superman a version of ideal corporeality raises a set of questions regarding class confidence and the representation of the body. How could the employee

75

class, aspiring to become bourgeois, invoke as the model of its own subjectivity a corporeality that throughout the previous century had been associated
with the brute force of the labouring classes? How can the petty bourgeois
himself appropriate this body without becoming engulfed in the class and
gender it had traditionally signified and rather see it as signifying an elitist
'aristocracy of blood'? What I will suggest is that once a large part of the
working male population was no longer engaged in manual labour or even on
the new assembly lines of the factories but rather employed as clerks and
'white collar' workers, there was no practical need for a physically strong
body. The body of the clerk was newly made available as a site of an alternative constellation of signs symbolising forces from personal integrity to
national power. His newly superfluous body, having ceased to become necessary to the actual work of production, had become the scene instead of
ideological contestation. In this spectacle, the return to a valorisation of a
physically strong body, which had formerly been the body of the labourer,
represented a strategic deployment of an archaism. It represented at once a
muted tribute to the clerk's origins, a betrayal of his fear of the power of the
class he had left behind, an attempt to outdo that class at its own self-display,
an acknowledgment of the unconscious appeal of the worker's sexuality, and
above all an attempt to inscribe new idioms of personal hegemony upon an
older spectacle of the physically strong body. Uniting this array of signs
inscribed upon the clerk's exercised body, the Nietzschean notion of the
superman allowed the clerk to transform what could be read as traces of the
labourer's body, and hence of the clerk's own origins, into a spectacle of a new
kind of aristocracy based on individual will. The clerk's unnecessarily muscled body could connote his new aspirations along with traces of the origins
he rejected: it was these two messages that the Nietzschean narrative could
absorb.

The particular quality of the superman's lingering monstrosity, the anxiety
about classes left behind that would continue to be implicit in the image of the
strong male body, had already been made evident in the way Emile Zola had
articulated the abnormal in his novel *La bête humaine* (The human beast) of
1890.[3] Part of Zola's Rougon-Macquart cycle, the novel is a net of interwoven
stories about *fin de siècle* French railroad life. As a social document, a story of
love and adultery and a thriller *noir*, *La bête humaine* was initially conceived
by its author as an investigation into the figure of the murderer as a type of
abnormal personality. The 'human beast' is Jacques Lantier, a young train
driver implicated in two murders, once as a witness and once as the perpetra-
tor. As the offspring of a family 'contaminated' by alcoholism, he is 'doomed'
by heredity to be a criminal with uncontrollable homicidal tendencies:
Jacques cannot make love to a woman without desiring to hurt and destroy
her body. Thus he kills his lover, Severine, driven by an inexplicable impulse,
incomprehensible to her and to himself.

Zola's construction of the beast relies on a view of sexuality as the channel where irrepressible drives as well as the 'poison' tainting Jacques's blood flow together. In this way, while the weakness of his flesh is presented as evil, it is at the same time pathologised, and – if not made acceptable – at least justified in biological terms that the eugenicists would have found familiar, that is, as 'hereditary taint': Jacques's homicidal impulses are specifically aimed at women. Depicted as an ancestral vengeance, his violence is defined as male; as such, it reinscribes a patriarchal paradigm of female submission. Notwithstanding its atrocity, the idea of a primordial 'voice of the blood'; is almost glamourised: 'Did it come from the remote past, some malady with which women had infected his race, the resentment passed down from male to male since the first betrayal in the depth of some cave?' (Zola, p. 67). The image of 'the blond beast of prey' employed at about the same time by Nietzsche is anticipated in the moment when the word 'male' slips into the place of 'beast'. 'He realised that the male in him … would push open that door and strangle that girl, lashed on by the instinct of rape and the urge to avenge the age-old outrage' (Zola, p. 69). But this is only a moment: 'Animality', monstrosity, and murder are posed as hereditary and pathological and given a precise class character. Jacques is a proletarian, the product of disadvantaged social conditions. Through this particular explanation of his 'instinct', Zola unravels his social agenda, transforming the reader's condemnation into possible empathy. Conversely, the sexual perversion of Grandmorin, the president of the railway company, and his own compulsive instinct to rape is foregrounded but never analysed by Zola.

By focusing on Lantier, the author ultimately works to medicalise and discursify the proletarian body and to declass its unruly sexuality while winning the reader to the cause of the protagonist. Jacques never ceases to be the figure of a 'good giant'; and the conclusion of the novel enforces this image by bringing together, at the core of a powerful, beast-like image of masculinity, a masochistic gesture of self-sacrifice among the sentimental figures of a troop of dying young soldiers. In what might be considered a final expiatory (and protofuturist) gesture, Jacques launches his train in a suicidal race while transporting a convoy of young soldiers to the German frontier. In this final scene, the 'human beast' atones for his criminal tendencies with his own violent death, and his image seems to be redeemed by the proximity of the young soldiers, the custodians of peace and of France's national security. Yet Lantier never acquires a sense of guilt or morality: Even his act of final expiation is another crime. As the Nietzschean 'blond beast of prey'; he never repents of his misdeeds.

This symptomatology of 'the beast within' is provided by Zola through his study of the abnormal male body of the dangerous proletarian – a member of the class of mechanics that was growing up alongside that of the clerks. It is foregrounded also in Nietzsche's texts, but here cleansed of the class anxiety that marks Zola's writing. In his rage, violence, and destructiveness, Lantier might be considered a protosuperman: his most Nietzschean quality is the *masculinity* of his violence. For Nietzsche too the beast is male: both in *Twilight of Idols* (1888) and in *On the Genealogy of Morals* (1887),[4] the German philosopher stages a breathtaking reversal of traditional tropes of gender, so that instinct is no longer coded as feminine and reason is not valorised as a male trait. In both texts, instinct, animality, and the body are now represented as masculine, whereas reason, morality, and the intellect are put under erasure and associated with feminised figures: priests, women, slaves, the herd, and the rabble. Yet comparing *la bête humaine* of Zola and 'the blond beast' of European philosophy, one discerns elements that unequivocally distance these two conceptions of the body: first, Nietzsche abandons Zola's social discourse; therefore, the blond beast is *not* the body of the proletarian. Further, Nietzsche elides class as an explicit social category; his hero belongs to a racial elite. Second, the superman's criminality is devoid of any immediate sexual overtones; his desire to kill is not centred primarily on women but rather is represented as a form of unchannelled and unspent energy. Nietzsche's view of criminality unequivocally reverses Zola's paradigm: what makes man criminally abnormal is not the wildness of the body and the distance from civilisation, denounced by Zola in the living conditions of the worker, but rather man's *being in* civilisation itself. The Nietzschean monstrosity cannot be explained by physical degeneration or heredity: the sick body of man, instead, has been produced through centuries of discipline, that of Judeo-Christian morality:

> The criminal type is the type of the strong human being under unfavourable circumstances: a strong human being made sick. He lacks the wildness, a somehow freer and more dangerous environment and form of existence. ... It is society, our tame, mediocre, emasculated society, in which a natural human being ... necessarily degenerates into a criminal.[5]

Deprived of a space where his wildness can be appropriately expressed, tied down by Christianity, this man has been reduced to one of the herd, and his body has grown ill.

In Nietzsche's schema, the superman's criminality and illness are *produced*: they are the material effects of an ideological activity, Christian morality, that has been at work in social and religious practices for centuries. Yet when Nietzsche moves to the *pars construens* of his theory – how to recuperate that which the priest has atrophied by discursifying it negatively, the body – he reverts to a language of origins, thus falling into what could be called an essentialist trap. The body as the place of instincts and nature is posed as an authentic and transhistorical category, always already present in the 'noble races' of the past and the present – 'the Roman, Arabian, Germanic, Japanese nobility, the Homeric heroes, the Scandinavian Vikings': as Nietzsche lists them in *The Genealogy of Morals*.[6] The 'blond beast' is dormant in man, but it can be 'awakened' at special moments and in special spaces:

> Once they go outside, where the strange, the stranger is found, they are not much better than uncaged beasts of prey. There they savour a freedom from all social constraints. ... They go back to the innocent conscience of the beast of prey, as triumphant monsters who perhaps emerge from a disgusting procession of murder, arson, rape and torture exhilarated and undisturbed of spirit. ... The hidden core has to erupt from time to time, the animal has to get out again and go back to the wilderness.[7]

The space 'outside' of civilisation, where man can become superman and recover all his feral and joyous freedom, here again functions as the employee's heterotopia,[8] his afterhours, the place where he thinks he can finally take off his encumbering social mask and become himself.

Just as Nietzsche represents the 'animal' in each man as a bedrock of authenticity, so he falls into the same form of essentialism when writing specifically about the body in *Thus Spoke Zarathustra* (1892). On the one hand, the body is presented as 'performing' subjectivity: 'Your intelligence, my brother, which you call "spirit" is also an instrument of your body. ... You say "I" and you are proud of this word. But greater than this ... is your body and its great intelligence, which does not say "I" but performs "I".'[9] On the other hand, the body is presented as the *source* of identity, authenticity, and truth, as no longer subverting but replacing reason and its function: 'Body I am and soul – thus speaks the child. ... But the awakened and knowing says: body I am entirely, and nothing else; and soul is only another world for something about the body.'[10] The Cartesian deletion and submission of the flesh is reversed into an almost Blakean triumph of the body over the soul. This central reversal became instrumental for the generational protest against the 'elders' and their authority, which made Nietzscheanism such a pervasive cultural force and animated German youth culture in particular in the early twentieth century. The image of the prophet Zarathustra, alone in nature, speaking his wisdom from a wild mountain landscape, inspired and reinforced the modern cult of *Bergeinsamkeit*, the 'solitude in the mountains', the desire to flee the city to 'find oneself' in the heterotopic space of nature or, subsequently, in the romanticised and heroically dangerous 'elsewhere' of the battlefield. At the outbreak of the war, *Thus Spoke Zarathustra* was the most popular book among literate German soldiers; copies were given free to the troops and commentators noted that it was even more popular in the trenches than the Bible.[11]

Nonetheless, the Nietzschean body is not lawless, nor does Nietzsche wish to do away with the subject: in the new subjectivity of the superman the body and its instincts are no longer held in check by reason but by will. Kant's question of the 'self-imposed tutelage' upon the individual self and of action through the individual's exercise of his own discernment – two elements through which the autonomy and free will of the bourgeois self had been historically predicated – is recast in terms of the individual's power over the body through the exercise of his will. As the locus of a 'material spirituality' no longer governed by the priests, the body is not allowed to dissipate itself in expenditure but rather becomes the testing ground for the subject's willpower. The most important evidence of this corporeal spirituality is 'not to react at once to a stimulus, but to gain control of all the inhibiting excluding instincts. ... [This] is what is called a strong will; the essential feature is precisely *not* to will, to be able to suspend desire. All unspirituality, all vulgar commonness depends on the inability to resist a stimulus.'[12] Notwithstanding the parallels in this concept with the masochistic logic of suspension of pleasure, here the Nietzschean superman's will to power has very little to do with the aesthete's 'disciplinary' self-indulgence. Whereas for Wilde, as a character in *The Picture of Dorian Gray* suggests, 'the only way to get rid of a temptation is to yield to it',[13] the superman considers the inability to resist a stimulus a sign of vulgarity and a lack of virility.

In employing the language of taste ('vulgar commonness') to define the aristocratic qualities of the superman, Nietzsche appears to share Gustave Le Bon's concern about the emotional crowd. The Nietzschean blond beast as another version of Le Bon's masculine individualist flaunts desire only in order to be able to display his mastery of it. What distinguishes the superman from the herd is his capability to control his flesh and its natural violence. Paradoxically, the blond beast's excessive body is constructed as an excess without desire and without any superfluousness. The superman is, as Nietzsche affirms in *Thus Spoke Zarathustra*, a 'necessary man' whose non-mundane qualities of self-mastery and frugality reinscribe his body in the economy of asceticism and, despite his independence, make him compatible with the bourgeois imperatives of order, restraint, functionality, and respectability.[14]

In order to become the prototype of the Aryan national figure, the blond beast and his violence had to be adapted to the moral principles of the middle class, chief upholders of the ideology of nationalism. The *embourgeoisement* of the superman and of his excessive body works on two levels: it serves the exclusive and xenophobic interest of the middle class and also represents a myth of identification for the petty bourgeois who wants to be part of that class. Through the image of the blond beast a discourse of elitist separation is spoken in a subtly interclassist language. In the end, the muscled body is taken from the manual labourer and the proletarian and given to the bourgeois male, who will care for it within the precepts of the Nietzschean protest, revised for popular application. Through a suitable domestication of Nietzschean ideas, so that the superman's grandiosity could also be a model for what Webb had termed 'those sections of the population that give proof of thrift and foresight', the petty bourgeois inherits this body with the charge that he care for it in the name of race and nation.

POPULARISING MANLINESS

In the decade before the First World War this antidecadent Nietzschean discourse of the body, which paradoxically championed the same neoclassical physique that the decadents had praised, was diffused in a range of activities that flourished with the increasing regimentation and militarisation of European society. Beside fostering more and more mass sports activities from lawn tennis to cycling and athletics, the maintenance of the healthy body made for fashions and fashionable crusades with dieting, vegetarianism, exercise, nudism, and abstention from alcohol and smoking all finding fierce advocates. Although these movements often did not immediately appear connected to each other, they all spoke a vitalistic and eugenicist jargon of renewal that functioned as an ideological Esperanto for masses of self-improvers. Most widespread was the mass organisation of sport. With the rise of sports as an industry akin to tourism by the turn of the century, athletics, gymnastics, football, and cycling became enormously popular.[15] In 1896 the first modern Olympic Games were held in Athens; their French organiser, Baron Pierre de Coubertin, spoke of sport as a means of national elevation, a spectacle that refines and improves both the character and the body of the nation. His model was the relation, noted again and again in this period, between the physical and moral education of British public schools and the power of the British Empire.[16] [...] In Germany in particular, the connection between athleticism, virility, and national renewal came to be particularly influential; the conditions were put in place in these years for the subsequent fascist colonisation of corporeality: 'The body'; as the Nazi sport theorist Alfred Baumler would declare in 1937, 'is a political concept/space' ('*Das Leib ist ein Politikum*').[17] The qualities of endurance, discipline, and strength suggested by the toned muscles of the national athlete anticipated and provided an image for the agonistic-sportive totalitarian state of thirty years later, in which ideological muscularity would be deliberately trumpeted against liberalism and its 'disembodied' weak politics.

The same concern with fitness, physical and cultural regeneration, coupled with a distrust of liberal institutions – in this case the family and the school – characterised the German Youth Movement, an early 'countercultural' phenomenon that spread nationally after its founding in a Berlin suburb in 1901. The slogan of the movement, 'youth for itself alone', pointed to its members' claim to independence from their elders and their values. The *Wandervogel* (the Ramblers), a movement of urban middle class boys who desired freedom from the tutelage of parents and teachers to create their own mode of life,[18] did not, however, invoke social change; rather, it constituted an unspecified rebellion against bourgeois values in the name of spontaneity and the Nietzschean ideal of self-creation. [...]

In uniting its fascination with elemental nature, youth, and an ideal of physical well-being to nationalist sentiments, the *Wandervogel* is symptomatic of the specific discourse taken in the early twentieth century rediscovery of the male body in European culture. The free and pure bodiliness for which these youths searched simultaneously challenged and reinforced bourgeois respectability: Whereas the group's emphasis on spontaneity and instinct taught that there was no shame in the body and in its activities, it also proposed a chivalric ideal of manliness through the image of a steeled, 'bronzed', and drilled body in which purity and self-mastery had deleted any trace of sexuality. This noble and natural body, in the words of Carl Boesch, the editor of the movement's publication *Der Vortrupp*, was defined in opposition to 'the ugly human being of modernity, the underdeveloped urban type, disfigured by debauchery, a hypocritical way of life and the spiritual paltriness of the employee'.[19] In Boesch's harangue, the language that the late Victorian commissions had used to describe the effects of slum living on proletarians is employed against modernity in general, with an added admonishment to the employee as the bearer of such modernity. What distinguished this paltry urban type from the 'real man' was the latter's capability to endure, to stick to physical discipline *and* enjoy it. In England these qualities of manly agonism had earlier been inculcated in the upper classes through the ethos and the athleticism (of 'prefects' and Kiplingesque gamesmanship) learned in the public schools. This ideal of manliness, both powerful and self-sacrificial, was popularised among boys of the 'lower classes' through the most popular youth movement of all, the Boy Scouts of Robert Baden-Powell, founded in 1908.

From the beginning, the British Boy Scout movement mixed Nietzschean ideals of individualism, will, and physical power with the patriotic concern of eugenics. Baden-Powell was deeply concerned with the 'boys' problem', which he saw as the waste of youthful bodies in the dissipated life of the city. His writing, as well as the summer camps, weekly meetings, and regime of exercise in nature that his movement instituted, aimed at producing a new type of young man, whose health and physical prowess could counteract the implicitly degenerative tendencies of modern England. 'God made men to be men', wrote Baden-Powell. 'We badly need some training for our lads, if we are to keep up manliness in our race instead of lapsing into a nation of soft, sloppy, cigarette-suckers.'[20] In a sketch that appeared in the first edition of *Scouting for Boys* (1908), Baden-Powell translated in visual terms the opposition between the 'real man' and the paltry urban creature: an upstanding, healthy-looking, self-possessed young man is contrasted with the 'streetcorner loafer' who, with his apathetic look, and curved shoulders, wastes himself away in smoking and in idling as a spectator of football matches. Baden-Powell's degenerate smoker is also wearing glasses: this detail signifies the author's disdain, shared by much German *Wandervogel* writing, for formal education and 'mental work'. Occasionally in his writing, Baden-Powell attacks intellectualism as a form of snobbery opposed to the vigour and the dynamism inscribed in the boy scout's body. [...]

In Baden-Powell's eugenicist discourse of national improvement, in the Youth Movement's romantic return to nature, and even in the spectacularised athleticism of sports, Nietzschean vitalism was transformed into a sentimentalised and heroical ethos of purposeful male endurance and even suffering. In fact, the young manliness of the athlete, boy scout, and soldier of this period was an icon of masculinity whose disciplinary character also included a transgressive and sexual edge. The way the body of the Nietzschean superman was 'marketed' and circulated in early twentieth century European culture as the natural foundation of a new form of normative masculinity was mostly the index of this culture's anxiety vis-à-vis the social and gender instabilities of the period. Because of its structural ambivalence, of its capability to speak both to bourgeois asceticism and self-control (the will) and to the desire to subvert these very bourgeois values through a language of excess (the instincts), the Nietzschean hyperbody constituted an ambiguous form of interpellation. While urging the New Man to master his own excess in a gesture of superior spirituality, as was visible both in the self-imposed discipline of the athlete and in the sacrificial self-expenditure of the patriotic soldier, the early twentieth century production of masculine corporeality also displayed the male body as an object of consumption. [...]

Thus the body of the superman, for Nietzsche a declassed icon of manliness that combined proletarian muscles and aristocratic will to power, came to be organised for mass consumption through the norms of visibility and propriety that had belonged to bourgeois representation. The new-style corporeality that the Boy Scouts' language of puritanism and renunciation produced was paradoxical: although the body was always foregrounded, even shown naked or semi-naked, sexuality had been wiped off its image. In this arena, the type of instinctuality Zola displayed through Jacques Lantier – but also the 'young man carbuncular's' playful expenditure – was banned altogether. The sexuality of the foregrounded body would be considered directly only in treatises of abnormal sexuality, such as Cesare Lombroso's *The Delinquent Woman* and Havelock Ellis's *Studies in the Psychology of Sex*,[21] or hidden beneath the quasi-mystic vitalism that can be traced from the utopias of Samuel Butler to D. H. Lawrence or dissimulated under the sign of 'the force of life' in vitalist texts such as G. B. Shaw's *Man and Superman*. This renewed splitting of the revealed body into an image akin to that of the Greek statue on the one hand and into outlaw wildness on the other was enforced by the two spheres where each fragment was confined and discursified. The healthy body became more and more the object of photographic inquiry, but in its images as they appeared in publications of the Youth Movement, such as Herman Popert's *Der Vortrupp*, or in the official journal of Baden-Powell's Boy Scouts, *The Headquarters Gazette*, particular, visual strategies assured that nakedness was not pornography: the young male body, almost always portrayed in movement against a natural background, was shown as disciplining itself and consuming its excess in the sportive gesture. This seminaked, sportive male body, precursor to the famous visual displays of the athlete's body in, for example, Lern Riefenstahl's 1936 film *Olympiad*, was made visible as nature to be contemplated. At the same time, the other body was medicalised in the inquiry of psychoanalysis and sexology by Havelock Ellis, Krafft-Ebing, Freud, and Hirschfield or transformed into a tourist attraction, as happened in occasional texts such as *Berlin drittes Geschlecht* (Berlin's third sex) (1904), a sort of Baedeker of the city's homosexual culture, listing all the major clubs, restaurants, cafés, and bathhouses where homosexuals could be found and joined but also watched as a curiosity.[22]

The split between visible and invisible bodiliness was articulated in terms of gender by such figures as the German cultural critic and racialist Otto Weininger. Weininger's *Sex and Character* of 1907, probably the most influential racial tract of the early twentieth century,[23] depicted the desexualised body as the perfect master of its instincts and as such 'spiritual' and male. Thanks to this mastery, the male subject was cast as the creator, the founder of civilisation. Women, in Weininger's scheme, preoccupied with their narcissistic sexuality, never matured socially: their biological emotionality relegated them to the private, infantile sphere of the home. True men, insisted Weininger, did not yield to their senses: their manliness, in a very Nietzschean way, resided exactly in their capability to practise self-restraint. As Lord Baden-Powell wrote in a sentence that might be considered a corollary to Weininger's theory, 'The energy that the primitive animal puts almost solely into sex, in the human is turned into all sorts of other activities, such as science. ...'[24] Women were excluded from such activities, and so were the 'inferior races': which, lacking a substantial portion of masculinity, were biologically constituted according to the feminine incapability of controlling their sexuality and emotions.

This view of sexuality as an unrestrainable and feminine quality helped Weininger to reaffirm, on a new ground, the patriarchal claims of a natural division of labour. If the opposition of man as breadwinner to woman as homemaker was less stable by the turn of the century, when women, such as [T.S.] Eliot's typist,[25] entered the European job market en masse, a new gendered distribution of public and private roles was now made possible through Weininger's argument: because of his physical qualities and spiritual characteristics man could conquer a new public space, further away from the newly feminised sphere of the office, by going to war. Women, whose bodies signified passivity and weakness, did not fight and remained caught in the private space of the city apartment and of civilian life. [...]

9

Male Bodies and the White Terror

Klaus Theweleit

THE BODY RECONSTRUCTED IN THE
MILITARY ACADEMY

By what means is a young boy made a soldier? How does he become what Canetti terms a 'stereometric figure'?[1] How does body armour attain its final form, what are its functions, how does the 'whole' man who wears it function – and above all – what is the nature of his ego, what is its site (which I believe must be identifiable)? And finally, what is the nature of the soldier's sexuality? What processes in the act of killing give him the pleasure he can apparently no longer find elsewhere?

As a rule, it was in the military academy – *the* German officer school – that the German officer acquired his finished form. One account of the changes undergone by the soldier body is given by Salomon.[2] The following precise reconstruction of his description should serve to highlight some of the differences between the language these men use in confrontation with what is alien (a language of reality destruction) and the language in which they describe their own bodily exterior – or, more specifically, the workings of their own musculature. Salomon at times waxes positively lyrical; apparently his musculature is not the site of his anxieties.

He describes the military academy as an 'institution' (*Anstalt*), a place where the cadet lives behind prison bars. He has no right of exit from the prison; it is granted only in reward for strict adherence to its governing laws.

Relationships between the inmates are, without exception, hierarchical. When the cadet enters the academy, his position in the hierarchy is initially determined by his age; he has to earn any subsequent position. All the cadets have a place within a direct order of rank. Each knows exactly which cadets are 'above' him and which 'below'. Each has the power to command and punish those below and a duty to obey those above. The occupant of the lowest position in the hierarchy must find another whom even he can dominate or he is finished.

If a cadet fails to exercise his rights over his inferiors, he is despised or demoted. Thus the situation never arises. Privilege is universally exercised.

There are no gaps in the cadet's daily round of duties. Only those who have sufficiently mastered the art of demand fulfilment can squeeze a few seconds for other activities.

Everything is planned and everything is public. Withdrawal is impossible, since there is no place to retreat to. Toilet doors leave the head and feet of the seated occupant exposed. Trousers have no pockets.

When the cadet receives a letter, he has to open it and present the signature for inspection. Letters signed by women are read by the officer distributing the mail and (usually) torn up. Only letters from mothers are handed on.

None of the cadets live in private. The dormitories have open doors. Talking from bed to bed is forbidden. The dormitory is kept under surveillance through a window in a wooden partition, behind which an officer sits and keeps watch.[3]

The beds are narrow, hard and damp. Any boy found hiding his head under the pillows is labelled a 'sissy' (*Schlappschwanz*). 'Sissies' are put on 'report'. There are reports for every infringement; but the only way a boy can carry out the extra duties they impose is by neglecting his existing duties. If his negligence is noticed, he is put on report again. One crime punishable by report is failure to keep equipment in order – which is unavoidable, since the regulations are too numerous to follow them all to the letter. Therefore after the first report, others are bound to follow.

Boys who want to go to the toilet at night have to wake the duty officer. In this case too, punishment invariably follows. Unusual behaviour of any kind is punished by forfeit; the boy is deprived of food, leave, or the opportunities for relaxation that are in any case minimal, no more than momentary easings of pressure.

In cadets who wish to remain such, all this very soon produces a 'quite extraordinarily thick skin'.[4] The 'thick skin' should not be understood metaphorically.

On his second day in the academy, Salomon had already sensed 'that here, for the first time in his life, he was not subject to arbitrary conditions, but to a single law'.[5] He experiences this as good fortune. He resolves to bear every punishment meted out to him, gives himself the necessary 'internal wrench', and stands stiffly erect. Everything up to now has been 'arbitrary' – and school continues to be so. School is an activity performed by teachers, powerless wielders of power – ridiculous. The boy enters the institution at the age of twelve. It is at the beginning of puberty and under the 'pressure' of its 'water' (Freud),[6] that he experiences the good fortune of subjection to a law. Freud saw puberty as a phase of transition to fully formed sexual organisation, the completion of which manifests itself in the capacity for heterosexual object-choice.[7] But the military academy transforms this 'unusually intense wave of the libido'[8] into something other than 'object-relationships'.

The cadet never receives instructions; he recognises his mistakes only in the moment of transgression from the reactions of others who already know the score. With slight variations according to his cleverness, each newcomer thus necessarily repeats the mistakes of his predecessors, who in turn recognise and welcome the apparent opportunity to treat their successors as they themselves have previously been treated. Justice works on the principle of equal torment for all. The principle is strictly adhered to; there are no grounds on which a mistake might be considered excusable.

The punishments meted out to fellow cadets are oriented exclusively to the body. For a minor transgression on his very first day, Salomon is made to balance a tray of knickknacks on his outstretched hands (and woe betide him should any of them fall). He is then made to crouch with an open pair of compasses wedged between his heels and buttocks. If he moves even infinitesimally upward or downward, the compasses will either stab him in the buttocks or drop on the floor. But if he succeeds in staying still, the reward, as always, will be immediate advancement. He will no longer be the lowest in the hierarchy of 'sacks' (*Säcke*) – 'sack' being the name for all newcomers who are treated accordingly, emptied out, punched into shape, and refilled.

Younger boys courageous enough to defend themselves gain respect. But even if they win the occasional fist-fight with older boys, punishment always remains the prerogative of their elders.

A further first day experience reported by Salomon: he recalls a talk by an officer on the importance of learning how to die.

Night, cold bed, cold blankets, the morning wash in cold water. The boy who hesitates, even momentarily, is immersed and showered by the others. Breakfast by hierarchy. The boy who grabs a roll before his turn gets nothing. For the last in the pecking order, there remains the smallest portion, a crumb. To be last is impermissible.

Physical exercise, even before breakfast:

> If I failed to pull myself up far enough for my nose to pass the bar, or to keep my knees straight while pulling my legs upward, the dormitory leader would give generous assistance by punching the tensed muscles of my upper arm with his clenched fist. This did indeed make it possible to identify the ultimate limits of my strength.[9]

Every exercise reaches the 'ultimate limits', the point where pain shifts to pleasure:

> The climbing apparatus was ten metres high; it had a ladder, various perches, and smooth wooden walls. We climbed up and jumped down, hesitating for one tense moment at the top, leaping blind, tasting the full weight of the drop, slamming into the ground with a force that sent a terrible shock reverberating from the heels through the lower back, then into the rest of the body.[10]

If the cadet has any kind of choice, it is one between different punishments. He is offered the alternative of a caning on the behind, or forfeiting leave – he chooses the beating. The body swallows attack after attack until it becomes addicted. Every exertion becomes a 'means of enhancing an already intoxicated consciousness, of adding strength to strength'.

The boy who fails to transform rituals of bodily pain into 'intoxicated consciousness'[11] (the mental intoxication of a head that crowns a powerful body) is cast out, as was the spy from the ritual speech or the unwilling participant from block parade-formations.

One passage in Salomon's book describes a certain cadet named Ulzig standing rigid with terror. He is the only nonswimmer to have failed to jump from a three-metre board. Many have already had to be pulled from the water to save them from drowning. But they continue to jump, half-blind, their limbs aching, until they can swim. Salomon learns to swim on the third day; but Ulzig leaves the institution – he is fetched away by his father, a 'mountain of a father', a major. The cadets would have liked to give him a good beating but were stopped by the officer in charge of the swimming (a leper is not for beating).

I had gradually adapted. The service no longer appeared to me as a machine racing along mysteriously, its actions unexpected and apparently unmotivated. Instead, a few figures with whom I had any kind of relationship were now clearly and concretely emerging from the confusion. I was as determined as ever to defend myself when necessary, but my resolve was now less often broken by perplexity. Slowly, I began to lift my head higher.[12]

As Salomon himself becomes a component in the machine, he no longer perceives it as racing on its way somewhere above him. Once the machine is no longer external to him and he himself is no longer its victim, it begins to protect him:

In the end, I found myself living a life of absolute solitude. At times, I surrendered with a zeal born of desperation and unhappiness to this most painful of feelings. The only common feature in all my unrelated perceptions was (...) the exceptional and universal ruthlessness that underlay them. This was the only indication of any purpose behind the whole machinery of the Academy. It was the basis on which it was constructed and imbued with life. My merciless subjection to the bitter reality of absolute isolation had originally seemed incongruous in a place where no one even momentarily escaped observation or control. But even the warmest comradeship remained far removed from simple friendship and from the brotherly stream that flows from hand to hand and heart to heart.[13]

At this point in the book, Salomon has been only partially assimilated. While he considers 'exceptional ruthlessness' an acceptable goal for the workings of the machinery, he himself remains half outside it, a lonely young man in search of 'the brotherly stream'. He then gradually comes to realise that the stream can be found only on the outside as a stream of pain. At this point, he integrates himself entirely.

It was, I believed, my own inadequacy that erected an iron barrier between myself and my comrades. I tried repeatedly to break it down; but even the most forceful expression of my lost yearning for human warmth and clumsy intimacy would have been useless. Even outside the academy, an air of sordidness surrounded such gestures; inside, they were still more likely to offend sensibilities. My pitiful efforts to struggle free of my cocoon rebounded against rubber walls; yet I continued to search for some escape. The futility of my efforts was made bitterly clear to me; yet at the same time, doors were opened as wide, at least, as they were able.[14]

The opportunity to escape from the 'cocoon' is presented on one occasion by a different kind of emission: a fart. In a rare conversation with the cadets, an officer suddenly becomes human as he remarks, in a not unfriendly tone, 'What a stench! Somebody open a window!' Salomon's desire for 'human warmth' grasps at this welcome evidence of a human interior, a smell that has broken the 'iron barrier'; he murmurs as in a trance: 'He who smelt it, dealt it'[15] – the moment the words slip from him, he realises they have made his isolation total ...

The officer orders Salomon to come to his room and grills him until he reveals the name of the boy who taught him the saying. Having 'ratted' on a fellow-cadet, Salomon is 'put in the shithouse' (*in Verschiss getan*) – the expression denotes the breaking off of all communication. Having spoken of something that no longer forms, or is permitted to form, part of the cadet's existence, he himself is treated as nonexistent, foul as the foulest air. 'Even my own brother was now inclined to give credence to my theory that I was a foundling. "No brother of mine" he said, "could do anything like this".'[16]

In the end, the culprit is released from the shithouse; the effect of this particular form of punishment seems insufficiently external. The penalty takes a new form as an assault on his bodily periphery. Payment is made in the only valid currency, which is pain:

The cadets stood around me in a semicircle. Each one held a knout in his hand, long leather thongs attached to a wooden stick that was used for beating the dirt out of clothes. Glasmacher stepped forward, took me by the arm, and led me over to the table. I climbed up, not without difficulty, and lay down on my stomach. Glasmacher took my head in his hands, pressed my eyes shut, and forced my skull hard against the surface of the table. I gritted my teeth and tensed my whole body. The first blow whistled. I jerked upward, but Glasmacher held me tight; the blows rained down on my back, shoulders, legs, a frenzied fire of hard, smacking blows. My hands were tightly gripped around the edge of the table, I beat out a rhythm with my knees, shins, and toes in an attempt to expel the excruciating pain. Now all the torment seemed to move through my body and implant itself in the table; again and again my hips and loins slammed against the wood and made it shudder with me; every blow recharged the bundle of muscles and skin, blood and bones and sinews, with slingshot force, till my whole body stretched under tension and threatened to burst in its lower regions. I gave my head over entirely to Glasmacher's hands, wrenched myself shut, and finally lay still and moaning. 'Stop!' Corporal First-Class Glöcklen commanded, and the assembled company jumped back instantly. I slid slowly from the table. Glasmacher stepped up to proffer his hand, and said, 'Peace! The affair is closed'.[17]

More than this, he has been accepted. He has experienced the sensations that indicate other men's affection; he now numbers among their beloved.

The only site at which feelings have legitimate existence is the body as a 'bundle of muscles and skin, blood and bones and sinews'. This is the message hammered out by the drill; each new exercise is structured around it, as is every punishment detail. No feeling or desire remains unclarified, all are transformed into clear perception: the desire for bodily warmth into a perception of the heat of bodily pain; the desire for contact into a perception of the whiplash.

And little by little the body accepts these painful interventions along its periphery as responses to its longing for pleasure. It receives them as experiences of satisfaction. The body is estranged from the pleasure principle, drilled and reorganised into a body ruled by the 'pain principle': what is nice is what hurts ...

And, finally, the 'sack' is given his equatorial baptism[18] – a form of torture that appears in German navy tales, unsurprisingly, as one of the high points in the life of a sailor:

There was an official ceremony to mark the end of one's days as a sack. On the appointed day, to the great joy of their older comrades, the sacks were individually summoned to the company room, where a dentist from the city would be busy with his instruments. Every sack then had to sit on a small stool, while the tooth-flicker (*Zahnfips*), as the comrades called him, messed around for a while in the poor offender's wide-open mouth with a long pair of pliers; he would then take a firm grip on all his remaining baby teeth and pull them one after the other. As I stood bent over the bucket, spitting blood beneath the wicked smile of the tooth-flicker, Glasmacher consoled me by saying that it had formerly been customary to take the sacks to the dispensary and fill them with the appropriate dose of castor oil to ensure they were purged both internally and externally.[19]

As his last baby teeth swim away in a bucket of blood, so too do the residues of his anchorage in mother-ocean and a rock stretches its head from the collar of his uniform.

I began to notice my body stiffening, my posture gaining in confidence. When I thought back to childhood games at home, I was filled with bitter shame. It had become quite impossible to move with anything other than dignity. On the rare occasions when a senseless desire for freedom surfaced, it invariably shattered against a new determination and will. My new-found capacity to follow orders to the letter was double compensation for losing the joys of roving unrestrained.[20]

Then the first visit home:

A deep chasm divided me from the habits and customs of my so-called parental home, a chasm I felt neither the desire nor the compulsion to bridge. I found any kind of solicitous care quite intolerable, and the broad stream of my mother's empathy only made me wish to breathe the harsher air of the corps again.[21]

In becoming *capable* of following orders to the letter – he is by this point no longer forced to do so – Salomon liberates himself from the family unit. His function is now to operate within a different formation – although the 'stream of his mother's empathy' is still able to reach him.

Does this stream have anything to do with the flow in the new machine of which Salomon has become a happily functioning component?

The machine's flow is continuous, a totality that maintains every component in appropriate and uninterrupted motion. It has no cut-off points. It never pauses: if the machinery of the military academy ever stops running, it is done for. To turn it off is impossible.

This machinery is the antithesis of the desiring-machine, whose principle – 'the joys of roving unrestrained' – Salomon explicitly renounces. The 'and now? ... so that was that' gives way to the pleasure of existing as a component within a whole machine, a macromachine, a power machine in which the component does not invest his own pleasure, but produces that of the powerful. The man pleasurably invests his self only as a thoroughly reliable part of the machine. His line from this point on: the machine must run, the faster the better; it breaks down, it won't be my fault ...

Remarkably enough: the component itself, in becoming a component, becomes whole – a whole that is simultaneously subordinate and dominant. It has precisely determined functions and very specific couplings to other parts; it no longer possesses its former functional multiplicity. There must have been some problem with multiplicity; its potential must have been threatening – for the component gladly accepts the wholeness it finds in the totality machine.

The machinery – and I think this is very important – transforms functions such as 'thinking', 'feeling', 'seeing' (potential multiplicity functions with the power to develop myriad couplings) into movement, movements of the body. Salomon's new thinking follows a very specific tempo:

> Here even the most improbable actions were redolent with significance. The simplest salute became a symbol of submission to an authority that bound both parties in mutually fruitful association. The slow march, tempo one hundred fourteen, became the physical and spiritual expression of discipline to the brink of death.[22]

THE TROOP AS TOTALITY-MACHINE

Canetti's description of the soldier as a 'stereometric figure' restricts attention to the individual soldier, to his body armour and the supporting armour surrounding it: the barrack walls, the block formations of the troop, etc. Since he neglects to consider the *function* of the soldier as machine component, he falls short of describing the construction of the machine *in toto*.[23]

> The colonel raised his hand to his helmet. The regiment began marking time, four thousand legs rising in unison and descending to stamp the ground; up and away, the first company pitched its legs high as if pulled by a single cord, then set them down on grass and soil, eighty centimetres between them, foot to foot – the flag approaches ... A single sword hurled itself upward, flashed, and dropped deep to the ground; the earth turned to dust under hundreds of marching feet; the earth rumbled and groaned; two hundred fifty men were passing, touching close one after another, two hundred fifty rifles on their shoulders, a line sequence straight as an arrow above a line of helmets, shoulders, knapsacks straight as an arrow; two hundred fifty hands hissing back and forth; two hundred fifty legs tearing bodies onward in cruel, relentless rhythm.[24]

The impression of a machine being set in motion as the 'finished' cadets march off to war is created quite intentionally by Salomon, as is the sense that the machine is both one of war and of sexuality ('bodies ... in cruel, relentless rhythm'). Salomon's description of bodies as 'tearing ... onward', emphasises the machine's violent nature.

Two aspects of its construction are stressed: the uniformity of its contours ('as if pulled by a single cord'; 'a line sequence straight as an arrow') and the large number of its functionally equivalent components ('four thousand legs rising in unison'; 'two hundred fifty hands hissing'; 'two hundred fifty legs tearing').

The soldier's limbs are described as if severed from their bodies; they are fused together to form new totalities. The leg of the individual has a closer functional connection to the leg of his neighbour than to his own torso. In the machine, then, new body-totalities are formed: bodies no longer identical with the bodies of individual human beings.

The brigade was a single body, destined to be bound in solidarity.[25] (H. Plaas, describing the Ehrhardt Naval Brigade.)

Each individual totality-component moves in precise unison with every other: 'One troop, one man and one rhythm' (Plaas).[26]

The principal goal of the machine seems to be to keep itself moving. It is entirely closed to the external world. Only in combination, with another machine absolutely like itself can it join together to create some larger formation.

What then produces the machine?

The second company, the third, the fourth. Endlessly, it rolled onward, a broad front advancing, never wavering, wall after wall, the whole regiment a machine with rows ranged deep, implacable, precise, four thousand human beings and one regiment, whipped by the hymn of martial music. Who could oppose it? Who would set himself against this power, youth, and discipline, this eager thousand formed in a single will? The forest border seemed to tremble and retreat; the earth shook and reared, clatter of weapons and crunch of leather, dark eyes under brims of helmets. The 109th Regimental Grenadiers: guards' piping, white wings, a four hundred year tradition. Formed and steeled through long years, sworn to the flag, practised in the art of death, plucked from the loins of a people and sent into war. And so the regiment marched, tempo one hundred fourteen, twelve companies, war strong, prepared for death, ninety rounds in the cartridge case of every man, hard biscuits and ammunition in his rucksack, coat rolled and boots new. Muscles like ropes, broad-chested, tough-jointed, wall of bodies born of discipline; this was the front, the frontier, the assault, the element of storm and resistance; and behind it stood Germany, nourishing the army with men and bread and ammunition.[27]

In the first instance, what the troop-machine produces is itself – itself as a totality that places the individual soldier in a new set of relations to other bodies; itself as a combination of innumerable identically polished components.

The troop also produces an expression: of determination, strength, precision; of the strict order of straight lines and rectangles; an expression of battle, and of a specific masculinity. Or to put it another way, the surplus value produced by the troop is a code that consolidates other totality-formations between men, such as the 'nation'.

As Salomon's text also shows with striking clarity, the troop-machine produces the front *before reaching it*: it *is* the front. As the troop sets itself in motion, the border itself is displaced. Even in peacetime, front and border are part of the troop. War is the condition of its being. It always has a border to defend, a front to advance (its own). The only thing that changes if war is declared is that the same process becomes easier and more satisfying. War offers an opportunity for discharge, for the front to be released from internal pressure. In peacetime, the front presses inward toward its own interior, compressing the individual components of the machine. It produces internal tensions of high intensity that press for discharge.

The crucial impulse behind the regeneration of the machine seems to be its desire for release – and release is achieved when the totality-machine and its components explode in battle. A strange productive principle: the machine produces its own new boundaries by transgressing the boundaries it erects around itself.

The troop-machine is not independent; it has no autonomous existence. It is connected to Germany by an umbilical cord that feeds it with bread, spare parts, and munitions. Its energy-machine is 'Germany'.

As long as the energy circuit symbiosis with 'Germany' continues to function, the machine marching to war can be presented as the supreme totality, the universal sum total. What Neruda says of the ocean ('And you lack nothing'), is realised for Jünger in the battle-machine: lack is transcended.

> ... there are times when we feel light and free in our heavy armour, sensing, despite the weight, the impetus and the power which drive us forward. We move most easily in battle-formation; for the power and will of the blood speaks most directly from the battle-machine. We are stirred as human beings are seldom stirred by (troops) marching by ... for they represent the will of a people to greatness and dominance, shaped in its most effective form, as steely hard implements. They contain all we have, all we think, all we are; modern man marching to battle is modern man in his most characteristic form. ... He is a whole, not one part only.[28]

The same utopian impulse was recognised by Foucault as part of a whole ion of representations of the military-machine.

Historians of ideas usually attribute the dream of a perfect society to the philosophers and jurists of the eighteenth century; its fundamental reference was not to the state of nature, but to the meticulously subordinated cogs of a machine, not to the primal social contract, but to permanent coercions, not to fundamental rights, but to indefinitely progressive forms of training, not to the general will but to automatic docility.[29]

THE TOTALITY-COMPONENT: FIGURE OF STEEL

Once in battle, the formation dissolves. The macromachine separates out into its components. Each component in the soldierly totality-body has been functional by the drill; battle gives it the opportunity to prove that its own function conform to the functioning principle of the machine itself. Each totality-component becomes a miniature of the machine.

This was a whole new race, energy incarnate, charged with supreme energy. Supple bodies, lean and sinewy, striking features, stone eyes petrified in a thousand terrors beneath their helmets. These were conquerors, men of steel tuned to the most grisly battle. Sweeping across a splintered landscape, they heralded the final triumph of all imagined horror. Unimaginable energies were released as these brave troops broke out to regain lost outposts where pale figures gaped at them with madness in their eyes. Jugglers of death, masters of explosive and flame, glorious predators, they sprang easily through the trenches. In the moment of encounter, they encapsulated the spirit of battle as no other human beings could. Theirs was the keenest assembly of bodies, intelligence, will, and sensation.[30]

Jünger's imaginary man is portrayed as a physical type devoid of drives and of psyche; he has no need of either since all his instinctual energies have been smoothly and frictionlessly transformed into functions of his steel body. This passage seems to me to crystallise a tendency that is evident throughout Jünger's writing: a tendency toward the utopia of the body machine.

In the body-machine the interior of the man is dominated and transformed in the same way as are the components of the macromachine of the troop. For Jünger, then, the fascination of the machine apparently lies in its capacity to show how a man might 'live' (move, kill, give expression) without emotion. Each and every feeling is tightly locked in steel armour.

The 'new man' sired in the drill (the drill as organised battle of the old men against himself) owes allegiance only to the machine that bore him.[31] He is a true child of the drill-machine, created without the help of a woman, parentless. His associations and relationships bind him instead to other specimens of the new man, with whom he allows himself to be united to form the macro-machine troop. All others belong only 'under' him – never alongside, behind, or in front.

The most urgent task of the man of steel is to pursue, to dam in, and to subdue any force that threatens to transform him back into the horribly disorganised jumble of flesh, hair, skin, bones, intestines, and feelings that calls itself human – the human being of old:

> These are the figures of steel whose eagle eyes dart between whirling propellers to pierce the cloud; who dare the hellish crossing through fields of roaring craters, gripped in the chaos of tank engines; who squat for days on end behind blazing machine-guns, who crouched against banks ranged high with corpses, surrounded, half-parched, only one step ahead of certain death. These are the best of the modern battlefield, men relentlessly saturated with the spirit of battle, men whose urgent wanting discharges itself in a single concentrated and determined release of energy.
>
> As I watch them noiselessly slicing alleyways into barbed wire, digging steps to storm outward, synchronising luminous watches, finding the North by the stars, the recognition flashes: this is the new man. The pioneers of storm, the elect of central Europe. A whole new race, intelligent, strong, men of will. Tomorrow, the phenomenon now manifesting itself in battle will be the axis around which life whirls ever faster. A thousand sweeping deeds will arch across their great cities as they stride down asphalt streets, supple predators straining with energy. They will be architects building on the ruined foundations of the world.[32]

The new man is a man whose physique has been machinised, his psyche eliminated – or in part displaced into his body armour, his 'predatory' suppleness. We are presented with a robot that can tell the time, find the North, stand his ground over a red-hot machine-gun, or cut wire without a sound. In the moment of action, he is as devoid of fear as of any other emotion. His knowledge of being able to do what he does is his only consciousness of self.

This, I believe, is the ideal man of the conservative utopia: a man with machinelike periphery, whose interior has lost its meaning (the technocrat is his contemporary manifestation).

This is not a utopia from the technologisation of the means of production; it has nothing to do with the development of machine technology. That development is simply used to express a quality specific to the bodies of these men. The mechanised body as conservative utopia derives instead from men's compulsion to subjugate and repulse what is specifically human within them – the id, the productive force of the unconscious. The soldier male responds to the successful damming in and chaoticising of his desiring-production from the moment of his birth (if not earlier) by fantasising himself as a figure of steel: a man of the new race.[33]

The armour of the soldier male may transform his incarcerated interior into the fuel that speeds him forward; or it may send it spinning outward. As something external to him, it can then be combatted; and it assails him constantly, as if it wished him back: it is a deluge, an invasion from Mars, the proletariat, contagious Jewish lust, sensuous woman.

The conservative utopia of the mechanised body, the body made machine in its totality, does not, then, derive from the development of the industrial means of production, but from the obstruction and transformation of human productive forces.

[...] The punishments of parents, teachers, masters, the punishment hierarchies of young boys and of the military, remind these men constantly of the existence of their periphery (showing them their boundaries), until they 'grow' a functioning and controlling body armour, and a body capable of seamless fusion into larger formations with armourlike peripheries. If my assumptions are correct, the armour of these men may be seen as constituting their ego.

A Freud distanced from the pleasure principle was able to write that:

the way in which we gain new knowledge of our organs during painful illnesses is perhaps a model of the way by which in general we arrive at the idea of our body.[34]

In a society that replaces the experience of pleasure in the body with its experience of pain this is irrefutably a statement of positivist truth. Drill and torture, it seems, are to be seen as the extremes of more general forms of bodily perception. (Now, in the process of being whipped, I know what my ass is capable of feeling and where exactly it's located. Now, as they kick me between the legs, I have my very first sense of my prick's enormous sensitivity ...)

I feel pain, therefore I am. Where pain is, there 'I' shall be – the psychic agency of the I as ego.

10

From 'The Fact of Blackness'

Frantz Fanon

'Dirty nigger!' Or simply, 'Look, a Negro!'

I came into the world imbued with the will to find a meaning in things, my spirit filled with the desire to attain to the source of the world, and then I found that I was an object in the midst of other objects.

Sealed into that crushing objecthood, I turned beseechingly to others. Their attention was a liberation, running over my body suddenly abraded into nonbeing, endowing me once more with an agility that I had thought lost, and by taking me out of the world, restoring me to it. But just as I reached the other side, I stumbled, and the movements, the attitudes, the glances of the other fixed me there, in the sense in which a chemical solution is fixed by a dye. I was indignant; I demanded an explanation. Nothing happened. I burst apart. Now the fragments have been put together again by another self.

As long as the black man is among his own, he will have no occasion, except in minor internal conflicts, to experience his being through others. There is of course the moment of 'being for others', of which Hegel speaks, but every ontology is made unattainable in a colonised and civilised society.[1] It would seem that this fact has not been given sufficient attention by those who have discussed the question. In the *Weltanschauung* [world outlook] of a colonised people there is an impurity, a flaw that outlaws any ontological explanation. Someone may object that this is the case with every individual, but such an objection merely conceals a basic problem. Ontology – once it is finally admitted as leaving existence by the wayside – does not permit us to understand the being of the black man. For not only must the black man be black; he must be black in relation to the white man. Some critics will take it on themselves to remind us that this proposition has a converse. I say that this is false. The black man has no ontological resistance in the eyes of the white man. Overnight the Negro has been given two frames of reference within which he has had to place himself. His metaphysics, or, less pretentiously, his customs and the sources on which they were based, were wiped out because they were in conflict with a civilisation that he did not know and that imposed itself on him.

The black man among his own in the twentieth century does not know at what moment his inferiority comes into being through the other. Of course I have talked about the black problem with friends, or, more rarely, with American Negroes. Together we protested, we asserted the equality of all men in the world. In the Antilles there was also that little gulf that exists among the almost-white, the mulatto, and the nigger. But I was satisfied with an intellectual understanding of these differences. It was not really dramatic. And then ...

And then the occasion arose when I had to meet the white man's eyes. An unfamiliar weight burdened me. The real world challenged my claims. In the white world the man of colour encounters difficulties in the development of his bodily schema. Consciousness of the body is solely a negating activity. It is a third-person consciousness. The body is surrounded by an atmosphere of certain uncertainty. I know that if I want to smoke, I shall have to reach out my right arm and take the pack of cigarettes lying at the other end of the table. The matches, however, are in the drawer on the left, and I shall have to lean back slightly. And all these movements are made not out of habit but out of implicit knowledge. A slow composition of my *self* as a body in the middle of a spatial and temporal world – such seems to be the schema. It does not impose itself on me; it is, rather, a definitive structuring of the self and of the world – definitive because it creates a real dialectic between my body and the world.

For several years certain laboratories have been trying to produce a serum for 'denegrification'; with all the earnestness in the world, laboratories have sterilised their test tubes, checked their scales, and embarked on researches that might make it possible for the miserable Negro to whiten himself and thus to throw off the burden of that corporeal malediction. Below the corporeal schema I had sketched a historico-racial schema. The elements that I used had been provided for me not by 'residual sensations and perceptions primarily of a tactile, vestibular, kinesthetic, and visual character',[2] but by the other, the white man, who had woven me out of a thousand details, anecdotes, stories. I thought that what I had in hand was to construct a physiological self, to balance space, to localise sensations, and here I was called on for more.

'Look, a Negro!' It was an external stimulus that flicked over me as I passed by. I made a tight smile.

'Look, a Negro!' It was true. It amused me.

'Look, a Negro!' The circle was drawing a bit tighter. I made no secret of my amusement.

'Mama, see the Negro! I'm frightened!' Frightened! Frightened! Now they were beginning to be afraid of me. I made up my mind to laugh myself to tears, but laughter had become impossible.

I could no longer laugh, because I already knew that there were legends, stories, history, and above all *historicity*. [...] Then, assailed at various points, the corporeal schema crumbled, its place taken by a racial epidermal schema.

In the train it was no longer a question of being aware of my body in the third person but in a triple person. In the train I was given not one but two, three places. I had already stopped being amused. It was not that I was finding febrile coordinates in the world. I existed triply: I occupied space. I moved toward the other ... and the evanescent other, hostile but not opaque, transparent, not there, disappeared. Nausea ...

I was responsible at the same time for my body, for my race, for my ancestors. I subjected myself to an objective examination, I discovered my blackness, my ethnic characteristics; and I was battered down by tom-toms, cannibalism, intellectual deficiency, fetishism, racial defects, slave-ships, and above all else, above all: 'Sho' good eatin'.'

On that day, completely dislocated, unable to be abroad with the other, the white man, who unmercifully imprisoned me, I took myself far off from my own presence, far indeed, and made myself an object. What else could it be for me but an amputation, an excision, a haemorrhage that spattered my whole body with black blood? But I did not want this revision, this thematisation. All I wanted was to be a man among other men. I wanted to come lithe and young into a world that was ours and to help to build it together.

But I rejected all immunisation of the emotions. I wanted to be a man, nothing but a man. Some identified me with ancestors of mine who had been enslaved or lynched: I decided to accept this. It was on the universal level of the intellect that I understood this inner kinship – I was the grandson of slaves in exactly the same way in which President Lebrun[3] was the grandson of tax-paying, hard-working peasants. In the main, the panic soon vanished.

In America, Negroes are segregated. In South America, Negroes are whipped in the streets, and Negro strikers are cut down by machine-guns. In West Africa, the Negro is an animal. And there beside me, my neighbour in the university, who was born in Algeria, told me: 'As long as the Arab is treated like a man, no solution is possible.'

'Understand, my dear boy, colour prejudice is something I find utterly foreign. ... But of course, come in, sir, there is no colour prejudice among us. ... Quite, the Negro is a man like ourselves. ... It is not because he is black that he is less intelligent than we are. ... I had a Senegalese buddy in the army who was really clever ...'

Where am I to be classified? Or, if you prefer, tucked away?

'A Martinican, a native of "our" old colonies.'

Where shall I hide?

'Look at the nigger! ... Mama, a Negro! ... Hell, he's getting mad. ... Take no notice, sir, he does not know that you are as civilised as we. ...'

My body was given back to me sprawled out, distorted, recoloured, clad in mourning in that white winter day. The Negro is an animal, the Negro is bad, the Negro is mean, the Negro is ugly; look, a nigger, it's cold, the nigger is shivering, the nigger is shivering because he is cold, the little boy is trembling because he is afraid of the nigger, the nigger is shivering with cold, that cold that goes through your bones, the handsome little boy is trembling because he thinks that the nigger is quivering with rage, the little white boy throws himself into his mother's arms: Mama, the nigger's going to eat me up.

All round me the white man, above the sky tears at its navel, the earth rasps under my feet, and there is a white song, a white song. All this whiteness that burns me. ...

I sit down at the fire and I become aware of my uniform. I had not seen it. It is indeed ugly. I stop there, for who can tell me what beauty is?

Where shall I find shelter from now on? I felt an easily identifiable flood mounting out of the countless facets of my being. I was about to be angry. The fire was long since out, and once more the nigger was trembling.

'Look how handsome that Negro is! ...'

'Kiss the handsome Negro's ass, madame!'

Shame flooded her face. At last I was set free from my rumination. At the same time I accomplished two things: I identified my enemies and I made a scene. A grand slam. Now one would be able to laugh.

The field of battle having been marked out, I entered the lists.

What? While I was forgetting, forgiving, and wanting only to love, my message was flung back in my face like a slap. The white world, the only honourable one, barred me from all participation. A man was expected to behave like a man. I was expected to behave like a black man – or at least like a nigger. I shouted a greeting to the world and the world slashed away my joy. I was told to stay within bounds, to go back where I belonged. [...]

I move slowly in the world, accustomed now to seek, no longer for upheaval. I progress by crawling. And already I am being dissected under white eyes, the only real eyes. I am *fixed*. Having adjusted their microtomes, they objectively cut away slices of my reality. I am laid bare. I feel, I see in those white faces that it is not a new man who has come in, but a new kind of man, a new genus. Why, it's a Negro!

I slip into corners, and my long antennae pick up the catch-phrases strewn over the surface of things – nigger underwear smells of nigger – nigger teeth are white – nigger feet are big – the nigger's barrel chest – I slip into corners, I remain silent, I strive for anonymity, for invisibility. Look, I will accept the lot, as long as no one notices me!

'Oh. I want you to meet my black friend. ... Aimé Césaire, a black man and a university graduate. ... Marian Anderson, the finest of Negro singers. ... Dr. Cobb, who invented white blood, is a Negro. ... Here, say hello to my friend from Martinique (be careful, he's extremely sensitive). ...'

Shame. Shame and self-contempt. Nausea. When people like me, they tell me it is in spite of my colour. When they dislike me, they point out that it is not because of my colour. Either way, I am locked into the infernal circle. [...]

I felt knife blades open within me. I resolved to defend myself. As a good tactician, I intended to rationalise the world and to show the white man that he was mistaken.

In the Jew, Jean-Paul Sartre says, there is

> a sort of impassioned imperialism of reason: for he wishes not only to convince others that he is right; his goal is to persuade them that there is an absolute and unconditioned value to rationalism. He feels himself to be a missionary of the universal; against the universality of the Catholic religion, from which he is excluded, he asserts the 'catholicity' of the rational, an instrument by which to attain to the truth and establish a spiritual bond among men.[4]

And, the author adds, though there may be Jews who have made intuition the basic category of their philosophy, their intuition

> has no resemblance to the Pascalian subtlety of spirit, and it is this latter – based on a thousand imperceptible perceptions – which to the Jew seems his worst enemy. As for Bergson, his philosophy offers the curious appearance of an anti-intellectualist doctrine constructed entirely by the most rational and most critical of intelligences. It is through argument that he establishes the existence of pure duration, of philosophic intuition; and that very intuition which discovers duration or life, is itself universal, since anyone may practise it, and it leads toward the universal, since its objects can be named and conceived.[5]

With enthusiasm I set to cataloguing and probing my surroundings. As times changed, one had seen the Catholic religion at first justify and then condemn slavery and prejudices. But by referring everything to the idea of the dignity of man, one had ripped prejudice to shreds. After much reluctance, the scientists had conceded that the Negro was a human being; *in viva* and *in vitro* the Negro had been proved analogous to the white man: the same morphology, the same histology. Reason was confident of victory on every level. I put all the parts back together. But I had to change my tune.

That victory played cat and mouse; it made a fool of me. As the other put it, when I was present, it was not; when it was there, I was no longer. In the abstract there was agreement: the Negro is a human being. That is to say, amended the less firmly convinced, that like us he has his heart on the left side. But on certain points the white man remained intractable. Under no conditions did he wish any intimacy between the races, for it is a truism that 'crossings between widely different races can lower the physical and mental level. ... Until we have a more definite knowledge of the effect of race-crossings we shall certainly do best to avoid crossings between widely different races.'[6]

For my own part, I would certainly know how to react. And in one sense, if I were asked for a definition of myself, I would say that I am one who waits; I investigate my surroundings, I interpret everything in terms of what I discover, I become sensitive.

In the first chapter of the history that the others have compiled for me, the foundation of cannibalism has been made eminently plain in order that I may not lose sight of it. My chromosomes were supposed to have a few thicker or thinner genes representing cannibalism, In addition to the *sex-linked*, the scholars had now discovered the racial-linked.[7] What a shameful science!

But I understand this 'psychological mechanism'. For it is a matter of common knowledge that the mechanism is only psychological. Two centuries ago, I was lost to humanity, I was a slave forever. And then came men who said that it all had gone on far too long. My tenaciousness did the rest; I was saved from the civilising deluge. I have gone forward. [...]

The Jew and I: Since I was not satisfied to be racialised, by a lucky turn of fate I was humanised. I joined the Jew, my brother in misery.

An outrage!

At first thought it may seem strange that the anti-Semite's outlook should be related to that of the Negrophobe. It was my philosophy professor, a native of the Antilles, who recalled the fact to me one day: 'Whenever you hear anyone abuse the Jews, pay attention, because he is talking about you.' And I found that he was universally right – by which I meant that I was answerable in my body and in my heart for what was done to my brother. Later I realised that he meant, quite simply, an anti-Semite is inevitably anti-Negro.

You come too late, much too late. There will always be a world – a white world – between you and us. ... The other's total inability to liquidate the past once and for all. In the face of this affective ankylosis of the white man, it is understandable that I could have made up my mind to utter my Negro cry.[8] Little by little, putting out pseudopodia here and there, I secreted a race. And that race staggered under the burden of a basic element. What was it? Rhythm! Listen to our singer, Léopold Senghor:

It is the thing that is most perceptible and least material. It is the archetype of the vital element. It is the first condition and the hallmark of Art, as breath is of life: breath, which accelerates or slows, which becomes even or agitated according to the tension in the individual, the degree and the nature of his emotion. This is rhythm in its primordial purity, this is rhythm in the masterpieces of Negro art, especially sculpture. It is composed of a theme-sculptural form – which is set in opposition to a sister theme, as inhalation is to exhalation, and that is repeated. It is not the kind of symmetry that gives rise to monotony; rhythm is alive, it is free. ... This is how rhythm affects what is least intellectual in us, tyrannically, to make us penetrate to the spirituality of the object; and that character of abandon which is ours is itself rhythmic.[9]

Had I read that right? I read it again with redoubled attention. From the opposite end of the white world a magical Negro culture was hailing me. Negro sculpture! I began to flush with pride. Was this our salvation?

I had rationalised the world and the world had rejected me on the basis of colour prejudice. Since no agreement was possible on the level of reason, I threw myself back toward unreason. It was up to the white man to be more irrational than I. Out of the necessities of my struggle I had chosen the method of regression, but the fact remained that it was an unfamiliar weapon; here I am at home; I am made of the irrational; I wade in the irrational. Up to the neck in the irrational. And now how my voice vibrates!

> Those who invented neither gunpowder nor the compass
> Those who never learned to conquer steam or electricity
> Those who never explored the seas or the skies
> But they know the farthest corners of the land of anguish
> Those who never knew any journey save that of abduction
> Those who learned to kneel in docility
> Those who were domesticated and Christianised
> Those who were injected with bastardy. ...

Yes, all those are my brothers – a 'bitter brotherhood' imprisons all of us alike. Having stated the minor thesis, I went overboard after something else.

> ... But those without whom the earth would not be
>   the earth
> Tumescence all the more fruitful
> than
> the empty land
> still more the land
> Storehouse to guard and ripen all
> on earth that is most earth
> My blackness is no stone, its deafness
> hurled against the clamour of the day
> My blackness is no drop of lifeless water
> on the dead eye of the world
> My blackness is neither a tower nor a cathedral
> It thrusts into the red flesh of the sun
> It thrusts into the burning flesh of the sky
> It hollows through the dense dismay of its own
>   pillar of patience.[10]

Eyah! the tom-tom chatters out the cosmic message. Only the Negro has the capacity to convey it, to decipher its meaning, its import. Astride the world, my strong heels spurring into the flanks of the world. I stare into the shoulders of the world as the celebrant stares at the midpoint between the eyes of the sacrificial victim. [...]

I walk on white nails. Sheets of water threaten my soul on fire. Face to face with these rites, I am doubly alert. Black magic! Orgies, witches' sabbaths, heathen ceremonies, amulets. Coitus is an occasion to call on the gods of the clan. It is a sacred act, pure, absolute, bringing invisible forces into action. What is one to think of all these manifestations, all these initiations, all these acts? From every direction I am assaulted by the obscenity of dances and of words [...] Black Magic, primitive mentality, animism, animal eroticism, it all floods over me. All of it is typical of peoples that have not kept pace with the evolution of the human race. Or, if one prefers, this is humanity at its lowest. Having reached this point, I was long reluctant to commit myself. Aggression was in the stars. I had to choose. What do I mean? I had no choice. ...

Yes, we are – we Negroes – backward, simple, free in our behaviour. That is because for us the body is not something opposed to what you call the mind. We are in the world. And long live the couple, Man and Earth! Besides, our men of letters helped me to convince you; your white civilisation overlooks subtle riches and sensitivity. Listen:

> Emotive sensitivity. *Emotion is completely Negro as reason is Greek.*[11] Water is rippled by every breeze? Un-sheltered soul is blown by every wind, whose fruit often drops before it is ripe? Yes, in one way, the Negro today is richer *in gifts than in works.*[12] But the tree thrusts its roots into the earth. The river runs deep, carrying precious seeds. And, the Afro-American poet, Langston Hughes, says:

> > I have known rivers
> > ancient dark rivers
> > my soul has grown deep
> > like the deep rivers.

> The very nature of the Negro's emotion, of his sensitivity, furthermore, explains his attitude toward the object perceived with such basic intensity. It is an abandon that becomes need, an active state of communion, indeed of identification, however negligible the action – I almost said the personality of the object. A rhythmic attitude: The adjective should be kept in mind.[13]

So here we have the Negro rehabilitated, 'standing before the bar', ruling the world with his intuition, the Negro recognised, set on his feet again, sought after, taken up, and he is a Negro – no, he is not a Negro but the Negro, exciting the fecund antennae of the world, placed in the foreground of the world, 'open to all the breaths of the world'. I embrace the world! I am the world! The white man has never understood this magic substitution. The white man wants the world; he wants it for himself alone. He finds himself predestined master of this world. He enslaves it. An acquisitive relation is established between the world and him. But there exist other values that fit only my forms. Like a magician, I robbed the white man of 'a certain world', forever after lost to him and his. [...]

I made myself a poet of the world. The white man had found a poetry in which there was nothing poetic. The soul of the white man was corrupted, and, as I was told by a friend who was a teacher in the United States, 'The presence of the Negroes beside the whites is in a way an insurance policy on humanness. When the whites feel that they have become too mechanised, they turn to the men of colour and ask them for a little human sustenance.' At last I had been recognised, I was no longer a zero.

I soon had to change my tune. Only momentarily at a loss, the white man explained to me that, genetically, I represented a stage of development: 'Your properties have been exhausted by us. We had earth mystics such as you will never approach. Study our history and you will see how far this fusion has gone.' Then I had the feeling that I was repeating a cycle. My originality had been torn out of me. I wept a long time, and then I began to live again. But I was haunted by a galaxy of erosive stereotypes: the Negro's *sui generis* odour ... the Negro's *sui generis* good nature ... the Negro's *sui generis* gullibility. ...

I had tried to flee myself through my kind, but the whites had thrown themselves on me and hamstrung me. I tested the limits of my essence; beyond all doubt there was not much of it left. It was here that I made my most remarkable discovery. Properly speaking, this discovery was a rediscovery.

I rummaged frenetically through all the antiquity of the black man. What I found there took away my breath. In his book *L'abolition de l'esclavage* Schoelcher presented us with compelling arguments. Since then, Frobenius, Westermann, Delafosse – all of them white – had joined the chorus: Segou, Djenne, cities of more than a hundred thousand people; accounts of learned blacks (doctors of theology who went to Mecca to interpret the Koran). All of that, exhumed from the past, spread with its insides out, made it possible for me to find a valid historic place. The white man was wrong, I was not a primitive, not even a half-man, I belonged to a race that had already been working in gold and silver two thousand years ago. [...]

I put the white man back into his place; growing bolder. I jostled him and told him point-blank, 'Get used to me, I am not getting used to anyone.' I shouted my laughter to the stars. The white man, I could see, was resentful. His reaction time lagged interminably. ... I had won. I was jubilant.

'Lay aside your history, your investigations of the past, and try to feel yourself into our rhythm. In a society such as ours, industrialised to the highest degree, dominated by scientism, there is no longer room for your sensitivity. One must be tough if one is to be allowed to live. What matters now is no longer play-ing the game of the world but subjugating it with integers and atoms. Oh, certainly, I will be told, now and then when we are worn out by our lives in big buildings, we will turn to you as we do to our children – to the innocent, the ingenuous, the spontaneous. We will turn to you as to the childhood of the world. You are so real in your life – so funny, that is. Let us run away for a little while from our ritualised, polite civilisation and let us relax, bend to those heads, those adorably expressive faces. In a way, you reconcile us "with ourselves".'

Thus my unreason was countered with reason, my reason with 'real reason'. Every hand was a losing hand for me. I analysed my heredity. I made a com-plete audit of my ailment. I wanted to be typically Negro – it was no longer possible. I wanted to be white – that was a joke. And, when I tried, on the level of ideas and intellectual activity, to reclaim my negritude, it was snatched away from me. Proof was presented that my effort was only a term in the dialectic:

> But there is something more important: The Negro, as we have said, creates an anti-racist racism for himself. In no sense does he wish to rule the world: He seeks the abolition of all ethnic privileges, wherever they come from; he asserts his solidarity with the oppressed of all colours. At once the subjec-tive, existential, ethnic idea of *negritude* 'passes', as Hegel puts it, into the objective, positive, exact idea of *proletariat*. 'For Césaire', Senghor says, 'the white man is the symbol of capital as the Negro is that of labour. ... Beyond the black-skinned men of his race it is the battle of the world proletariat that is his song.'
>
> That is easy to say, but less easy to think out. And undoubtedly it is no coincidence that the most ardent poets of negritude are at the same time militant Marxists.
>
> But that does not prevent the idea of race from mingling with that of class: The first is concrete and particular, the second is universal and abstract; the one stems from what Jaspers calls understanding and the other from intellection; the first is the result of a psychobiological syn-cretism and the second is a methodical construction based on experience. In fact, negritude appears as the minor term of a dialectical progression: The theoretical and practical assertion of the supremacy of the white man is its thesis; the position of negritude as an antithetical value is the moment of negativity. But this negative moment is insufficient by itself, and the Negroes who employ it know this very well; they know that it is intended to prepare the synthesis or realisation of the human in a society without races. This negritude is the root of its own destruction, it is a translation and not a conclusion, a means and not an ultimate end.[14]

When I read that page, I felt that I had been robbed of my last chance. I said to my friends, 'The generation of the younger black poets has just suffered a blow that can never be forgiven.' Help had been sought from a friend of the coloured peoples, and that friend had found no better response than to point out the relativity of what they were doing. For once, that born Hegelian had forgotten that consciousness has to lose itself in the night of the absolute, the only condition to attain to consciousness of self. In opposition to rationalism, he summoned up the negative side, but he forgot that this negativity draws its worth from an almost substantive absoluteness. A consciousness committed to experience is ignorant, has to be ignorant, of the essences and the determinations of its being. [...]

From time to time one would like to stop. To state reality is a wearing task. But, when one has taken it into one's head to try to express existence, one runs the risk of finding only the nonexistent. What is certain is that, at the very moment when I was trying to grasp my own being, Sartre, who remained The Other, gave me a name and thus shattered my last illusion. While I was saying to him:

'My negritude is neither a tower nor a cathedral.
it thrusts into the red flesh of the sun,
it thrusts into the burning flesh of the sky,
it hollows through the dense dismay of its own pillar
    of patience ...'

while I was shouting that, in the paroxysm of my being and my fury, he was reminding me that my blackness was only a minor term. In all truth, in all truth I tell you, my shoulders slipped out of the framework of the world, my feet could no longer feel the touch of the ground. Without a Negro past, without a Negro future, it was impossible for me to live my Negrohood. Not yet white, no longer wholly black, I was damned. Jean-Paul Sartre had forgotten that the Negro suffers in his body quite differently from the white man.[15] Between the white man and me the connection was irrevocably one of transcendence.[16]

But the constancy of my love had been forgotten. I defined myself as an absolute intensity of beginning. So I took up my negritude, and with tears in my eyes I put its machinery together again. What had been broken to pieces was rebuilt, reconstructed by the intuitive lianas of my hands.

My cry grew more violent: I am a Negro, I am a Negro, I am a Negro. ...

And there was my poor brother – living out his neurosis to the extreme and finding himself paralysed:

THE NEGRO: I can't, ma'am.
LIZZIE: Why not?
THE NEGRO: I can't shoot white folks.
LIZZIE: Really! That would bother them, wouldn't it?

THE NEGRO: They're white folks, ma'am.

LIZZIE: So what? Maybe they got a right to bleed you like a pig just because they're white?

THE NEGRO: But they're white folks.[17]

A feeling of inferiority? No, a feeling of nonexistence. Sin is Negro as virtue is white. All those white men in a group, guns in their hands, cannot be wrong. I am guilty. I do not know of what, but I know that I am no good. [...]

So it is with the character in *If He Hollers Let Him Go*[18] – who does precisely what he did not want to do. That big blonde who was always in his way, weak, sensual, offered, open, fearing (desiring) rape, became his mistress in the end.

The Negro is a toy in the white man's hands; so, in order to shatter the hellish cycle, he explodes. I cannot go to a film without seeing myself. I wait for me. In the interval, just before the film starts, I wait for me. The people in the theatre are watching me, examining me, waiting for me. A Negro groom is going to appear. My heart makes my head swim.

The crippled veteran of the Pacific war says to my brother, 'Resign yourself to your colour the way I got used to my stump; we're both victims.'[19]

Nevertheless with all my strength I refuse to accept that amputation. I feel in myself a soul as immense as the world, truly a soul as deep as the deepest of rivers, my chest has the power to expand without limit. I am a master and I am advised to adopt the humility of the cripple. Yesterday, awakening to the world, I saw the sky turn upon itself utterly and wholly. I wanted to rise, but the disembowelled silence fell back upon me, its wings paralysed. Without responsibility, straddling Nothingness and Infinity, I began to weep.

11

Womanliness as a Masquerade[1]

Joan Riviere

Every direction in which psychoanalytic research has pointed seems in its turn to have attracted the interest of Ernest Jones, and now that of recent years investigation has slowly spread to the development of the sexual life of women, we find as a matter of course one by him among the most important contributions to the subject.[2] As always, he throws great light on his material, with his peculiar gift of both clarifying the knowledge we had already and also adding to it fresh observations of his own.

In his paper on 'The early development of female sexuality'[3] he sketches out a rough scheme of types of female development which he first divides into heterosexual and homosexual, subsequently subdividing the latter homosexual group into two types. He acknowledges the roughly schematic nature of his classification and postulates a number of intermediate types. It is with one of these intermediate types that I am today concerned. In daily life types of men and women are constantly met with who, while mainly heterosexual in their development, plainly display strong features of the other sex. This has been judged to be an expression of the bisexuality inherent in us all; and analysis has shown that what appears as homosexual or heterosexual character-traits, or sexual manifestations, is the end-result of the interplay of conflicts and not necessarily evidence of a radical or fundamental tendency. The difference between homosexual and heterosexual development results from differences in the degree of anxiety, with the corresponding effect this has on development. Ferenczi pointed out a similar reaction in behaviour,[4] namely, that homosexual men exaggerate their heterosexuality as a 'defence' against their homosexuality. I shall attempt to show that women who wish for masculinity may put on a mask of womanliness to avert anxiety and the retribution feared from men.

It is with a particular type of intellectual woman that I have to deal. Not long ago intellectual pursuits for women were associated almost exclusively with an overtly masculine type of woman, who in pronounced cases made no secret of her wish or claim to be a man. This has now changed. Of all the women engaged in professional work today, it would be hard to say whether

110

the greater number are more feminine than masculine in their mode of life and character. In university life, in scientific professions and in business, one constantly meets women who seem to fulfil every criterion of complete feminine development. They are excellent wives and mothers, capable housewives; they maintain social life and assist culture; they have no lack of feminine interests, e.g. in their personal appearance, and when called upon they can still find time to play the part of devoted and disinterested mother-substitutes among a wide circle of relatives and friends. At the same time they fulfil the duties of their profession at least as well as the average man. It is really a puzzle to know how to classify this type psychologically.

Some time ago, in the course of an analysis of a woman of this kind, I came upon some interesting discoveries. She conformed in almost every particular to the description just given; her excellent relations with her husband included a very intimate affectionate attachment between them and full and frequent sexual enjoyment; she prided herself on her proficiency as a housewife. She had followed her profession with marked success all her life. She had a high degree of adaptation to reality and managed to sustain good and appropriate relations with almost everyone with whom she came in contact.

Certain reactions in her life showed, however, that her stability was not as flawless as it appeared; one of these will illustrate my theme. She was an American woman engaged in work of a propagandist nature which consisted principally in speaking and writing. All her life a certain degree of anxiety, sometimes very severe, was experienced after every public performance, such as speaking to an audience. In spite of her unquestionable success and ability, both intellectual and practical, and her capacity for managing an audience and dealing with discussions, etc., she would be excited and apprehensive all night after, with misgivings whether she had done anything inappropriate, and obsessed by a need for reassurance. This need for reassurance led her compulsively on any such occasion to seek some attention or complimentary notice from a man or men at the close of the proceedings in which she had taken part or been the principal figure; and it soon became evident that the men chosen for the purpose were always unmistakable father-figures, although often not persons whose judgement on her performance would in reality carry much weight. There were clearly two types of reassurance sought from these father-figures: first, direct reassurance of the nature of compliments about her performance; secondly, and more important, indirect reassurance of the nature of sexual attentions from these men. To speak broadly, analysis of her behaviour after her performance showed that she was attempting to obtain sexual advances from the particular type of men by means of flirting and coquetting with them in a more or less veiled manner. The extraordinary incongruity of this attitude with her highly impersonal and objective attitude during her intellectual performance, which it succeeded so rapidly in time, was a problem.

Analysis showed that the Oedipus situation of rivalry with the mother was extremely acute and had never been satisfactorily solved. I shall come back to this later. But beside the conflict in regard to the mother, the rivalry with the father was also very great. Her intellectual work, which took the form of speaking and writing, was based on an evident identification with her father, who had first been a literary man and later had taken to political life; her adolescence had been characterised by conscious revolt against him, with rivalry and contempt of him. Dreams and phantasies[5] of this nature, castrating the husband, were frequently uncovered by analysis. She had quite conscious feelings of rivalry and claims to superiority over many of the 'father-figures' whose favour she would then woo after her own performances! She bitterly resented any assumption that she was not equal to them, and (in private) would reject the idea of being subject to their judgement or criticism. In this she corresponded clearly to one type Ernest Jones has sketched: his first group of homosexual women who, while taking no interest in the other women, wish for 'recognition' of their masculinity from men and claim to be the equals of men, or in other words, to be men themselves. Her resentment, however, was not openly expressed; publicly she acknowledged her condition of womanhood.

Analysis then revealed that the explanation of her compulsive ogling and coquetting – which actually she was herself hardly aware of till analysis made it manifest – was as follows: it was an unconscious attempt to ward off the anxiety which would ensue on account of the reprisals she anticipated from the father-figures after her intellectual performance. The exhibition in public of her intellectual proficiency, which was in itself carried through successfully, signified an exhibition of herself in possession of the father's penis, having castrated him. The display once over, she was seized by horrible dread of the retribution the father would then exact. Obviously it was a step towards propitiating the avenger to endeavour to offer herself to him sexually. This phantasy, it then appeared, had been very common in her childhood and youth, which had been spent in the Southern States of America; if a negro came to attack her, she planned to defend herself by making him kiss her and make love to her (ultimately so that she could then deliver him over to justice). But there was a further determinant of the obsessive behaviour. In a dream which had a rather similar content to this childhood phantasy, she was in terror alone in the house; then a negro came in and found her washing clothes, with her sleeves rolled up and arms exposed. She resisted him, with the secret intention of attracting him sexually, and he began to admire her arms and caress them and her breasts. The meaning was that she had killed father and mother and obtained everything for herself (alone in the house), became terrified of their retribution (expected shots through the window), and defended herself by taking on a menial rôle (washing clothes) and by *washing off* dirt and sweat, guilt and blood, everything she had obtained by the deed, and 'disguising herself' as merely a castrated woman. In that guise the man found no stolen property on her which he need attack her to recover and, further, found her attractive as an object of love. Thus the aim of the compulsion was not merely to secure reassurance by evoking friendly feelings towards her in the man; it was chiefly to make sure of safety by masquerading as guiltless and innocent. It was a compulsive reversal of her intellectual performance; and the two together formed the 'double-action' of an obsessive act, just as her life as a whole consisted alternately of masculine and feminine activities.

Before this dream she had had dreams of people putting masks on their faces in order to avert disaster. One of these dreams was of a high tower on a hill being pushed over and falling down on the inhabitants of a village below, but the people put on masks and escaped injury!

Womanliness therefore could be assumed and worn as a mask, both to hide the possession of masculinity and to avert the reprisals expected if she was found to possess it – much as a thief will turn out his pockets and ask to be searched to prove that he has not the stolen goods. The reader may now ask how I define womanliness or where I draw the line between genuine womanliness and the 'masquerade'. My suggestion is not, however, that there is any such difference; whether radical or superficial, they are the same thing. The capacity for womanliness was there in this woman – and one might even say it exists in the most completely homosexual woman – but owing to her conflicts it did not represent her main development and was used far more as a device for avoiding anxiety than as a primary mode of sexual enjoyment. [...]

In everyday life one may observe the mask of femininity taking curious forms. One capable housewife of my acquaintance is a woman of great ability, and can herself attend to typically masculine matters. But when, e.g., any builder or upholsterer is called in, she has a compulsion to hide all her technical knowledge from him and show deference to the workman, making her suggestions in an innocent and artless manner, as if they were 'lucky guesses'. She has confessed to me that even with the butcher and baker, whom she rules in reality with a rod of iron, she cannot openly take up a firm straightforward stand; she feels herself as it were 'acting a part', she puts on the semblance of a rather uneducated, foolish and bewildered woman, yet in the end always making her point. In all other relations in life this woman is a gracious, cultured lady, competent and well-informed, and can manage her affairs by sensible rational behaviour without any subterfuges. This woman is now aged 50, but she tells me that as a young woman she had great anxiety in dealings with men such as porters, waiters, cabmen, tradesmen, or any other potentially hostile father-figures, such as doctors, builders and lawyers; moreover, she often quarrelled with such men and had altercations with them, accusing them of defrauding her and so forth.

Another case from everyday observation is that of a clever woman, wife and mother, a university lecturer in an abstruse subject which seldom attracts

women. When lecturing, not to students but to colleagues, she chooses
particularly feminine clothes. Her behaviour on these occasions is also
marked by an inappropriate feature: she becomes flippant and joking, so
much so that it has caused comment and rebuke. She has to treat the situation
of displaying her masculinity to men as a 'game', as something *not real*, as a
'joke'. She cannot treat herself and her subject seriously, cannot seriously
contemplate herself as on equal terms with men; moreover, the flippant
attitude enables some of her sadism to escape, hence the offence it causes. [...]

To return to the case I first described. Underneath her apparently satisfac-
tory heterosexuality it is clear that this woman displayed well-known manifestations of the castration complex. [Karen] Horney was the first among
others to point out the sources of that complex in the Oedipus situation; my
belief is that the fact that womanliness may be assumed as a mask may
contribute further in this direction to the analysis of female development. [...]

12

The Anorexic Body: Reading Disorders

Abigail Bray

Anorexia nervosa and the less 'spectacular' eating disorder bulimia have engendered a multiplicity of discourses on the female body. In particular, the public fascination with the figure of the anorexic amounts to a fetishisation; like the mute and malleable fetish object, the anorexic body has been inscribed, diagnosed and translated by various interpretive technologies. Following Paula Treichler's (1987) ironic listing of the almost limitless interpretations of the AIDS body, the list below exemplifies the ways in which eating disorders are constituted by an 'epidemic of signification'.[1]

Eating disorders are:

1. A slimmers' epidemic which is destroying the lives of mostly young, intelligent, white, middle-class women.
2. 'A kind of mourning for a pre-Oedipal (i.e. precastrated body and a corporeal connection to the mother that women in patriarchy are required to abandon).'[2]
3. Evidence of the mass media's sadistic brainwashing of women into complying with unrealistic beauty ideals.[3,4]
4. A form of perverse feminine narcissism.[5]
5. The shadow of the astronaut's body.[6]
6. A non-productive, reactive body without organs.[7]
7. A psychosomatic phenomenon which articulates the pathologies of the patriarchal capitalist nuclear family.[8,9]
8. An obsessive–compulsive disorder best treated with benzodiazepines, haloperidol, thioridazine, trazodone, maprotiline, bilateral ECT or, if all else fails, a stereotactic limbic leucotomy (aka lobotomy).[10]
9. A rejection of the role of adult femininity and a retreat into the asexual body of a child.[11,12]
10. A pathology which flourishes in matriarchal households.[13]
11. A mental illness created by gay fashion designers who want women to look like young boys.
12. A pathological fear of menarches and the implications of fertility.[14]

13. A mass-marketed dieting disorder.[15]
14. Phallogocentrism's brutal marginalisation of the female imaginary and the materiality of the body.[16,17]
15. The introjection of a bad object and the consequent internalisation of a 'false body'.[18]
16. An emblem of twentieth-century *fin-de-siècle* decadence. Hunger art.[19]
17. An experimental becoming.[20]
18. Something women catch from television, the disease of the McLuhan age.[21,22]
19. A reading disorder.

This taxonomy demonstrates that the body of the woman who practises eating disorders presents a coding problem. As the 'dark continent of femininity', the territory of the anorexic body has been colonised by a motley group of discourses contesting the truth of anorexic lack.[23] Furthermore, biomedical professionals have yet to locate an unequivocal aetiology for practices such as self-starvation, and as Matra Robertson observes, treatment effectivity has not improved in the last fifty years.[24]

Rather than reproducing yet another prescriptive diagnosis of women's eating disorders, I shall investigate the formation of a dominant paradox which has been mapped onto the anorexic subject. The paradox articulates itself through a theorisation of food refusal as the direct result of the consumption of media representations of idealised thin femininity. An excessive consumption of media images is perceived to activate a pathological fear of corporeal consumption: over-reading produces under-eating. This paradoxical description of consumption, I will argue, represents the imagined reading practices of female audiences within modernity as quintessentially irrational.

At stake in the analysis of anorexic reading practices is a contestation over the relationship between representation and material reality, epistemology and the female body, and, in turn, economies of reading and eating as they are articulated through the metaphor of consumption. As Treichler asserts, 'illness *is* metaphor',[25] and in relation to eating disorders the metaphor most at work is that of 'consumption'.

In order to situate my argument within a conceptual history, I offer a critical appraisal of some feminist approaches to anorexic reading practices. I will not attempt to account for all feminist interpretations of eating disorders; to do so would be reductive and misleading. What I do want to foreground, however, are specific accounts of anorexic reading practices within this dispersed field. Second, I will analyse the potential correspondences between feminist conceptualisations of anorexic reading practices and representations of the mass audience within the history of cultural criticism. Finally, I will question the assumption that anorexic identity is a fixed construction and suggest that this agency also produces oppositional inscriptions. In this context I argue for an attention to the genealogy of everyday practices of weight-loss regimens.

TOXIC TEXTS AND POISONED BODIES

Janice Radway has alerted us to the rhetorical operations of the metaphor of consumption as a way of devaluing the reception of mass-produced texts.[26] The analogy between eating and reading evoked in this metaphor fictionalises (and displaces) cerebral activity as a simple alimentary process. Lacking the discerning palate of the educated elite, the masses uncritically consume anything and everything produced by the media. It is interesting to note in this context that Bernard Rosenberg's description of mass culture does indeed evoke an association with eating disorders.[27] In effect, Rosenberg describes a habit-forming diet of little nourishment which, rather than satiating, produces greater hunger: the 'masses' suffer from a reading (eating) disorder.

Furthermore, it becomes apparent that mass cultural artefacts such as popular women's magazines or romances are endowed with the ability to poison their consumers. As Radway notes, not only is popular fiction metaphorised as 'rubbish', 'trash' or 'junk', but it is perceived as a toxic pollutant, corrupting a pure premodern body. Moreover, the literal meaning of the verb 'consume' as denoting the annihilation or exhaustion of an object takes on a strange twist in relation to the imagined reading practices of anorexics; they are thought to consume representations of their gender only to suffer from a literal, corporeal, consumption as their bodies are 'eaten away'. In other words, the consumption of images of an idealised and commodified self is interpreted as an autophagic process in which the subject is transformed into the object of narcissistic consumption.

TOXIC BODIES AND POISONED TEXTS

The contaminating relationship of textuality and materiality, representations and real bodies, is powerfully evoked in the recent controversy around the fashion industry's 'waif' look. The popularity of this new 'thin' look prompted many to argue that it would cause a further escalation in what is already seen as an epidemic of eating disorders. Thus thin models are frequently pathologised as suffering from eating disorders to such an extent that their appearance in popular culture texts is hailed as dangerously contagious.

The Australian magazine *Who* recently addressed this issue with the help of a psychiatrist, who diagnosed such models as anorexic and warned that these popular representations were potentially fatal to the women who consume them. Arguing that Twiggy caused an escalation in anorexia, Professor Ross

Kelucy is quoted as saying that if the waif look 'follows the Twiggy trend, [there will be] a worsening of what is already a big problem in the next 18 months'.[28] On Australian television the news programme *Lateline* also addressed this question and spoke to psychiatric experts in the field, who similarly diagnosed the consumption of popular representations of thin women as a strong cause of eating disorders among the female audience.

Moreover, this particular understanding of the causal relationship between representations and material bodies is so much a part of the 'common sense' of popular women's magazines that we are currently witnessing attempts to counteract the valorisation of this contaminating 'thin' ideal. A plethora of articles dealing with the problem of eating disorders and the fatal desire to actualise a fashionable thinness circulated within women's magazines and campus papers during the early 1990s.[29] The public confession of anorexia by celebrities became a common motif within these magazines. Indeed, the idea that advertisements representing thin models coerce women into anorexia has passed from a form of oppositional sense to common sense. To articulate this position is to sign oneself as occupying a critical space in relation to the oppressive influences of the mass media – as being in the know, in this case, about the operations of patriarchal power. The prevalence of the anorexic stereotype in the popular media and the circulation of this psychiatric label as a 'folk' term attests to the way this figure is folded into the discursive construction of contemporary femininity.

IRRATIONAL CONSUMPTION

As Matra Robertson points out in *Starving in the Silences*, the diagnostic category 'anorexia nervosa' invokes the authority of medical discourse over experiences of female embodiment.[30] The medicalisation of self-starvation is far from innocent; rather, as Robertson argues, it is caught up in the operations of power at the site of the body. Central to these operations is the act of diagnosis, where symptoms are read through an established grid which functions to fix the truth of the subject. [...]

Far from being neutral, biomedical discourses are historically situated representations of human behaviour that are irrevocably connected to and influenced by wider representations of sex, class and ethnicity. The classification of insanity relies on the image of a normal healthy body that is often equated, as various feminists have argued, with a white adult male body.[31,32] Corporeal practices which deviate from this normative ideal function as a synecdoche for the non-healthy and the non-rational, such that, for example, hysteria and eating disorders are translated as representative of female irrationality in general.

Ironically, perhaps, this process is also noticeable in some of the early feminist interpretations of eating disorders. M. Boskind-White, for example, argues that 'bulimarexics' 'have devoted their lives to fulfilling the feminine role rather than the individual person'.[33] Depicting anorexia as an hyperbolic expression of an alienated femininity, the author diagnoses the 'bulimarexic' as the perfect victim of discourses which attempt to coerce all women into occupying the shrunken space of a childlike femininity. Indeed, as Robertson observes, eating disorders are frequently theorised by feminists as a quintessential symbol of the oppression of all women,[34] such that the anorexic functions as a synecdoche for women's alienated body image in general. More recently, accounts of anorexia within Australian 'corporeal feminism' have tended to argue from a similar position.[35,36] The anti-rationalist, anti-Cartesian project of thinking through the body views all representational systems as phallocentric and thus as denials of the positive specificity of female embodiment. Within these terms it is possible to argue that women's body image is modelled on lack, and even that women consider themselves to be castrated.[37] Thus the incorporation of phallocentric representations leads to an inauthentic and potentially lethal body image in all women.

Feminist theorists have also focused on issues of social and psychical space. Kim Chernin, Susie Orbach, Linda Brown, and to a lesser extent, Naomi Wolf have all argued that the aestheticisation of thin femininity reflects a fear of female power. [...] The celebration of the slender body is thus seen as a direct political weapon against women, even as fat becomes a symbol of prohibited female power and fertility. Susie Orbach argues that fat is used by women as a protective barrier against an oppressive patriarchal environment,[38] while Linda Brown agrees that feminine frailty is privileged by patriarchy because it represents the conquest of female power.[39] Many of these arguments were recycled and developed in Naomi Wolf's bestselling book *The Beauty Myth*; according to Wolf, anorexia should be recognised as 'political damage' and women who diet are 'politically castrated'.[40]

While these texts offer important critiques of the formation of the female body image, they tend to present culture as a monolithic patriarchal system while romanticising the pre-cultural as the space of non-alienated female embodiment. Chernin, for example, argues that a connection with the 'primordial female' (representing the soul of mother earth and an Edenic pre-patriarchal past) has been sacrificed in a modernised patriarchal culture.[41] The essentialist dichotomy between authenticity–femininity–nature and inauthenticity–masculinity–culture leads to a reductive account of women's oppression and fails to explain why not all women suffer from eating disorders.

READING/EATING DISORDERS

The idea that representations are harmful to women's bodies became popular during the nineteenth century, when biomedical professionals entered into the

debate over women's education. Hysteria and neurasthenia were framed as
the 'new woman's' diseases: the more educated the woman, the more likely she
was to suffer from nervous complaints. Indeed it was even argued that the
education of women would lead to the atrophy of the reproductive organs
and the degeneration of the human race. The consumption of popular literature and magazines was also linked to the enfeeblement of the mind and body.
In her discussion of the medical, physiological and psychoanalytic accounts
of the woman reader during this time, Kate Flint writes that 'no body was
perceived as being more vulnerable to impure mental foods than that of the
young woman'.[42] In other words, the infantilisation of women's reading
practices as necessarily detrimental to their minds and bodies has an extensive
history within modernity.

More recently, the consumption of mass media images is depicted as
having a similar effect on the female viewer or reader. Television in particular
is frequently cited as the most dangerous influence in arguments about eating
disorders. For example, Orbach's analysis of anorexia nervosa in *Hunger
Strike* posits anorexia as an unconscious protest against patriarchal oppression.[43] However, Orbach suggests that the female experience of embodiment
is formed through the consumption of representations of femininity within
the mass media, and that this process of consumption largely determines the
protest of anorexia.[44] Orbach's description of female embodiment as an interpellation of media representations suggests that women only come to know
themselves through the media, ignoring the significance of work, sexual relationships or motherhood as means to corporeal knowledge and relying on an
image of a docile and childlike female viewer.

Hilde Bruch, the author of the influential study on anorexia nervosa *The
Golden Cage*,[45] also interprets self-starvation as a reading disease. Briefly,
Bruch argues that anorexia nervosa is a response to the contradictory roles of
adult, white, middle-class femininity. As an attempt to reconcile the cultural
dictate to be economically independent while remaining emotionally
dependent, anorexia is interpreted as a retreat into a childlike body. Unable to
synthesise cultural double-binds, anorexics opt for an excessive control of
their own bodies in an attempt to exercise sovereignty. Bruch argues that the
fashion industry's valorisation of the slender body coerces women into this
response. 'Magazines and movies carry the same message, but the most
persistent is television, drumming it in, day in day out, that one can only be
loved and respected when slender.'[46] Anorexia is therefore an example of
being interpellated as the ideal reader. Furthermore, in *Conversations with
Anorectics* Bruch suggests that the popular dissemination of anorexia and
bulimia in the mass media acts pedagogically insofar as these representations
instruct women on how to reproduce the symptoms of eating disorders.[47]
As Maud Ellmann comments, 'the fact that they believe they have contracted
their disorder from the media suggests that *anorexia is the disease of*

the McLuhan age, disseminated by telecommunications rather than by contact'.[48]

This notion that forms of telecommunication are viral is a seductive one. [...] The protectionist and paternalistic rhetoric operative in traditional cultural criticism regarding the negative effects of television is taken to an absurd level: to argue that women contract psychiatric diseases from television is to enter the realm of science fiction. [...] And yet the force of this idea remains remarkably unchallenged. In 'Anorexia nervosa: psychopathology as the crystallisation of culture', Susan Bordo concludes with a description of 'anorexic' reading practices as necessarily negative.[49] Locating television advertisements as the perfect medium for the indoctrination of body insecurity, Bordo describes the female audience as passively consuming poisonous messages about female embodiment. The apocalyptic tone of her writing is noticeable in the following:

> Watching the commercials are thousands of anxiety-ridden women and adolescents. ... And watching the commercials is the anorexic, who associates her relentless pursuit of thinness with power and control, but who in fact destroys her health and imprisons her imagination. She is surely the most startling and stark illustration of how cavalier power relations are with respect to the motivations and goals of individuals, yet how deeply they are etched on our bodies, and how well our bodies serve them.[50]

Bordo's positioning of the female audience as potential anorexics paints an unbearably oppressive social environment. Audience pleasure would in this case be diagnosed merely as a form of masochism. Indeed, it is no surprise to discover that Bordo is the author of a paper entitled 'How television teaches women to hate their hungers'.[51] While eating disorders are clearly sociopolitical problems, to devalue women's abilities to resist media interpellation is to frame the female audience (and thus women in general) as weak-minded, docile bodies. The anorexic body is thus simply read as an example of a deep etching of power on the 'paedocratised' bodies of the female audience.

Within this critical paradigm, anorexia is the result of consuming too many ideologically unsound representations of women on television. In this way, the anorexic is either performing an over-determined (hysterical) reaction to ideology, or occupying the space of the ideal reader in a response to dominant injunctions to be thin. The causal logic of this argument understands anorexia as merely another example of being interpellated and coerced into occupying preferred reading positions. Elspeth Probyn argues that *'what we can clearly hear from these descriptions is that women are pathologically susceptible to media images'*.[52]

Indeed, one of the more insidious, and perhaps unintentional, consequences of these arguments is that they potentially pathologise the female audience *en masse*. For, if all women are perceived to be preoccupied with their weight, primarily because of their consumption of mass-produced images of idealised thin femininity, then the female audience is framed as neurotically vulnerable to late twentieth-century media representations. This assumption can be seen as a continuation of a paternalistic and moralistic history of academic research into the assumed effects of television violence on women and children. It is no coincidence that women and children are frequently cited as subjects peculiarly vulnerable to the effects of television. Censorship is never for the protection of white, middle-class men, as though the economic security of their citizenship were somehow to inoculate them against the contaminating effects of media representations.

It is also interesting to note that advertisements are frequently targeted by critics such as Bordo as highly influential in the production of eating disorders. Describing the evangelical logic underpinning cultural criticism of advertising, Helen Irving contends that it is typically seen to produce false consciousness by clouding the material reality of viewers' lives.[53] However, it is often the occupant of Karl Popper's 'Third World',[54] the impossibly pure critic, who pontificates on false and true consciousness, fabricated and authentic needs, without any self-reflexive consideration of the materiality of their own everyday life as part of the 'masses'. To privilege the mass media as the most effective means of moulding minds is to ignore the multiplicity of social contexts operating in the everyday. It is this disregard for wider and less consignable contexts which is so lacking in the theorisation of anorexia. As Irving asks, 'Can we never escape from the legacy of the Frankfurt School which saw the individual in mass capitalist culture as having lost all powers of critical perspectives, as moronically equating movies "directly with reality?" '.[55]

In her discussion of the assumptions embedded within nineteenth-century criticisms of consumer culture and its perceived negative effects on the (apparently asexual) social body, Rita Felski argues that, 'given a prevalent equation of bourgeois masculinity with reason and self-restraint, it was above all through the representation of the consuming woman that writers criticised the crass materialism brought about by capitalist development.'[56] As a popular stereotypical representation of the 'consuming woman', the woman who practises eating/reading disorders is similarly imbricated within the pathologising discourse of psychiatry. The perverse irrationality of 'anorexic' reading practices, whereby consumption facilitates autophagy, serves to highlight this critical agenda; the effects of crass materialism are identified with a perverted feminine appetite. The image of women consuming television advertisements presented by Bordo unfortunately perpetuates this stereotype.

Given the degree of cultural paranoia attached to the object of television, eating disorders thus become merely another item on the list of social problems caused by the medium. Patrice Petro argues that this critical paradigm leads to a devaluing of television through recourse to gendered binaries in which the passive consumption of the popular is feminised in opposition to the active and thus masculine consumption of art.[57] Such a gendered division privileges distanced critical judgement over a sensual engagement with the object. The female subject's purported close identification with the text is read as undermining impartial judgement and the capacity for objective and rational reading. At issue within this paradigm is the conception of female desire within modernity as the expression of an uncritical hunger for representations of a commodified self.

'How can feminists challenge the power structures of male-stream knowledge', asks Matra Robertson, 'without at the same time becoming entangled in reductionist concepts of the object, i.e. the anorexic?'[58] Probyn suggests that we examine the local specificity of everyday anorexic practices and the ways in which anorexia articulates various discourses of femininity.[59] While eating disorders are arguably inscribed by phallocentric power at the site of the body, it is reductive to argue that anorexia is a synecdoche for all women's pathological vulnerability to phallocentric representational systems, or that the perfect medium for the articulation of this oppression is television or mass culture.

REWRITING 'ANOREXIA'

Several points can be drawn from this brief analysis of the discourses in operation within the formation of anorexia nervosa as the disease of the McLuhan age. First, the idea that women 'catch' psychiatric diseases from the media constitutes a form of (scientifically sanctioned) common sense. Second, given the prevalence of what psychiatrists are now terming 'normative eating disorders' among women, this common-sense understanding (in which the reading practices of women with eating disorders are framed as perversely autophagic) demonstrates an infantilisation of the female audience as pathologically suggestible to media representations. Participation as readers in the late twentieth-century media-scape is thus imagined to be a potentially lethal activity for women in general. However, the problem of how to approach the subject of eating disorders remains.

The following sections have a dual purpose: first, to render problematic totalising definitions of the identity of the anorexic subject, and second, to investigate the genealogy of the everyday techniques of eating disorders. It is not my intention to suggest that anorexia or self-starvation can be read as the positive articulation of a resistive agency. Such a task would obviously be insensitive – self-starvation is a deadly activity. Nor is it my intention to offer an account of anorexia which collapses the historical differences between its medieval and contemporary actualisations: the self-starvation of

St Catherine of Siena, for instance, has little in common with contemporary anorexia, apart from the fact that both involve relinquishing food. The forms of such practices are articulated according to the techniques provided by historical and cultural contexts. The purpose of this section is not to establish a new methodology as such, but rather to suggest questions for future analysis.

In *Sexing the Self*, Probyn describes the reception of her article 'The anorexic body', and remarks on the fact that her passing words 'I became anorexic' functioned to contaminate the text as a confession.[60] For example, Eva Szekely argues that Probyn's article neglected to foreground the 'body, in its vitality, emotionality, sweat and trepidation', and openly criticises Probyn for absenting her own anorexic body from the text.[61] On the other hand, Arthur Frank interpreted Probyn's article simply as a 'confession of anorexia' and an example of a postmodern American ethnology of the self.[62] Both interpretations assumed that Probyn was confessing to an essential and static truth of her personal identity.

Against these readings Probyn describes the articulation of the self as a situated narrative of becoming rather than an indication of a fixed identity: while the self is clearly constructed, it is not closed by that same construction. Similarly, in *Gender Trouble* Judith Butler points out that while identity is constructed, which is to say signified, it does not follow that identity is therefore fully determined by this construction – such an argument would deny the possibility of agency. 'Construction is not opposed to agency', Butler writes, 'it is the necessary scene of agency, the very terms in which agency is articulated and becomes culturally intelligible'.[63] Instead of attempting to locate anorexic identity, a project which seems embedded in the reductionist quest for the truth of the anorexic lack, one might recognise that the subject who practises self-starvation exemplifies a point of agency which is not fully commensurable with the psychiatric label 'anorexia nervosa'.

This is not to affirm the existence of a pre-discursive body which is beyond signification, but rather to recognise that agency is a performative act constructed but not fully determined by discursive contexts. For example, the psychiatric label *anorexia nervosa* identifies a group of indistinguishable subjects; the imagined repetition of the anorexic identity which is assumed to occur under this sign needs to be contested if the stasis of such an identity is to be challenged. It is not enough, however, to oppose sameness with a multiplicity of differences; such an approach risks a relativism resulting in empty rhetoric rather than intervention. For example, an instance of anorexia in an elderly, blind, working-class man might very well trouble the common-sense understanding of the anorexic identity, and produce potentially interesting psychoanalytic, postmodern, sociological or cultural critiques, but it would do little to explain why the majority of anorexics are women.

Rather, the point is to locate a subversive repetition within the signifying practices which construct gender identity.[64] In other words, transformations occur through the repetition of elements, such that 'agency is to be located within the possibility of a variation on that repetition'.[65] For Butler, agency is thus only possible in relation to the signifying practices which enable and constrain identity. An articulation of agency within the psychiatric formation of the anorexic identity would therefore involve a subversive re-signification of that same psychiatric discourse.

To clarify this point, it is worth recalling an example from the nineteenth century. Charlotte Perkins Gilman's 'The yellow wallpaper' (1892) is a semi-autobiographical account of the experience of a woman diagnosed as hysterical.[66] The text describes Silas Weir Mitchell's popular rest-cure of enforced passivity and confinement, and represents the effects of his instruction to Gilman to avoid all forms of intellectual stimulation. Indeed, Gilman's text actively criticises the very terms used by the medical profession in the diagnosis of hysteria, while also condemning prevailing methods of treatment. The hysterical woman in Gilman's text suffers from the construction of her identity as merely hysterical; any understanding of her identity in alternative terms is excluded, including her own perception that she is in fact imprisoned by the sentence of hysteria. Gilman's text has since become a feminist classic precisely because of its chilling depiction of the effects of androcentric medical discourses on female identity.

While anorexia is not simply the contemporary equivalent of hysteria, Gilman's narrative exemplifies the ways in which biomedical or psychiatric constructions of identity can be re-signified by the very subjects which they claim to define. In relation to anorexia, one might locate a similar pattern of subversion in both confessional genres and general fiction written by women who have been coded as practising eating disorders. As I have argued elsewhere, one of the consistent criticisms voiced by such women in popular women's magazines is a dissatisfaction with the clinical definition of the anorexic identity and its use to justify problematic forms of medical interventions.[67]

In her confessional narrative, Fiona Place argues that the clinical definition of anorexia nervosa creates the identity of the subject who practises self-starvation by excluding everyday language: any other understanding of the anorexic's identity is marginalised.[68] Likewise, the anorexic 'Ellen West' wrote of her experience of being psychoanalysed: 'the anal-erotic connection is purely theoretical. It is completely incomprehensible to me. I don't understand my self at all … I confront myself as a strange person.'[69] West's critical description of the identity constructed for her by psychoanalysis suggests, at least, a signifying practice not fully determined by its terms. A re-signification of anorexia might entail an intervention into the discourses which construct it, of which biomedical knowledge is arguably the most authoritative, and the production of a counter-discourse on the biomedical formation of anorexic identities. This is not a romantic project: that electroshock treatment and the surgical mutilation of the brain known politely as 'stereotactic limbic leucotomy' are still used on women who practise eating disorders should be cause for concern. By contesting the neutrality of biomedical knowledge and recognising that scientific representations of the body have calculable effects, it might be possible to transform the normative discourses which form anorexia nervosa.

However, I also want to resist rarefying anorexic practices as a 'new' pathology. While seemingly existing outside normal regimens of food consumption, they exemplify a grammar similar to other contemporary dietetic discourses. I am not suggesting here that all women are latent anorexics, or that contemporary forms of diet management lead inexorably to self-starvation. Rather, I am interested in the question of the cultural conditions which enable the practice of contemporary eating disorders. In order to explore this question it is necessary to turn to a consideration of the historical specificity of contemporary dietetic regimens.

THE METABOLIC BODY

The genealogy of the formation of weight-loss regimens as everyday practices, whether or not they are considered to be disordered, thus needs to be addressed if a clearer understanding of the everyday constructions of anorexic identity is to be achieved. After all, a preoccupation with losing weight is not restricted to women with eating disorders; the weight-loss industry extracted around $5 billion from its American consumers in 1985 alone.[70] Thus calorie counting and the weighing and measuring of the body are prevalent techniques not only in self-starvation but also in contemporary popular practices of weight control.

In *The Uses of Pleasure* Foucault argues that the practice of specific dietetic and exercise regimens is a central organising principle in the formation of ethical subjects and constitutes an art of living or an ascetics of the self.[71] These techniques of ascetic and ethical self-transformation rely on a meticulous measuring and regulation: the measurement of corporeal activities is coded as a moral activity.[72] In classical Greece an attention to this type of measurement enabled an 'equilibrium of the body' which 'was one of the conditions for the proper hierarchy of the soul'.[73] Without denying the historical differences between ancient 'pagan' practices and our own time, one might also recognise that contemporary weight-loss regimens deploy related techniques in the name of an ethics of self-care, involving a similar transformation of the self through processes of measurement.

The biomedical discourse of metabolism serves to organise such everyday techniques of weight loss within modernity. Its cultural prevalence is evident in popular women's magazines, diet books, television programmes and multinational weight-loss clinics, which function pedagogically to instruct women how to eat and manage their weight. 'Burn fat faster' is the title of a recent article in a women's magazine; the reader is informed that 'when dieting won't shift stubborn kilos, you may need to beat your sluggish metabolism', and that 'the latest research proves there's plenty we can do to increase our ability to burn kilojoules and excess body fat faster.'[74] Indeed, the colloquialism 'going for the burn' describes the catabolism of fat. The article lists methods for achieving a faster metabolism, while criticising 'crash' diets that purportedly slow down metabolic rates. The key to achieving the thin ideal is described as the attainment of an ideal metabolic equilibrium, defined in terms of a harmony between the 'fuel' consumed and the 'fuel' exerted in work. Excess fat is represented in this discourse as marking an asymmetrical relation between working and consuming; it is a sign both of an unruly metabolism and of a subject's inability to maintain a specified balance between production and consumption. I am not implying here that women are indoctrinated by the evil discourse of metabolism, but simply noting that weight-loss regimens within modernity are organised around this concept, which provides the biomedical grammar through which such regimens are expressed in the everyday.

The calorie or kilojoule which measures heat and food is central to contemporary forms of weight control. Popularised by the chemistry professor Wilbur O. Atwater in 1895 during the progressive era in America, the introduction of the calorific unit into the everyday lives of women recodified consumption.[75] Thus the calculation of calories became an important methodological technique within the discourse of contemporary dietetics. In this way the private sphere of the kitchen/dining room was transformed into a quasi-chemical laboratory, where middle-class women juggled with various kinds of scientifically coded food or fuel in order to produce meals which would ensure the normalisation of their families' body weight and health. Concurrently, public schools participated in massive weighing programmes.[76] The first best-selling weight control book, published in America in 1918, not only demonstrated that weight loss was a popular concern among women but that counting calories was central to the operation of these regimens. In the words of the book's author, Lulu Hunt Peters, 'hereafter you are going to eat calories of food. Instead of saying one slice of bread, or a piece of pie, you will say 100 calories of bread, 350 calories of pie.'[77] Furthermore, the description of calorie-counting in this same book depicts it as an act of patriotism and humanitarianism, informed by a meritocratic ideology of consumption.

Brumberg neatly summarises the effects of the popularisation of calorie-counting when she writes that 'physical features once regarded as natural – such as appetite and body weight – were designated as objects of conscious control'.[78] Indeed, this particular type of calculation enabled new forms of bodily surveillance. In *Eating Our Hearts Out: Personal Accounts of Women's Relationships to Food*, for example, Jan Wienpahl discusses the practice of calorie-counting in weight-loss regimens, describing the self-management of the body as a 'calorie-balance machine, counting calories in and calories out'.[79] The pervasiveness of such calculation has now assumed absurd limits, as food and drink is packaged and sold according to its low-calorific merits. The bottlers of Evian water, for example, find it necessary to reassure their consumers that water contains no calories, as if they imagine that these consumers suffer from a form of arithnomania, whereby they are compelled to measure the consumption of every *single* calorie.

This obsessive attention to the calculation of calories, alongside what appears to be a compulsion to fetishise the measuring of body weight and dress size, indicates that weight-loss regimens, disordered or otherwise, articulate the body through a numerical grammar involved in an eschatology of the flesh. The counting down of this body and that which it consumes is acted out with deathly rigour in anorexia. Furthermore, the frenetic exercise which often accompanies anorexia can be read as caught up with this same discourse of metabolism. Burning fat faster, or increasing the basal metabolic rate, is the expressed goal, not only of the anorexic who eventually catabolises much more than just fat, but also of contemporary weight-loss regimens as a whole.

Here one might usefully explore Paul Virilio's claim in *The Aesthetics of Disappearance* that the body within modernity *is* speed.[80] The cultural preoccupation with the rate at which fat is consumed points to the suggestive historical interconnections between the trope of speed and an aesthetics of disappearing flesh. Further attention to the archaeology of metabolism and its impact on weight-loss regimens might clarify the ways in which the feminine body is organised and rendered legible in modernity. The impact of the seemingly innocent and trivial calorie, for example, recodified consumption and body weight to the extent that every single calorie is calculated in the act of consumption just as *every* pound lost or gained is measured.

13

Introduction to *Bodies That Matter*

Judith Butler

Why should our bodies end at the skin, or include at best other beings encapsulated by skin?

(Donna Haraway, *A Manifesto for Cyborgs*)

If one really thinks about the body as such, there is no possible outline of the body as such. There are thinkings of the systematicity of the body, there are value codings of the body. The body, as such, cannot be thought, and I certainly cannot approach it.

(Gayatri Chakravorty Spivak, 'In a Word', interview with Ellen Rooney)

There is no nature, only the effects of nature: denaturalisation or naturalisation.

(Jacques Derrida, *Donner le Temps*)

Is there a way to link the question of the materiality of the body to the performativity of gender? And how does the category of 'sex' figure within such a relationship? Consider first that sexual difference is often invoked as an issue of material differences. Sexual difference, however, is never simply a function of material differences which are not in some way both marked and formed by discursive practices. Further, to claim that sexual differences are indissociable from discursive demarcations is not the same as claiming that discourse causes sexual difference. The category of 'sex' is, from the start, normative; it is what Foucault has called a 'regulatory ideal'. In this sense, then, 'sex' not only functions as a norm, but is part of a regulatory practice that produces the bodies it governs, that is, whose regulatory force is made clear as a kind of productive power, the power to produce – demarcate, circulate, differentiate – the bodies it controls. Thus, 'sex' is a regulatory ideal whose materialisation is compelled, and this materialisation takes place (or fails to take place) through certain highly regulated practices. In other words, 'sex' is an ideal construct which is forcibly materialised through time. It is not a simple fact or static condition of a body, but a process whereby regulatory norms materialise 'sex' and achieve this materialisation through a forcible reiteration of those norms. That this reiteration is necessary is a sign that materialisation is never quite complete, that bodies never quite comply with the norms by which their materialisation is impelled. Indeed, it is the instabilities, the possibilities for rematerialisation, opened up by this process that mark one domain in which the force of the regulatory law can be turned against itself to spawn rearticulations that call into question the hegemonic force of that very regulatory law.

But how, then, does the notion of gender performativity relate to this conception of materialisation? In the first instance, performativity must be understood not as a singular or deliberate 'act', but, rather, as the reiterative and citational practice by which discourse produces the effects that it names. What will, I hope, become clear in what follows is that the regulatory norms of 'sex' work in a performative fashion to constitute the materiality of bodies and, more specifically, to materialise the body's sex, to materialise sexual difference in the service of the consolidation of the heterosexual imperative.

In this sense, what constitutes the fixity of the body, its contours, its movements, will be fully material, but materiality will be rethought as the effect of power, as power's most productive effect. And there will be no way to understand 'gender' as a cultural construct which is imposed upon the surface of matter, understood either as 'the body' or its given sex. Rather, once 'sex' itself is understood in its normativity, the materiality of the body will not be thinkable apart from the materialisation of that regulatory norm. 'Sex' is, thus, not simply what one has, or a static description of what one is: it will be one of the norms by which the 'one' becomes viable at all, that which qualifies a body for life within the domain of cultural intelligibility.[1]

At stake in such a reformulation of the materiality of bodies will be the following: (1) the recasting of the matter of bodies as the effect of a dynamic of power, such that the matter of bodies will be indissociable from the regulatory norms that govern their materialisation and the signification of those material effects; (2) the understanding of performativity not as the act by which a subject brings into being what she/he names, but, rather, as that reiterative power of discourse to produce the phenomena that it regulates and constrains; (3) the construal of 'sex' no longer as a bodily given on which the construct of gender is artificially imposed, but as a cultural norm which governs the materialisation of bodies; (4) a rethinking of the process by which a bodily norm is assumed, appropriated, taken on as not, strictly speaking, undergone *by a subject*, but rather that the subject, the speaking 'I', is formed by virtue of having gone through such a process of assuming a sex; and (5) a linking of this process of 'assuming' a sex with the question of *identification*, and with the discursive means by which the heterosexual imperative enables certain sexed identifications and forecloses and/or disavows other identifications. This exclusionary matrix by which subjects are formed thus requires the simultaneous production of a domain of abject beings, those who are not yet 'subjects', but who form the constitutive outside to the domain of the subject. The abject[2] designates here precisely those 'unlivable' and 'uninhabitable' zones of social life which are nevertheless densely populated by those who do not enjoy the status of the subject, but whose living under the sign of the 'unlivable' is required to circumscribe the domain of the subject. This zone of uninhabitability will constitute the defining limit of the subject's domain; it will constitute that site of dreaded identification against which – and by virtue of which – the domain of the subject will circumscribe its own claim to autonomy and to life. In this sense, then, the subject is constituted through the force of exclusion and abjection, one which produces a constitutive outside to the subject, an abjected outside, which is, after all, 'inside' the subject as its own founding repudiation.

The forming of a subject requires identification with the normative phantasm of 'sex', and this identification takes place through a repudiation which produces a domain of abjection, a repudiation without which the subject cannot emerge. This is a repudiation which creates the valence of 'abjection' and its status for the subject as a threatening spectre. Further, the materialisation of a given sex will centrally concern *the regulation of identificatory practices* such that the identification with the abjection of sex will be persistently disavowed. And yet, this disavowed abjection will threaten to expose the self-grounding presumptions of the sexed subject, grounded as that subject is in a repudiation whose consequences it cannot fully control. The task will be to consider this threat and disruption not as a permanent contestation of social norms condemned to the pathos of perpetual failure, but rather as a critical resource in the struggle to rearticulate the very terms of symbolic legitimacy and intelligibility.

Lastly, the mobilisation of the categories of sex within political discourse will be haunted in some ways by the very instabilities that the categories effectively produce and foreclose. Although the political discourses that mobilise identity categories tend to cultivate identifications in the service of a political goal, it may be that the persistence of *dis*identification is equally crucial to the rearticulation of democratic contestation. Indeed, it may be precisely through practices which underscore disidentification with those regulatory norms by which sexual difference is materialised that both feminist and queer politics are mobilised. Such collective disidentifications can facilitate a reconceptualisation of which bodies matter, and which bodies are yet to emerge as critical matters of concern.

FROM CONSTRUCTION TO MATERIALISATION

The relation between culture and nature presupposed by some models of gender 'construction' implies a culture or an agency of the social which acts upon a nature, which is itself presupposed as a passive surface, outside the social and yet its necessary counterpart. One question that feminists have raised, then, is whether the discourse which figures the action of construction as a kind of imprinting or imposition is not tacitly masculinist, whereas the figure of the passive surface, awaiting that penetrating act whereby meaning is endowed, is not tacitly or – perhaps – quite obviously feminine. Is sex to gender as feminine is to masculine?[3]

Other feminist scholars have argued that the very concept of nature needs to be rethought, for the concept of nature has a history, and the figuring of nature as the blank and lifeless page, as that which is, as it were, always already dead, is decidedly modern, linked perhaps to the emergence of technological means of domination. Indeed, some have argued that a rethinking of 'nature' as a set of dynamic interrelations suits both feminist and ecological aims (and has for some produced an otherwise unlikely alliance with the work of Gilles Deleuze). This rethinking also calls into question the model of construction whereby the social unilaterally acts on the natural and invests it with its parameters and its meanings. Indeed, as much as the radical distinction between sex and gender has been crucial to the de Beauvoirian version of feminism, it has come under criticism in more recent years for degrading the natural as that which is 'before' intelligibility, in need of the mark, if not the mar, of the social to signify, to be known, to acquire value. This misses the point that nature has a history, and not merely a social one, but, also, that sex is positioned ambiguously in relation to that concept and its history. The concept of 'sex' is itself troubled terrain, formed through a series of contestations over what ought to be a decisive criterion for distinguishing between the two sexes; the concept of sex has a history that is covered over by the figure of the site or surface of inscription. Figured as such a site or surface, however, the natural is construed as that which is also without value; moreover, it assumes its value at the same time that it assumes its social character, that is, at the same time that nature relinquishes itself as the natural. According to this view, then, the social construction of the natural presupposes the cancellation of the natural by the social. Insofar as it relies on this construal, the sex/gender distinction founders along parallel lines; if gender is the social significance that sex assumes within a given culture – and for the sake of argument we will let 'social' and 'cultural' stand in an uneasy interchangeability – then what, if anything, is left of 'sex' once it has assumed its social character as gender? At issue is the meaning of 'assumption', where to be 'assumed' is to be taken up into a more elevated sphere, as in 'the Assumption of the Virgin'. If gender consists of the social meanings that sex assumes, then sex does not *accrue* social meanings as additive properties but, rather, *is replaced by* the social meanings it takes on; sex is relinquished in the course of that assumption, and gender emerges, not as a term in a continued relationship of opposition to sex, but as the term which absorbs and displaces 'sex', the mark of its full substantiation into gender or what, from a materialist point of view, might constitute a full *de*substantiation.

When the sex/gender distinction is joined with a notion of radical linguistic constructivism, the problem becomes even worse, for the 'sex' which is referred to as prior to gender will itself be a postulation, a construction, offered within language, as that which is prior to language, prior to construction. But this sex posited as prior to construction will, by virtue of being posited, become the effect of that very positing, the construction of construction. If gender is the social construction of sex, and if there is no access to this 'sex' except by means of its construction, then it appears not only that sex is absorbed by gender, but that 'sex' becomes something like a fiction, perhaps a fantasy, retroactively installed at a prelinguistic site to which there is no direct access.

But is it right to claim that 'sex' vanishes altogether, that it is a fiction over and against what is true, that it is a fantasy over and against what is reality? Or do these very oppositions need to be rethought such that if 'sex' is a fiction, it is one within whose necessities we live, without which life itself would be unthinkable? And if 'sex' is a fantasy, is it perhaps a phantasmatic field that constitutes the very terrain of cultural intelligibility? Would such a rethinking of such conventional oppositions entail a rethinking of 'constructivism' in its usual sense?

The radical constructivist position has tended to produce the premise that both refutes and confirms its own enterprise. If such a theory cannot take account of sex as the site or surface on which it acts, then it ends up presuming sex as the unconstructed, and so concedes the limits of linguistic constructivism, inadvertently circumscribing that which remains unaccountable within the terms of construction. If, on the other hand, sex is a contrived premise, a fiction, then gender does not presume a sex which it acts upon, but rather, gender produces the misnomer of a prediscursive 'sex', and the meaning of construction becomes that of linguistic monism, whereby everything is only and always language. Then, what ensues is an exasperated debate which many of us have tired of hearing: Either (1) constructivism is reduced to a position of linguistic monism, whereby linguistic construction is understood to be generative and deterministic. Critics making that presumption can be heard to say, 'If everything is discourse, what about the body?' or (2) when construction is figuratively reduced to a verbal action which appears to presuppose a subject, critics working within such a presumption can be heard to say, 'If gender is constructed, then who is doing the constructing?'; though, of course, (3) the most pertinent formulation of this question is the following: 'If the subject is constructed, then who is constructing the subject?' In the first case, construction has taken the place of a godlike agency which not only causes but composes everything which is its object; it is the divine performative, bringing into being and exhaustively constituting that which it names, or, rather, it is that kind of transitive referring which names and inaugurates at once. For something to be constructed, according to this view of construction, is for it to be created and determined through that process.

In the second and third cases, the seductions of grammar appear to hold sway; the critic asks, Must there not be a human agent, a subject, if you will, who guides the course of construction? If the first version of constructivism presumes that construction operates deterministically, making a mockery of human agency, the second understands constructivism as presupposing a voluntarist subject who makes its gender through an instrumental action. A construction is understood in this latter case to be a kind of manipulable artifice, a conception that not only presupposes a subject, but rehabilitates precisely the voluntarist subject of humanism that constructivism has, on occasion, sought to put into question.

If gender is a construction, must there be an 'I' or a 'we' who enacts or performs that construction? How can there be an activity, a constructing, without presupposing an agent who precedes and performs that activity? How would we account for the motivation and direction of construction without such a subject? As a rejoinder, I would suggest that it takes a certain suspicion toward grammar to reconceive the matter in a different light. For if gender is constructed, it is not necessarily constructed by an 'I' or a 'we' who stands before that construction in any spatial or temporal sense of 'before'. Indeed, it is unclear that there can be an 'I' or a 'we' who has not been submitted, subjected to gender, where gendering is, among other things, the differentiating relations by which speaking subjects come into being. Subjected to gender, but subjectivated by gender, the 'I' neither precedes nor follows the process of this gendering, but emerges only within and as the matrix of gender relations themselves.

This then returns us to the second objection, the one which claims that constructivism forecloses agency, pre-empts the agency of the subject, and finds itself presupposing the subject that it calls into question. To claim that the subject is itself produced in and as a gendered matrix of relations is not to do away with the subject, but only to ask after the conditions of its emergence and operation. The 'activity' of this gendering cannot, strictly speaking, be a human act or expression, a wilful appropriation, and it is certainly *not* a question of taking on a mask; it is the matrix through which all willing first becomes possible, its enabling cultural condition. In this sense, the matrix of gender relations is prior to the emergence of the 'human'. Consider the medical interpellation which (the recent emergence of the sonogram notwithstanding) shifts an infant from an 'it' to a 'she' or a 'he', and in that naming, the girl is 'girled', brought into the domain of language and kinship through the interpellation of gender. But that 'girling' of the girl does not end there; on the contrary, that founding interpellation is reiterated by various authorities and throughout various intervals of time to re-enforce or contest this naturalised effect. The naming is at once the setting of a boundary, and also the repeated inculcation of a norm.

Such attributions or interpellations contribute to that field of discourse and power that orchestrates, delimits, and sustains that which qualifies as 'the human'. We see this most clearly in the examples of those abjected beings who do not appear properly gendered; it is their very humanness that comes into question. Indeed, the construction of gender operates through *exclusionary* means, such that the human is not only produced over and against the inhuman, but through a set of foreclosures, radical erasures, that are, strictly speaking, refused the possibility of cultural articulation. Hence, it is not enough to claim that human subjects are constructed, for the construction of the human is a differential operation that produces the more and the less 'human', the inhuman, the humanly unthinkable. These excluded sites come to bound the 'human' as its constitutive outside, and to haunt those boundaries as the persistent possibility of their disruption and rearticulation.[4]

Paradoxically, the inquiry into the kinds of erasures and exclusions by which the construction of the subject operates is no longer constructivism, but neither is it essentialism. For there is an 'outside' to what is constructed by discourse, but this is not an absolute 'outside', an ontological thereness that exceeds or counters the boundaries of discourse,[5] as a constitutive 'outside', it is that which can only be thought – when it can – in relation to that discourse, at and as its most tenuous borders. The debate between constructivism and essentialism thus misses the point of deconstruction altogether, for the point has never been that 'everything is discursively constructed'; that point, when and where it is made, belongs to a kind of discursive monism or linguisticism that refuses the constitutive force of exclusion, erasure, violent foreclosure, abjection and its disruptive return within the very terms of discursive legitimacy.

And to say that there is a matrix of gender relations that institutes and sustains the subject is not to claim that there is a singular matrix that acts in a singular and deterministic way to produce a subject as its effect. That is to install the 'matrix' in the subject-position within a grammatical formulation which itself needs to be rethought. Indeed, the prepositional form 'Discourse constructs the subject' retains the subject-position of the grammatical formulation even as it reverses the place of subject and discourse. Construction must mean more than such a simple reversal of terms.

There are defenders and critics of construction, who construe that position along structuralist lines. They often claim that there are structures that construct the subject, impersonal forces, such as Culture or Discourse or Power, where these terms occupy the grammatical site of the subject after the 'human' has been dislodged from its place. In such a view, the grammatical and metaphysical place of the subject is retained even as the candidate that occupies that place appears to rotate. As a result, construction is still understood as a unilateral process initiated by a prior subject, fortifying that presumption of the metaphysics of the subject that where there is activity, there lurks behind it an initiating and wilful subject. On such a view, discourse or language or the social becomes personified, and in the personification the metaphysics of the subject is reconsolidated.

In this second view, construction is not an activity, but an act, one which happens once and whose effects are firmly fixed. Thus, constructivism is reduced to determinism and implies the evacuation or displacement of human agency.

This view informs the misreading by which Foucault is criticised for 'personifying' power: if power is misconstrued as a grammatical and metaphysical subject, and if that metaphysical site within humanist discourse has been the privileged site of the human, then power appears to have displaced the human as the origin of activity. But if Foucault's view of power is understood as the disruption and subversion of this grammar and metaphysics of the subject, if power orchestrates the formation and sustenance of subjects, then it cannot be accounted for in terms of the 'subject' which is its effect. And here it would be no more right to claim that the term 'construction' belongs at the grammatical site of subject, for construction is neither a subject nor its act, but a process of reiteration by which both 'subjects' and 'acts' come to appear at all. There is no power that acts, but only a reiterated acting that is power in its persistence and instability.

What I would propose in place of these conceptions of construction is a return to the notion of matter, not as site or surface, but as *a process of materialisation that stabilises over time to produce the effect of boundary, fixity, and surface we call matter*. That matter is always materialised has, I think, to be thought in relation to the productive and, indeed, materialising effects of regulatory power in the Foucaultian sense.[6] Thus, the question is no longer, How is gender constituted as and through a certain interpretation of sex? (a question that leaves the 'matter' of sex untheorised), but rather, Through what regulatory norms is sex itself materialised? And how is it that treating the materiality of sex as a given presupposes and consolidates the normative conditions of its own emergence?

Crucially, then, construction is neither a single act nor a causal process initiated by a subject and culminating in a set of fixed effects. Construction not only takes place *in* time, but is itself a temporal process which operates through the reiteration of norms; sex is both produced and destabilised in the course of this reiteration.[7] As a sedimented effect of a reiterative or ritual practice, sex acquires its naturalised effect, and, yet, it is also by virtue of this reiteration that gaps and fissures are opened up as the constitutive instabilities in such constructions, as that which escapes or exceeds the norm, as that which cannot be wholly defined or fixed by the repetitive labour of that norm. This instability is the *de*constituting possibility in the very process of repetition, the power that undoes the very effects by which 'sex' is stabilised, the possibility to put the consolidation of the norms of 'sex' into a potentially productive crisis.[8]

Certain formulations of the radical constructivist position appear almost compulsively to produce a moment of recurrent exasperation, for it seems that when the constructivist is construed as a linguistic idealist, the constructivist refutes the reality of bodies, the relevance of science, the alleged facts of birth, ageing, illness, and death. The critic might also suspect the constructivist of a certain somatophobia and seek assurances that this abstracted theorist will admit that there are, minimally, sexually differentiated parts, activities, capacities, hormonal and chromosomal differences that can be conceded without reference to 'construction'. Although at this moment I want to offer an absolute reassurance to my interlocutor, some anxiety prevails. To 'concede' the undeniability of 'sex' or its 'materiality' is always to concede some version of 'sex', some formation of 'materiality'. Is the discourse in and through which that concession occurs – and, yes, that concession invariably does occur – not itself formative of the very phenomenon that it concedes? To claim that discourse is formative is not to claim that it originates, causes, or exhaustively composes that which it concedes; rather, it is to claim that there is no reference to a pure body which is not at the same time a further formation of that body. In this sense, the linguistic capacity to refer to sexed bodies is not denied, but the very meaning of 'referentiality' is altered. In philosophical terms, the constative claim is always to some degree performative.

In relation to sex, then, if one concedes the materiality of sex or of the body, does that very conceding operate – performatively – to materialise that sex? And further, how is it that the reiterated concession of that sex – one which need not take place in speech or writing but might be 'signalled' in a much more inchoate way – constitutes the sedimentation and production of that material effect?

The moderate critic might concede that *some part* of 'sex' is constructed, but some other is certainly not, and then, of course, find him or herself not only under some obligation to draw the line between what is and is not constructed, but to explain how it is that 'sex' comes in parts whose differentiation is not a matter of construction. But as that line of demarcation between such ostensible parts gets drawn, the 'unconstructed' becomes bounded once again through a signifying practice, and the very boundary which is meant to protect some part of sex from the taint of constructivism is now defined by the anti-constructivist's own construction. Is construction something which happens to a ready-made object, a pregiven thing, and does it happen *in degrees*? Or are we perhaps referring on both sides of the debate to an inevitable practice of signification, of demarcating and delimiting that to which we then 'refer', such that our 'references' always presuppose – and often conceal – this prior delimitation? Indeed, to 'refer' naïvely or directly to such an extra-discursive object will always require the prior delimitation of the extra-discursive. And insofar as the extra-discursive is delimited, it is formed by the very discourse from which it seeks to free itself. This delimitation, which often is enacted as an untheorised presupposition in any act of description, marks a boundary that includes and excludes, that decides, as it were, what will and will not be the stuff of the object to which we then refer. This marking off will have some normative force and, indeed, some violence, for it can construct only through erasing; it can bound a thing only through enforcing a certain criterion, a principle of selectivity.

What will and will not be included within the boundaries of 'sex' will be set by a more or less tacit operation of exclusion. If we call into question the fixity of the structuralist law that divides and bounds the 'sexes' by virtue of their dyadic differentiation within the heterosexual matrix, it will be from the exterior regions of that boundary (not from a 'position', but from the discursive possibilities opened up by the constitutive outside of hegemonic positions), and it will constitute the disruptive return of the excluded from within the very logic of the heterosexual symbolic.

The trajectory of this text, then, will pursue the possibility of such disruption, but proceed indirectly by responding to two interrelated questions that have been posed to constructivist accounts of gender, not to defend constructivism per se, but to interrogate the erasures and exclusions that constitute its limits. These criticisms presuppose a set of metaphysical oppositions between materialism and idealism embedded in received grammar which, I will argue, are critically redefined by a poststructuralist rewriting of discursive performativity as it operates in the materialisation of sex.

PERFORMATIVITY AS CITATIONALITY

When, in Lacanian parlance, one is said to assume a 'sex', the grammar of the phrase creates the expectation that there is a 'one' who, upon waking, looks up and deliberates on which 'sex' it will assume today, a grammar in which 'assumption' is quickly assimilated to the notion of a highly reflective choice. But if this 'assumption' is *compelled* by a regulatory apparatus of heterosexuality, one which reiterates itself through the forcible production of 'sex', then the 'assumption' of sex is constrained from the start. And if there is *agency*, it is to be found, paradoxically, in the possibilities opened up in and by that constrained appropriation of the regulatory law, by the materialisation of that law, the compulsory appropriation and identification with those normative demands. The forming, crafting, bearing, circulation, signification of that sexed body will not be a set of actions performed in compliance with the law; on the contrary, they will be a set of actions mobilised by the law, the citational accumulation and dissimulation of the law that produces material effects, the lived necessity of those effects as well as the lived contestation of that necessity.

Performativity is thus not a singular 'act', for it is always a reiteration of a norm or set of norms, and to the extent that it acquires an act-like status in the present, it conceals or dissimulates the conventions of which it is a repetition. Moreover, this act is not primarily theatrical; indeed, its apparent theatricality is produced to the extent that its historicity remains dissimulated (and, conversely, its theatricality gains a certain inevitability given the impossibility of a full disclosure of its historicity). Within speech act theory, a performative is that discursive practice that enacts or produces that which it names.[9] According to the biblical rendition of the performative, i.e., 'Let there be light!', it appears that it is by virtue of *the power of a subject or its will* that a phenomenon is named into being. In a critical reformulation of the performative, Derrida makes clear that this power is not the function of an originating will, but is always derivative:

> Could a performative utterance succeed if its formulation did not repeat a 'coded' or iterable utterance, or in other words, if the formula I pronounce in order to open a meeting, launch a ship or a marriage were not identifiable as conforming with an iterable model, if it were not then identifiable in some way as a 'citation'? ... in such a typology, the category of intention will not disappear; it will have its place, but from that place it will no longer be able to govern the entire scene and system of utterance [*l'énonciation*].[10]

To what extent does discourse gain the authority to bring about what it names through citing the conventions of authority? And does a subject appear as the author of its discursive effects to the extent that the citational practice by which he/she is conditioned and mobilised remains unmarked? Indeed, could it be that the production of the subject as originator of his/her effects is precisely a consequence of this dissimulated citationality? Further, if a subject comes to be through a subjection to the norms of sex, a subjection which requires an assumption of the norms of sex, can we read that 'assumption' as precisely a modality of this kind of citationality? In other words, the norm of sex takes hold to the extent that it is 'cited' as such a norm, but it also derives its power through the citations that it compels. And how it is that we might read the 'citing' of the norms of sex as the process of approximating or 'identifying with' such norms?

Further, to what extent within psychoanalysis is the sexed body secured through identificatory practices governed by regulatory schemas? Identification is used here not as an imitative activity by which a conscious being models itself after another; on the contrary, identification is the assimilating passion by which an ego first emerges.[11] Freud argues that 'the ego is first and foremost a bodily ego', that this ego is, further, 'a projection of a surface',[12] what we might redescribe as an imaginary morphology. Moreover, I would argue, this imaginary morphology is not a presocial or presymbolic operation, but is itself orchestrated through regulatory schemas that produce intelligible morphological possibilities. These regulatory schemas are not timeless structures, but historically revisable criteria of intelligibility which produce and vanquish bodies that matter.

If the formulation of a bodily ego, a sense of stable contour, and the fixing of spatial boundary is achieved through identificatory practices, and if psychoanalysis documents the hegemonic workings of those identifications, can we then read psychoanalysis for the inculcation of the heterosexual matrix at the level of bodily morphogenesis? What Lacan calls the 'assumption' or 'accession' to the symbolic law can be read as a kind of *citing* of the law, and so offers an opportunity to link the question of the materialisation of 'sex' with the reworking of performativity as citationality. Although Lacan claims that the symbolic law has a semi-autonomous status prior to the assumption of sexed positions by a subject, these normative positions, i.e., the 'sexes', are only known through the approximations that they occasion. The force and necessity of these norms ('sex' as a symbolic function is to be understood as a kind of commandment or injunction) is thus functionally *dependent on* the approximation and citation of the law; the law without its approximation is no law or, rather, it remains a governing law only for those who would affirm it on the basis of religious faith. If 'sex' is assumed in the same way that a law is cited – an analogy which will be supported later in this text – then 'the law of sex' is repeatedly fortified and idealised as the law only to the extent that it is reiterated as the law, produced as the law, the anterior and inapproximable ideal, by the very citations it is said to command. Reading the meaning of 'assumption' in Lacan as citation, the law is no longer given in a fixed form *prior* to its citation, but is produced through citation as that which precedes and exceeds the mortal approximations enacted by the subject.

In this way, the symbolic law in Lacan can be subject to the same kind of critique that Nietzsche formulated of the notion of God: the power attributed to this prior and ideal power is derived and deflected from the attribution itself.[13] It is this insight into the illegitimacy of the symbolic law of sex that is dramatised to a certain degree in the contemporary film *Paris Is Burning*:[14] the ideal that is mirrored depends on that very mirroring to be sustained as an ideal. And though the symbolic appears to be a force that cannot be contravened without psychosis, the symbolic ought to be rethought as a series of normativising injunctions that secure the borders of sex through the threat of psychosis, abjection, psychic unlivability. And further, that this 'law' can only remain a law to the extent that it compels the differentiated citations and approximations called 'feminine' and 'masculine'. The presumption that the symbolic law of sex enjoys a separable ontology prior and autonomous to its assumption is contravened by the notion that the citation of the law is the very mechanism of its production and articulation. What is 'forced' by the symbolic, then, is a citation of its law that reiterates and consolidates the ruse of its own force. What would it mean to 'cite' the law to produce it differently, to 'cite' the law in order to reiterate and coopt its power, to expose the heterosexual matrix and to displace the effect of its necessity?

The process of that sedimentation or what we might call *materialisation* will be a kind of citationality, the acquisition of being through the citing of power, a citing that establishes an originary complicity with power in the formation of the 'I'.

In this sense, the agency denoted by the performativity of 'sex' will be directly counter to any notion of a voluntarist subject who exists quite apart from the regulatory norms which she/he opposes. The paradox of subjectivation (*assujetissement*) is precisely that the subject who would resist such norms is itself enabled, if not produced, by such norms. Although this constitutive constraint does not foreclose the possibility of agency, it does locate agency as a reiterative or rearticulatory practice, immanent to power, and not a relation of external opposition to power.

As a result of this reformulation of performativity, (a) gender performativity cannot be theorised apart from the forcible and reiterative practice of regulatory sexual regimes; (b) the account of agency conditioned by those very regimes of discourse/power cannot be conflated with voluntarism or individualism, much less with consumerism, and in no way presupposes a choosing subject; (c) the regime of heterosexuality operates to circumscribe and contour the 'materiality' of sex, and that 'materiality' is formed and sustained through and as a materialisation of regulatory norms that are in part those of heterosexual hegemony; (d) the materialisation of norms requires those identificatory processes by which norms are assumed or appropriated, and these identifications precede and enable the formation of a subject, but are not, strictly speaking, performed by a subject; and (e) the limits of constructivism are exposed at those boundaries of bodily life where abjected or delegitimated bodies fail to count as 'bodies'. If the materiality of sex is demarcated in discourse, then this demarcation will produce a domain of excluded and delegitimated 'sex'. Hence, it will be as important to think about how and to what end bodies are constructed as it will be to think about how and to what end bodies are *not* constructed and, further, to ask after how bodies which fail to materialise provide the necessary 'outside', if not the necessary support, for the bodies which, in materialising the norm, qualify as bodies that matter.

14

From 'Intensities and Flows'

Elizabeth Grosz

There is no ideology and never has been.
(Gilles Deleuze and Félix Guattari,
A Thousand Plateaus)[1]

[...] Can accounts of subjectivity and the psychical interior be adequately explained in terms of the body? Can depths, the interior, the subjective, and the private instead be seen in terms of surfaces, bodies, and material relations? Can the mind/body dualism be overcome using the concepts associated with the devalued term of the binary pair of mind and body, that is, are the body and corporeality the (disavowed) grounds and terms on which the opposition is erected and made possible? What happens to conceptual frameworks if the body stands in place of the mind or displaces it from its privileged position defining humanity against its various others? What happens in the bifurcation of sexed bodies – which is, in my opinion, an irreducible cultural universal – that is inevitably part of our understanding of bodies? If mind or subjectivity can be adequately and without reduction explained in terms of bodies, bodies understood in their historicocultural specificity, does this mean that sexual specificity – sexual difference – will be finally understood as a necessary (even if not sufficient) condition of our understanding of subjectivity? Can various key issues and concepts in feminist theory – including women's experience, subjectivity, desire, pleasure – be reconceived in corporeal terms, whether these are provided by the theoretical frameworks of Nietzsche, Foucault, Deleuze, or others? Is there a possibility of transposing the terms of consciousness and the entire psychical topography into those of body mapping and social tattooing? What is lost in this process? Or gained? Why is it necessary to transform these terms? Here I propose a provisional reconstruction of Deleuze and Guattari's understanding of corporeality in *A Thousand Plateaus* – a text that could be regarded as their (anti-)opus – in terms of the flatness, surfaces, intensities, investments, i.e., in the terms other than those provided by dichotomous thought, capable of outstripping, overturning, or exceeding binary logics.

142

FEMINISM AND RHIZOMATICS

It is significant that all the male theorists of the body I have explored [in *Volatile Bodies*] have a highly contentious position in feminist theory; all of them have generated considerable debate regarding their ostensibly sexist remarks, their apparent derision of women or femininity; and all of them have been defended by other feminists in terms of their strategic and provisional usefulness in explaining the operations of a phallocentric[2] culture and patriarchal representational models. Deleuze and Guattari's status in feminist evaluations seems rather more shaky than others'. Most feminists have said virtually nothing about them, although there are a few significant exceptions.[3] They seem to have been generally ignored by those who are otherwise quite sympathetic to French theory: their works have thus far generated little of the controversy and impact accorded to the writings of Lacan, Foucault, or Derrida. This is rather surprising given the privileged position they – or at least Deleuze – hold in radical French thought. And even those feminists who do engage with their writings have tended to be critical or at least suspicious of their apparent appropriations, of feminist theory and, politics, in similar ways to feminist suspicions regarding Derrida's metaphorics of invagination.[4]

Alice Jardine, for example, expresses a series of misgivings about their work and its possible value or usefulness for feminist purposes. She claims that

> to the extent that women must 'become woman' first ... might that not mean that she must also be the first to disappear? Is it not possible that the process of 'becoming woman' is but a new variation of an old allegory for the process of women becoming obsolete? There would remain only her simulacrum: a female figure caught in a whirling sea of male configurations. A silent, mutable, head-less, desireless spatial surface necessary only for his metamorphosis?[5]

The notion of the flattening of subjectivity, the disorganisation of the organism ('headless'), the destabilisation of political order and social organisation, poses a theoretical anxiety for Jardine that, in this passage at least, is almost as strong as her worries about the appropriation of the metaphorics of 'becoming woman' as a new label for male self-expansion. Jardine articulates clearly the anxieties posed for feminists by Deleuze's radical refiguring of ontology in terms of planes, intensities, flows, becomings, linkages, rather than being, objects, qualities, pairs, and correlations, through the figure of woman and femininity. Her anxieties seem related to the apparent bypassing or detour around the very issues with which feminist theory has tended to concern itself: 'identity', otherness, gender, oppression, the binary divisions of male and female – all central and driving preoccupations of feminist thought.[6] [...]

Between them, Jardine, Irigaray, and Braidotti voice a number of reservations that seem to chart a more general attitude on the part of many feminists
toward the project Deleuze has described as rhizomatics.[7] I will briefly list
these objections, adding that it is not always clear to me that these objections
are justified.

First, the metaphor of 'becoming woman' is a male appropriation of
women's politics, struggles, theories, knowledges, insofar as it 'borrows' from
them while depoliticising their radicality. At the least, Deleuze and Guattari
can be accused of aestheticising and romanticising women's struggles,[8] while
in stronger terms, they may be accused of depoliticising women's various
political struggles and using them precisely to neutralise, to render human
(and thus to rephallicise), women's specificity, which they have struggled so
hard to produce and represent.

Second, these metaphors not only neutralise women's sexual specificity,
but, more insidiously, they also neutralise and thereby mask men's specifici-
ties, interests, and perspectives. This means that the question of becoming
itself becomes a broadly human, and indeed an even more general, phenomenon, a defining characteristic of life itself, a manoeuvre that desexualises and
obfuscates one of the major features of phallocentric thought – its subsumption of two sexual symmetries under a single norm. It is not clear that a
'feminine' becoming woman would be the same as the one Deleuze and
Guattari describe. It remains a block both to women's explorations and inter-
rogations of their own specific, nongeneralisable modes of becoming and
desiring production and to men's acceptance of the corporeal specificity of
their own positions of becoming and desiring production.

Third, in both *Anti-Oedipus*[9] and *A Thousand Plateaus*, Deleuze and
Guattari invest in a romantic elevation of psychoses, schizophrenia, becoming, which on one hand ignores the very real torment of suffering individuals
and, on the other hand, positions it as an unlivable ideal for others. Moreover,
in making becoming woman the privileged site of all becomings, Deleuze and
Guattari confirm a long historical association between femininity and
madness which ignores the sexually specific forms that madness takes.

Fourth, in invoking metaphors of machinic functioning, in utilising the
terminology of the technocratic order, Deleuze and Guattari, like other masculinist philosophers, utilise tropes and terms made possible only through
women's exclusion and denigration; while not inherently and irremediably
masculinist, technocracies are in fact masculinist insofar as technological developments have thus far been historically predicated on women's
exclusion.

These are of course very serious objections or reservations, ones which
cannot be simply cast aside. They will be returned to. [...] [But] it is significant
that the 'reversal of Platonism' Deleuze and Guattari seek shares the concern
of many feminists to overcome the binary polarisations so pervasive in

Western thought. Not only do they seek alternatives to contest or bypass the metaphysical bases of Western philosophy; they seek to position traditional metaphysical identities in a context which renders them effects or surface phenomena in an ontology conceived quite otherwise. [...] Even if their procedures and methods do not actively affirm or support feminist struggles around women's autonomy and self-determination, their work may help to clear the ground of metaphysical oppositions and concepts so that women may be able to devise their own knowledges, accounts of themselves and the world. [...]

Their notion of the body as a discontinuous, nontotalisable series of processes, organs, flows, energies, corporeal substances and incorporeal events, speeds and durations, may be of great value to feminists attempting to reconceive bodies outside the binary oppositions imposed on the body by the mind/body, nature/culture, subject/object and interior/exterior oppositions. They provide an altogether different way of understanding the body in its connections with other bodies, both human and nonhuman, animate and inanimate, linking organs and biological processes to material objects and social practices while refusing to subordinate the body to a unity or a homogeneity of the kind provided by the body's subordination to consciousness or to biological organisation. Following Spinoza, the body is regarded as neither a locus for a consciousness nor an organically determined entity; it is understood more in terms of what it can do, the things it can perform, the linkages it establishes, the transformations and becomings it undergoes, and the machinic connections it forms with other bodies, what it can link with, how it can proliferate its capacities – a rare, affirmative understanding of the body.[10]

Not only do they develop alternative notions of corporeality and materiality; they also propose quite different, active, affirmative conceptions of desire. It has been argued[11] that while psychoanalysis relies on a notion of desire as a lack, an absence that strives to be filled through the attainment of an impossible object, desire can instead be seen as what produces, what connects, what makes machinic alliances. Instead of aligning desire with fantasy and opposing it to the real, instead of seeing it as a yearning, desire is an actualisation, a series of practices, bringing things together or separating them, making machines, making reality. Desire does not take for itself a particular object whose attainment it requires; rather, it aims at nothing above its own proliferation or self-expansion. It assembles things out of singularities and breaks things, assemblages, down into their singularities. It moves; it does. Such a notion of desire cannot but be of interest to feminist theory insofar as women have been the traditional repositories and guardians of the lack constitutive of desire, and insofar as the opposition between presence and absence, reality and fantasy, has traditionally defined and constrained woman to inhabit the place of man's other. Lack only makes sense insofar as some other, woman, personifies and embodies it for man. Any model of desire that dispenses with the primacy of lack in conceiving desire seems to be a positive step forward and, for that reason alone, worthy of careful investigation. But the surpassing of the model of lack does not, should not, return us to the affirmation of pure plenitude or presence. Presence and absence are coupled in and to the same framework. In place of plenitude, being, fullness or self-identity is not lack, absence, rupture, but rather becoming.

Deleuze's writings may provide unexpectedly powerful weapons of analysis, critique, transgression, and transformation. They may demonstrate that other kinds of theoretical approaches, other intellectual paradigms, new ways of conceptualising knowledge, power, bodies, representations, other than the kind of Freudo-Marxism that dominated and perhaps still dominates much of feminist theory in spite of Freudo-Marxism's well-recognised problems (the centrality of the phallus for psychoanalysis; the centrality of relations of production; monolithic, cohesive forms for Marxism). [...]

BODIES, BODIES WITHOUT ORGANS, BECOMINGS

My goal here is not to be in any way 'faithful' to the Deleuzian oeuvre but, on the contrary, and more in keeping with its spirit, to use it, to make it work, to develop and experiment with it in order to further develop theories and concepts that Deleuze and Guattari do not. In particular, I intend to develop only those elements of their work, only those plateaus, that are useful for feminist reconceptions of the body, for rethinking materiality, and for retranscribing the mind/body opposition – clearly a highly selective reading. Given that Deleuze and Guattari do not have a systematic account of the body, this will involve not only a selective reading of their elusive and immensely complex text *A Thousand Plateaus* but also a reconstruction which is inevitably more cohesive, more 'arboreal' (systematic, centralised, ordered, and organised), than their own nomadic or rhizomatic understanding.[12] I will concentrate on a small number of concepts that I believe overlap with the concerns of feminist theories of the body: the rhizome, assemblage, machine, desire, multiplicity, becoming, and the Body without Organs (BwO). These concepts seem loosely linked together in an attempt to reject or displace prevailing centrisms, unities, and rigid strata.

In Deleuze and Guattari's work, subject and object can no longer be understood as discrete entities or binary opposites. Things, material or psychical, can no longer be seen in terms of rigid boundaries, clear demarcations; nor, on an opposite track, can they be seen as inherently united, singular or holistic. Subject and object are series of flows, energies, movements, strata, segments, organs, intensities – fragments capable of being linked together or served in potentially infinite ways other than those which congeal them into identities. Production consists of those processes which create linkages between fragments, fragments of bodies and fragments of objects. Assemblages or machines are heterogeneous, disparate, discontinuous alignments or linkages brought together in conjunctions (x plus y plus z) or severed through disjunctions and breaks. But significantly, an assemblage follows no central or hierarchical order, organisation, or distribution; rather, it is, like the contraption or gadget, a conjunction of different elements on the same level:

> An assemblage has neither base nor superstructure, neither deep structure nor superficial structure; it flattens all of its dimensions onto a single place of consistency upon which reciprocal presuppositions and mutual insertions play themselves out.　(p. 90)[13]

Assemblages are the provisional linkages of elements, fragments, flows, of disparate status and substance: ideas, things – human, animate, and inanimate – all have the same onotological status. There is no hierarchy of being, no preordained order to the collection and conjunction of these various fragments, no central organisation or plan to which they must conform. Their 'law' is rather the imperative of endless experimentation, metamorphosis, or transmutation, alignment and realignment. It is not that the world is without strata, totally flattened; rather, the hierarchies are not result of substances and their nature and value but of modes of organisation of disparate substances. They are composed of lines, of movements, speeds and intensities, rather than of things and their relations. Assemblages or multiplicities, then, because they are essentially in movement, in action, are always made, not found. They are the consequences of a practice, whether it be that of the bee in relation to the flower and the hive or of a subject making something using tools or implements. They are necessarily finite in space and time, provisional and temporary in status; they always have an outside; they do not, or need not, belong to a higher-order machine. Machines, for Deleuze and Guattari, are not simply mechanical replacements or corporeal prosthetics (as Freud suggests). They are not standardised, conforming to a plan or blueprint, the 'application' of principles. Machines are opposed to mechanism. They are the condition as well as the effect of any making, any producing.

A 'desiring machine' opposes the notion of unity or oneness: the elements or discontinuities that compose it do not belong to either an original totality that has been lost or one which finalises or completes it, a telos. They do not re-present the real, for their function is not a signifying one: they produce and they themselves are real. They constitute, without distinction, individual, collective, and social reality. Desire does not create permanent multiplicities; it experiments, producing ever-new alignments, linkages, and connections, making things. It is fundamentally nomadic not teleological, meandering, creative, nonrepetitive, proliferative, unpredictable.

Insofar as the body can no longer be seen as a unified and unifying organism, an organism centred either biologically or psychically, organised in terms of an overarching consciousness or unconscious, cohesive through its intentionality or its capacity for reflection and self-reflection, Deleuze and Guattari see the body as elements or fragments of a desiring machine and themselves as composed of a series of desiring machines. When the body is freely amenable to the flows and intensities of the desiring machines that compose it, Deleuze and Guattari, following Antonin Artaud, call it 'the Body-without Organs', the BwO. The BwO is the body in abundance of its (biological, psychical, and signifying) organisation and organs:

> The body without organs is not a dead body but a living body all the more alive and teeming once it has blown apart the organism and its organization. ... The full body without organs is a body populated by multiplicities.   (p. 30)

Their notion of the BwO is Deleuze and Guattari's attempt to denaturalise human bodies and to place them in direct relations with the flows or particles of other bodies or things. In presuming a Spinozist conception of the univocity of being ('Spinozist's ethics is a *physics*', Deleuze and Parnet write),[14] in which all things, regardless of their type, have the same ontological status, the BwO refers indistinguishably to human, animal, textual, sociocultural, and physical bodies. That is why they seem less interested in the general question of embodiment than in the question of the capacities and unknown potential of the body to do things, to engage in practices:

> ... Spinoza's question: *what is a body capable of?* What affects is it capable of? Affects are becomings: somewhere they awaken us to the extent they diminish our strength of action and decompose our relations (sadness), sometimes they make us stronger through augmenting our force, and make us enter into a faster and higher individual (joy). Spinoza never ceases to be astonished at the body: not of having a body, but at what the body is capable of. Bodies are defined not by their genus and species, nor by their origins and functions, but by what they can do, the affects they are capable of, in passion as in action.   (p. 74)[15]

Unlike psychoanalysis, which regards the body as a development union or aggregate of partial objects, organs, drives, orifices, each with their own significance, their own modalities of pleasure which, through the processes of Oedipal reorganisation, bring these partial objects and erotogenic bodily zones into alignment in the service of a higher goal than their immediate, local gratification (the ultimate goal being reproduction), the BwO invokes a conception of the body that is disinvested of fantasy, images, projections, representations, a body without a psychical or secret interior, without internal cohesion and latent significance. Deleuze and Guattari speak of it as a surface of speeds and intensities before it is stratified, unified, organised, and hierarchised.

As they describe it, the BwO is not a body evacuated of all psychical interiority, a kind of blanket rewriting or remapping of the body. The BwO is a tendency to which all bodies, whatever their organisation, aspire. Deleuze and Guattari speak of it as an egg, which instead of being composed of three kinds of substances is fluid throughout (neither Lacan's scrambled egg of a subject, the 'hommelette', nor the egg in its differential properties, hard shell, clear white, and yellow yolk), an unimpeded flow:

> The BwO is made in such a way that it can be occupied, populated, only by intensities. Only intensities pass and circulate. Still, the BwO is a scene, a place, or even a support on which something comes to pass. It has nothing to do with phantasy, there is nothing to interpret. The BwO causes intensities to pass: it produces and distributes them in a *spatium* that is itself intensive, lacking extension. It is not a space nor is it in space; it is matter that occupies space to a given degree – to the degree corresponding to the intensities produced. It is non-stratified, unformed, intense matter. The matrix of intensity, intensity $= 0$. ... That is why we treat the BwO as the full egg before the extension of the organism and the organisation of the organs, before the formation of the strata. ... Is not Spinoza's *Ethics* the great book of the BwO? (p. 153)

The BwO does not oppose or reject organs but is opposed to the structure or organisation of bodies, the body as it is stratified, regulated, ordered, and functional, as it is subordinated to the exigencies of property and propriety. The BwO is the body before and in excess of the coalescence of its intensities and their sedimentation into meaningful, organised, transcendent totalities constituting the unity of the subject and of signification. The BwO is 'the *field of immanence* of desire, the *plane of consistency* specific to desire (with desire defined as a process of production without reference to any exterior agency, whether it be a lack that hollows it out or a pleasure that fills it)' (p. 154). It resists transcendence; it refuses the sedimentation and hierarchisation required for the movement of transcendence, resists the stratifications and layerings and overcodings that produce the three great strata or identities: the union constituting the organism, the unification that constitutes the subject, and the structure of significance. It refuses all propriety: 'The BwO is never yours or mine. It is always *a* body' (p. 164).

We come to the gradual realisation that the BwO is not at all the opposite of the organs. The organs are not its enemies. The enemy is the organism.

The BwO is opposed not to the organs but to that organisation of the organs called the organism. It is true that Artaud wages a struggle against the organs, but at the same time what he is going after, what he has it in for, is the organism: the *body is the body. Alone it stands. And in no need of organs. Organism it never is. Organisms are the enemy of the body.* The BwO is not opposed to organs; rather, the BwO and its 'true organs', which must be composed and positioned, are opposed to the organism, the organic organisation of the organ.   (p. 158)

The BwO is not uniform, a singular, definable 'type' or structure. Rather, for Deleuze and Guattari one BwO can be differentiated from another in terms of the types or modalities of circulation, the movement and flow of intensities that it allows or produces on its surface. It is thus not a question of what the BwO is, what composes it, but what it does, how it functions, what it affects, what it produces. For example, they distinguish between two kinds of BwO: the emptied BwO of the drug addict, the masochist, and the hypochondriac and the full BwO in and through which intensities flow and circulate, where productions are engendered:

What is certain is that the masochist has made himself a BwO under such conditions that the BwO can no longer be populated by anything but the intensities of pain, *pain waves*. It is false to say that the masochist is looking for pain but just as false to say that he is looking for pleasure in a particularly suspensive or roundabout way. The masochist is looking for a type of BwO that only pain can fill, or travel over, due to the very conditions under which that BwO was constituted.   (p. 152)

In the case of the empty BwO, the body is evacuated not only of organs and organisation but also of its intensities and forces. This body does not lack; its problem is the opposite: it fills itself to the point where nothing further can circulate. It is empty only in the sense that if a body is made up of proliferations, connections, and linkages, the empty BwO has ceased to flow. The hypochondriac destroys both organs and the circulation of matter and intensities, vitrifying the body, rendering it fragile, amenable to invasion, inducing certain flows – flows of pain and pleasure – while at the same time disconnecting it from others. In destabilising the correlation of desire with pleasure and substituting pain for pleasure, the masochist creates new flows and movements, but only at the cost of self-enclosure, only by all other forms of openness being smothered or counteracted by what Deleuze and Guattari call pain waves. This is not a moral attitude or judgment regarding masochism but a description of its 'microphysics', of its sub-subjective components in their relations among themselves and with objects or implements and even sadistic subjects or sources of torture.[16] Where the masochist emits 'pain waves' to enliven and numb the body, the junkie is filled with 'refrigerator-waves', with the numbing-enlivening Cold:

> [A junkie] wants The Cold like he wants his Junk – Not OUTSIDE where it does him no good but INSIDE so he can sit around with a spine like a frozen hydraulic jack ... his metabolism approaching Absolute Zero.[17]

The empty BwO seems to have emptied itself too fast, too definitively. Instead of disconnecting some of its organisation and putting it to work in other reconnections, the empty BwO empties itself too quickly, disarrays itself too much, so that it closes in on itself, unable to transmit its intensities differently, stuck in repetition. It does not deny becoming; rather, it establishes a line of flight that is unable to free the circulation of intensities, making other, further connections with other BwOs impossible. It is a line of flight that ends in its own annihilation:

> Instead of making a body without organs sufficiently rich or full for the passage of intensities, drug addicts erect a vitrified and emptied body, or a cancerous one: the causal line, creative line or line of flight immediately turns into a line of death and abolition.   (p. 285)

While being neither a place nor a plane nor a scene nor a fantasy, the BwO is a field for the production, circulation, and intensification of desire, the locus of the immanence of desire. Although it is the field for the circulation of intensities and although it induces deterritorialisations at its lines of flight, movements of becoming, the ability to sustain itself is the condition that seems to be missing in the empty BwO. There must, it seems, be a minimal level of cohesion and integration in the BwO in order to prevent its obliteration; there must be small pockets of subjectivity and signification left in order for the BwOs to survive in the face of the onslaughts of power and reality. A complete destratification renders even the BwO disconnected:

> You have to keep enough of the organism for it to reform each dawn; and you have to keep small supplies of significance and subjectification, if only to turn them against their own systems when the circumstances demand it, when things, persons, even situations, force you to; and you have to keep small rations of subjectivity in sufficient quantity to enable you to respond to the dominant reality. Mimic the strata. You don't reach the BwO, and its plane of consistency, by wildly destratifying. That is why we encountered the paradox of those emptied and dreary bodies at the very beginning: *they had emptied themselves of their organs* instead of looking for the point at which they could patiently and momentarily dismantle the organisation of the organs we call the organism. There are, in fact, several ways of botching

the BwO: either one fails to produce it, or one produces it more or less, but nothing is produced on it, intensities do not pass or are blocked. This is because the BwO is always swinging between the surfaces that stratify it and the plane that sets it free. If you free it with too violent an action, if you blow apart the strata without taking precautions, then instead of drawing a plane you will be plunged into a black hole, or even dragged toward catastrophe.   (pp. 160–1)

Destratification, freeing lines of flight, the production of connections, the movements of intensities and flows through and beyond the BwO, is thus a direction or movement rather than a fixed state or final position. Deleuze and Guattari do not advocate a dissolution of identity, a complete destabilisation and defamiliarisation of identity; rather, micro-destratifications, intensifications of some but clearly not all interactions, are necessary:

Staying stratified – organised, signified, subjected – is not the worst that can happen; the worst that can happen is that you throw the strata into demented or suicidal collapse, which brings them back down on us heavier than ever.   (p. 161)

Deleuze and Guattari distinguish the BwO from the singular, organised, self-contained organic body; they also distinguish between molar and molecular arrangements of flows and minoritarian and majoritarian organisational modes. Becomings are always molecular, traversing and realigning molar unities:

If we consider the great binary aggregates, such as the sexes or classes, it is evident that they also cross over into molecular assemblages of a different nature, and that there is a double reciprocal dependency between them. For the two sexes imply a multiplicity of molecular combinations bringing into play not only the man in the woman and the woman in the man, but the relation of each to the animal, the plant etc.   (p. 213)

If molar unities, like the divisions of classes, rates, and sexes, attempt to form and stabilise an identity, a fixity, a system that functions homeostatically, sealing in its energies and intensities, molecular becomings traverse, create a path, destabilise, energise instabilities, vulnerabilities of the molar unities. It is clear that this de-massification of the great divisions of social power in culture must at first sight appear to undermine the power and justification of various oppressed groups – women, the working class, people of colour, gays and lesbians, religious or cultural minorities and their struggles: it is not that Deleuze and Guattari are trying to explain away the great divisions and global categories that have thus far helped categorise and provide political positions for various social groups. Instead, as I read them, they seem to be rendering more complex the nature and forms that these oppressions take. I must admit that it makes me feel uncomfortable that Deleuze and Guattari choose to refer to the 'man in the woman and the woman in the man', which tends to obliterate the very real bodily differences and experiences of the two sexes. Once again it is crucial to note that the man 'in the woman' is not the same man as the man 'in the man'! But in their defence, it is also crucial to recognise the micro-segmentarities we seize from or connect with in others which give us traits of 'masculinity' and 'femininity' whether we 'are' men or women. In my opinion, this is politically dangerous ground to walk on, but if we do not walk in dangerous places and different types of terrain, nothing new will be found, no explorations are possible, and things remain the same. The risks seem to me worth taking: risking rethinking global oppositions and macroscopic hierarchies in order to have more optimistic prospects for effecting transformations and realignments of these global relations, and moreover, seeing their capacity to infiltrate microscopic recesses which may appear immune to or outside of their influence. Thus, if the division or the binary opposition of sexes or, for that matter, the global system constituting patriarchy can be considered as molar lines, then traversing and interrupting them and transforming, breaking them down is what Deleuze and Guattari describe as the processes of 'becoming woman'. [...]

Becoming-woman means going beyond identity and subjectivity, fragmenting and freeing up lines of flight, 'liberating' multiplicities, corporeal and otherwise, that identity subsumes under the one. Woman's becoming-woman is a movement for and of all subjects insofar as it is the putting into play of a series of microfemininities, impulses, wills, in all subjects: her becoming-woman carries all humanity's, in a striking reversal (but exact replication) of phallocentrism:

> A woman has to become-woman, but in a becoming-woman of all men ... A becoming-minoritarian exists only by virtue of a deterritorialised medium and subject that are like its elements. There is no subject of the becoming except as a deterritorialised variable of a majority; there is no medium of becoming except as a deterritorialised variable of a minority. We can be thrown into a becoming by anything at all, by the most unexpected, most insignificant of things. You don't deviate from the majority unless there is a little detail that starts to swell and carries you off.   (p. 292)

If becoming-woman is the medium through which all becomings must pass, it is however only a provisional becoming or a stage, a trajectory or movement that in fact has an (asymptotic) 'end', the most microscopic and fragmenting of becomings, which they describe as 'becoming-imperceptible'. This line of flight, this particular desiring-machine is the breakdown or shrinkage of all identities, molar and molecular, majoritarian and minoritarian, the freeing of infinitely microscopic lines, a process whose end is achieved only with complete dissolution, the production of the incredible ever-shrinking 'man'.

> If becoming-woman is the first quantum, or molecular segment with the becomings-animal that link up with it coming next, what are they all rushing towards? Without a doubt, toward becoming-imperceptible. The imperceptible is the immanent end of becoming, its cosmic formula. For example, Matheson's *Shrinking Man* passes through the kingdoms of nature, slips between molecules, to become an unfindable particle in infinite meditation on the infinite. (p. 279)

Implicit here is the claim that there is a kind of direction to the quantum leap required by becomings, a labyrinthine but nonetheless goal-orientated movement in which becoming-woman is, for all subjects, a first trajectory. Becoming-woman desediments the masculinity of identity; becoming-child, the modes of cohesion and control of the adult; becoming-animal, the anthropocentrism of philosophical thought; and becoming-imperceptible replaces, dismantles, problematises the most elementary notions of entity, thingness. Indiscernibility, imperceptability, and impersonality remain the end points of becoming, their immanent orientation or internal impetus, the freeing of absolutely minuscule micro-intensities to the nth degree. Feminist struggles around the question of 'woman's identities', 'woman's rights', are thus only part of a stage setting for the processes of becoming woman; and becoming-woman is in turn the condition of human-becomings, which in their turn must deterritorialise and become-animal. This is a path toward 'being like everybody else' (p. 279), an absolute, indiscernible annonymity. Not the obliteration of all characteristics – which, of course, is annihilation – but the resonance of all kinds of machines with each other, the imperceptibility of traits, characteristics, identities, positions. It need no longer be woman who functions as the figure of radical otherness for identity. Deleuze and Guattari produce a radical antihumanism that renders animals, nature atoms, even quasars as modes of radical alterity.

There are worrisome implications here. The ordering of these becomings is unmistakable in the language ('first', 'coming next', etc.) and in its tone ('without a doubt'). Deleuze and Guattari describe here a process of the blowing apart of the fragments into smaller fragments and so on ad infinitum. How this occurs is nomadic, random, or contingent; but Deleuze and Guattari imply a clear movement toward imperceptibility that is in many ways similar to the quest of physics for the microscopic structures of matter, the smallest component, the most elementary particle. If it remains materialist at this level, it is a materialism that is far beyond or different from the body, or bodies: their work is like an acidic dissolution of the body, and the subject along with it.

Moreover, the presumption that women's molar struggles for identity are merely a stage or stepping stone in a broader struggle must be viewed with great suspicion, for Deleuze and Guattari begin to sound alarmingly similar to a number of (male) political groups that have supported feminism on condition that it be regarded as the stage, phase, element, or subdivisions of a broader cause. These are very common claims, claims which have been used to tie woman to struggles that in fact have little to do with them, or rather, to which women have been tied through generalised 'humanity' which in no way represents their interests, which is a projection or representation of men's specific fantasies about what it is to be human. The Marxist subordination of women's struggles to the class struggle or struggles for cultural identity, the subsumption of women's call for identities as women under a general call for the dissolution of all identities (Kristeva), the positing of women's pleasures and desires as the means of access to the Other (Lacan and Levinas), all serve as relatively current examples of such phallocentrism. But perhaps Deleuze and Guattari fit less easily into this category than it seems on a first reading. [...]

15

Beyond Food/Sex: Eating and an Ethics of Existence

Elspeth Probyn

Appetite is nothing but the very essence of man.
(Spinoza, *The Ethics*)[1]

WHAT'S EATING US?

It seems like a strange time to be arguing that the primacy of sex may be passing. After all, the world has watched in horror and mostly disbelief as Bill's concept of sexuality was disclosed.[2] In fact, my horror was caused less by the Monicagate ensemble than by the idea that this article would be totally out of sync with the times. But as commentators (perhaps especially outside the US) constantly complained about being bored with sex, and as the sex-non-sex definitions were aired, it became legitimate to wonder whether this scandal constituted the last gasp of the reign of sex. (It also led me to wonder if oral sex wasn't sex, was it eating?) Possible epistemological ruptures aside, in this article, and under the rubric of the question that Foucault[3] takes from Kant ('*Was ist die Aufkärung?*' ['What is Enlightenment?']), I want to ask 'What's eating us now?' As you will recall, this is to question 'who we are in the present'; to engage with passion in 'stalking the elusive singularity of the present'.[4] In my own small quest to figure the present, I try to follow the line of sex as it intersects with that of food. My argument takes from research that I have been conducting in Australia on the role that food now occupies in re-articulating national identity. More generally, I am interested in thinking about a new ethics of existence, one which is theoretically indebted to Foucault and his work on the dietetic regimen, or as Deleuze puts it, the alimentary-sexual regime.[5] Along with others, I want to try to push at our ways of thinking sexuality in order to get beyond the impasse that threatens studies of sexuality. Simply put, I will argue that thinking sex through food is compelling for the ways that it focuses our attention on the interrelation of various corporeal dimensions: that constituting oneself as an ethical subject involves conjugating the forces of sex along with those of food, exercise, sleeping, writing and thinking.

156

Like a rhizomatic line that always turns into something else, the vector of food soon leads into other areas, and along the way I have been struck by the ways in which the boundaries between food and sex are currently being blurred. As others have argued, food has a propensity for hazing the frontiers of categories. For instance, Georg Simmel argues that food encapsulates the paradox of absolute individuality and complete universality: 'Of everything that people have in common, the most common is that they must eat and drink. It is precisely this which is, oddly enough, the most egoistic, and the most unconditionally and most immediately linked to each individual.'[6] Food here is both what we all share and forms the absolute limit to any commonality. Simmel writes that 'what the individual eats, no one else can eat under any circumstance'.[7] By this rather strange statement, Simmel gestures to what we might call the brute physicality of food: as the morsel is going into my mouth, pricking up my tongue and taste buds, and then sliding down on its route to digestion and finally defecation, you cannot be anything more than a witness. In the face of this fundamental alienation of one from the other, it is only 'the shared meal [that] lifts an event of physiological primitivity and inescapable commonality into the sphere of social interaction'.[8]

As that which both viscerally segregates us and radically brings us together, without doubt food is a hugely powerful system of values, regulations and beliefs; in short a system of representation that hides its nature in appeals to immediacy, and non-mediation. One of the difficulties that faces any investigation of food is its enormity, and the ways in which it spills into every aspect of life. As it lends itself to easy metaphor, the chances are that any sociological specificity will be lost. Mary Douglas quite rightly warned against the propensity to privilege an overly cultural or symbolic reading of food, stating that 'Food is not only a metaphor or vehicle of communication; a meal is a physical event'.[9] In a similar fashion, Arjun Appadurai argues that 'Food may generally possess a special semiotic force because of certain universal properties. ... But this special force must always remain tacit until it is animated by particular cultural concepts and mobilised by particular social contexts.'[10] Appadurai qualifies the rush to celebrate food's innate universal qualities by arguing that 'the cultural notion that food has an inherently homogenising capacity ... is itself converted from a metonymic hazard into a metaphoric convenience in the contexts where sharing, equality, solidarity, and communality are, within limits, perceived as desirable results'.[11]

The problems that arise from either 'a metonymic hazard' or a 'metaphoric convenience' are especially troubling if one wants to use food to think through different relations of sociality. To name but a few, food is imbricated in nation-building, the reproduction of the family, constitutes a major site of the division of labour, and is central in the production of geo-political inequalities. But if food statements commonly contain a metonymic connection ('you are what you eat'), the peculiarities of what and how you are eating and the connections to who or what you are soon get lost. As Appadurai reminds us, food seems to possess inherent tropic qualities. Simply put, food moves about all the time. It constantly shifts registers: from the sacred to the everyday, from metaphor to materiality, it is the most common and elusive of matters. This is, of course, not 'natural' to food, and as Roland Barthes has argued 'food has a constant tendency to transform itself into situation'.[12] For as he states, food is always 'bound to values of power', revealing the fact that 'a representation of contemporary existence is implied in the consciousness we have of the function of food'.[13]

I will now turn to several sites that highlight the scrambling of sex, gender and food. I use these somewhat idiosyncratic examples to sketch out the possibilities that food may offer in rethinking the limits of sex deployed as the sole or privileged object within the theorisation of identity. I should be clear that this is not a polemic against those theories (queer and feminist) that have centred on sex, and which I have myself used. Rather, it is my wish to *extend* the reach of sexuality by looking first at the way that sex now spills on to food, and, second, at accounts of food that compel us to think in terms of another ethics of living. While I realise the enormity of the term, here I take Foucault's fairly simple if demanding line on ethics in order to concentrate on modes of living already in existence, 'to learn from and strengthen these, not to discover or "invent" others'.[14] If 'ethics' cannot be reified as an object, but rather it is always a mode of relating to oneself and to others, then the task of thinking ethics will necessarily be a doubled one. On the one hand, it enjoins us to seek out the singularities marking our present, and on the other hand to engage with them as they mark us. The promise of thinking food/sex is that it requires attention to what Foucault calls 'attitude': 'a way of thinking and feeling; a way too of acting and behaving that at one and the same time marks a relation of belonging and presents itself as task'.[15] The question I put to myself, then, is in what ways might food and sex come to constitute the outlines of another way of thinking and feeling, one that is fuelled by what the novelist Antoine Laurent calls 'sympathy': 'Sympathy for where she is, for who she's with, and for what's feasible at any time or place. For the ingredients themselves, the people she's cooking for, all play a part.'[16] In this sense, sympathy highlights an ethical practice, not a passive acceptance of life. In what follows, I will first sketch out certain overdetermined ways of constituting food/sex, and then focus on the ethical possibilities that food and sex offer when practised with care, restraint and good timing.

FOOD CHIC

To start, come with me to Sydney in order to experience the sights and smells. It is a hazy summer evening in the fashionable enclave of Potts Point, and around the corner from the flesh spots of King's Cross things were getting hot and sticky at the Paramount restaurant. The buzz spilled on to the pavement as a veritable who's who of Australian power-queers sipped a concoction called 'passion pops'. In terms of the Sydney Gay and Lesbian Mardi Gras, 'Eat our Words', a queer fiction and food fest, was the hottest ticket and sold out in minutes. The event had gay and lesbian writers squashed in like mere membranes of a *millefeuille*, digestive fodder in between the sumptuous courses. The real star of the night was Christine Manfield who, along with her partner Margie Harris, owns the Paramount. The mistress of ceremonies introduced her as 'the dominatrix of the kitchen', 'sex on a plate', and described one of Manfield's famous dishes, 'Creaming Cock' which compels the eater to go down on large *tuile* cones with apple-ginger custard and Tokay caramel. In turn, Manfield said grace, telling us 'to eat the words that you are given and if you want to go down, go ahead'. The *piece de resistance* was not a cigar but Manfield's signature dish, the 'slice of pride', a beautiful pink and white ice cream triangle which in true commensal fashion we were to share.

Let me turn now from the restaurant to television. In one of the weirder series, two large women regale with tales of derring-do among the landed gentry of Scotland, ham it up with the members of a girls' school lacrosse team, flirt with boy scouts, and play at being Annie Oakley on the moors as they shoot small birds. In between titbits about cooking testicles in Benghazi (in cream of course), or musings about their 'kitchenalia fetish', one of the ladies plunges her beringed fingers complete with long red nails into a bowl of raw mince and egg, the other passes scathing remarks about vegetarians, microwave ovens and supermarket bought chicken, the conversation is peppered with remarks about 'real faggots' (meatballs), instructions to wrap your meatloaf in bacon so it looks like a Union Jack, and we learn that 'pan Asian' is really Australian. This is all lubricated with asides about 'slap-up meals', 'toothsome meat', and odd refrains of songs: 'The playing fields of Eton have made us frightfully brave' croons the one, as the other declines Latin verbs.[17]

The programme is the phenomenally successful BBC cooking show *Two Fat Ladies*, starring the decidedly upper-class Clarissa Dickson Wright who apparently owes her girth to a destroyed thyroid brought about by an excess of gin, and the worldly and at times rather 'pukka' Jennifer Paterson; she of the long red nails to be found at the end of an episode clutching cigarette and gin and tonic. Talking to others, it wasn't surprising to find that many found this show decidedly queer. Certainly, Jennifer's arch comments belie a Cowardesque inclination (her immediate advice to the young female producer was 'to find yourself a nice poof'). And the easy banter of the two ladies is evidence of a female homosociality, which may also be a mellowed version of the edgy homoerotism rampant in private girls' schools. If the Ladies were good on their first series, in the second they get down and have a great time with each other. Perhaps being centrefolds in the British gay mag, *Attitude*

(November, 1997) has given them the cue to show off that they are as queer as a bent sixpence in a rich fruit loaf (lavished with cream no doubt). While the interviewer, Nick Taylor, had them pegged ('Eccentric, shameless and unmarried? They're clearly lesbians'), they will only admit to being vegetarian-phobic, and very *fond* of men. But as they drool over the young boys from King's College, Cambridge, remarking on the fact that the white ruffles around the singers' necks make them look like deliciously edible little lamb chops, it is their pronounced taste for all forms of flesh that tantalises.

In their latest cookbook, *Two Fat Ladies Full Throttle*, we're told that 'the whole of the USA seemed to have developed Fatladymania'.[18] Given the fact that Clarissa 'holds the home of the hamburger responsible for everything that's wrong with the modern world – including fast food, political correctness and plastic surgery', they may be deluding themselves about their status in the States. However, certainly in Britain they move with the powerful, and dine with the Blairs. In short, they inhabit the world where, as a recent columnist writes, 'Chefs are the new rock 'n' roll stars, cookbooks are the new pornography'. Wendy Harmer concludes that 'When the difference between a boring Saturday night alone and an evening of mind-blowing erotic adventure is a backlit picture of a chargrilled eggplant ... you've got it made'.[19] In the boudoir, the kitchen, or more likely in a trendy restaurant, it seems that food has become more exciting than sex. As a case in point, the *Sydney Morning Herald* recently instructed that we should 'Forget sex sells – these days food sells. Replace the motor show dolly birds with a plate of stuffed squid draped over the car bonnet and see what happens' (9 February 1998). The article focuses on the new smart restaurant in Sydney, 'MC Garage' which offers 'extravagant petrol heads a sportscar as a side with their octopus ... snapper and mussel stew with saffron, tomato and rouille'. Apparently, replacing girlies with sexy and expensive food has resulted in a doubling of the sales of MGs which start at $45,000. Food also seems to sell queer mags. The Australian gay glossy *Blue* recently published a display of the popular Manfield doing 'rude food'. According to a breathless newspaper report, this featured an *s/m* scene with two models in meringue, raspberry sauce, nipple rings, and 'plenty of black leather'. In actual fact, the scenes were pretty tame with a rather sweet looking Manfield in black lurex and spikes. While one can only agree with Manfield's motto that 'Life's too short for bad food, bad sex or no sex at all',[20] her recipes and food are, in fact, a lot sexier than the photos. [...]

So what *is* this food fetishism all about? Could it be simply that food is now replacing sex as the ground of identities, be they gendered, national, postcolonial, collective or individual? If this is so, what happens to the purchase of all those theories – feminist, gay, lesbian, queer, psychoanalytic, etc. – that have privileged sex in one way or another as either constituting the very truth of ourselves; or those that have invested in endlessly deconstructing that supposed truth? While it is tempting to categorically proclaim that sex is dead, long live the cook as queen, this is not only hasty but would, I think, miss the insights that the current popular cultural food scene provides. While there are numerous analytic lines that flow from food, here I want to consider whether in the celebration of food as sex and sex as food we can see some of the limitations of dominant theoretical uses of sex. For instance, certain examples of food porn forcefully reveal the limits of thinking in terms of transgression, be it about food or sex.

Bluntly put, the conflation of food/sex may be simply convenient (the use of easy metaphors), or sloppy (the type of inversion that makes meat equal masculinity). Either way, these appropriations of food miss their mark. For surely sexuality, like food, is only of interest insofar as it allows us to see new connections between individuals, collectivities: to ask what sex and food allow and disallow. Whether it be food or sex, or a doubled reconfiguration of both, what matters is how they enable precise connections to be thought and enacted. In Deleuze and Guattari's words, 'What regulates the obligatory, necessary, or permitted interminglings of bodies is above all an alimentary regime and a sexual regime'.[21] In turn, I also want to question what types of ethical bodies the intermingling of sex and food might produce.

This is at the heart of Foucault's argument in the second volume of *The History of Sexuality*, where he is interested not in sex per se but rather in the conception of corporeal ethics that the Greeks practised. As a way of defining 'the uses of pleasure ... in terms of a certain way of caring for one's body', diet, or the notion of the regimen was central.[22] Foucault argues that regimen was dietetic not therapeutic, thus signalling an important difference between a Greek conception of ethics and sex, and how the ensuing history of Western thought and practice would deal with sex. Thus, 'diet', what, how, when and where one eats 'characterised the way in which one managed one's existence ... a mode of problematisation of behaviour. ... Regimen was a whole art of living.'[23] If one were interested in generalisations of history, one could say that sex became the object of what Foucault describes as the Christian motif of 'knowing oneself', whereas food and diet continued as the way in which one cared for oneself.

THE MORAL OF THE FLESH

Of course, things are not quite so clear cut. The long tradition within anthropology reminds us that food has also functioned as a privileged way by which we know and categorise the other. For instance, the preoccupation with cannibalism within anthropology reveals much about the colonial imagination as well as the constitution of the discipline.[24] 'Eating the other' is both a metaphor for imperial violence, and the point where knowing the self and caring for the self merge, where food and sex intersect.[25, 26] Either way we are faced with the elemental fact of the flesh. In a bare manner, flesh confuses the limits of what we are and what we eat, what or who we want; flesh encapsulates the quandary of whether the body in question is edible, fuckable, or both. As Derrida so famously states, it is 'a question no longer of knowing if it is "good" to eat the other or if the other is "good" to eat. One eats him regardless and lets himself be eaten by him.'[27] Breast or thigh, dark or white meat, or a sweaty sexy entanglement of limbs? Angela Carter's early feminist critique of the function of sex in Sade mines the possibilities as well as the limits of flesh. As she writes, 'The word "fleisch", in German, provokes me to an involuntary shudder. In the English language, we make a fine distinction between flesh, which is usually alive and typically, human; and meat, which is dead, inert, animal and intended for consumption'.[28] Her musings set off others: in French, '*La chair*' evokes the delicious intermingling of species as well as the variety of human form. '*La chair*' equally refers to animal, human and vegetable flesh, but also always brings to mind the image of a woman '*bien en chair*', rounded, voluptuous, or again in the superbly evocative French adjective, '*plantureuse*' – copious, lavish, buxom, fertile, of an ample *poitrine*. In French one dives into the expansiveness of flesh, describing penetration as '*entrer dans les chairs*', and firm young flesh is seemingly of necessity exemplified in the dictionary as '*aimer la chair fraîche*', for indeed how could anyone not *aimer entrer dans les chairs fraîches*, not wish to enter into young firm flesh.

Carter uses the semiotic slides between body/flesh/meat to give a compelling critique of Sade, and by extension of certain modern understandings of sexuality. She draws out the ways that a mechanics of transgression based solely in the inversion of body and meat is at the core of Sade's work. Against either celebration or simple condemnation, Carter shows how his mania for sexual transgression as inversion was fundamentally uninteresting. Her argument constitutes an early warning against an overvalorisation of sex as transgressive when she proposes that Sade provides a model of sex that in the end is devoid of complication. For all his physical exertion, sex is rigidly compartmentalised and serves to confine the leakages between categories. 'Sade is a great puritan and will disinfect of sensuality anything he can lay his hands on; therefore he writes about sexual relations in terms of butchery and meat.'[29]

In Carter's argument, sexual pleasure through transgression maintains a sovereign position for the transgressor and serves only to reinforce the inward-looking, isolated and alienated subject. It is the very principle of containment, with sex as 'nothing but a private and individual shock of the nerves'. As such, 'sexual pleasure is not experienced *as* experience; it does not modify the subject'. When sex is a cerebral, knowing act of transgression, 'where desire is a function of the act rather than the act a function of desire,

desire loses its troubling otherness'.[30] It becomes a way of reterritorialising the subject rather than sending it into lines of flight. In other words, this model of transgression fundamentally reterritorialises the body in sex. Instead of being the fusion of bodies that confuses their limits, sex as meat becomes the principle to reintegrate.

In a wonderful line, Carter writes that the bed is 'as public as the dinner table and governed by the same rules of formal confrontation'.[31] Carter's reading of Sade clarifies for me why I find much of the current food-porn boring. Call me the Sheila Jeffreys of food-sex, but representations of sex combined with food are not per se transgressive (although of course that would not be the complaint that anti-porn campaigners would use).[32] In a recent example of transgression as inversion, Linda Jaivin's bestselling novel and soon to be film, *Eat Me*, uses food to disguise the ways sex is rendered as the very principle of normalisation. In the opening story, one of the heroines, Ava, is in the supermarket stuffing different kinds of fruit up her cunt. To be more precise, figs, strawberries, grapes, and a kiwi fruit before the store detective stops her and is ordered to eat her out. He then fucks her with a banana. She then fucks him with a Lebanese cucumber. The store closes, and as they leave it turns out that this is a regular routine: 'See you next week, honey pot?' asked Adam. 'Usual time, usual place?' 'You bet, sweet pea', answers Ava.[33]

What emerges from Jaivin's novel is the sense that sex on its own is no longer terribly interesting. And to be fair, she is not alone in this regard. Indeed the issue of 'sex on its own' is implicitly raised by 'the ampersand problem' of sexual politics, a problem that queer was supposed to fix by its expansive inclusiveness, but may have instead aggravated. While Jaivin's account is fundamentally about heterosex, she seeks to queer it by hyphenating sex and food. But surely the queerness of sex is not to be found in merely adding on another bit; does it not lie in the way in which it compels other combinations, sends lines out to seemingly distant realms and brings other worlds into dizzying proximity. When queer becomes content merely to *be* sex, is it possible that it may actually hinder our capacities to make connections? Posed as the answer, we need to question whether sex can really explain everything.

THE REPRESSIVE HYPOTHESIS OF MEAT

Within certain cultures of eating it seems that sex can explain everything. When it comes to *not* eating meat, it also seems that the repressive hypothesis is well and truly alive. If we no longer say 'no' to sex, in some articulations of eating, 'no' is the way to go. Carole Adams is the guru of such thought, and takes a radical feminist anti-porn line into the realm of eating, equating s/m and butchery in a sort of weird return to Sade. In her book, *The Sexual*

Politics of Meat, women and animals are the 'voiceless' victims of patriarchy. She reiterates endlessly that 'Eating animals acts as a mirror and representation of patriarchal values'.[34] In fact it doesn't seem to matter whether it is animal or woman that is the object of consumption because 'Meat eating is the re-inscription of male power at every meal'. This yields a direct equation of the terms meat and men, which then can be inverted at will: 'The killed and slaughtered animal yields ... imagery of ferociousness, territorial imperative, armed hunting, aggressive behavior, the vitality and virility of meat eating.'[35]

Strangely enough Adams' unreconstructed rad-fem analysis of sexual politics is similarly structured to the wannabe 'bad girl' Jaivin's orgy of heterosex dished with fruit and veg. To use Carter's phrase, in neither does the combination of food and sex fulfil the capacity of the flesh for the 'fusion to confuse'. In Jaivin's story, it is clear that she 'knows' what sex is, and the addition of vegetables and fruit merely serves to enforce this knowingness. And in a congruent fashion, Adams wants to police the troubling fusion of flesh eating flesh. In her rage against meat-eaters and, worse, those 'bad' vegetarians who eat fish, we hear not ethics but the maintenance of strict predetermined boundaries.[36]

In these scenarios, the importation of food into sex tends to close down the troubling possibilities of sex – as well as those of food. I would suggest that these examples show up some of the limits of sex, or at least the limited possibilities of an ampersand model of sex, whereby addition doesn't alter the other term. As Foucault argued throughout his work, the point was to lose oneself, to have oneself rearranged through sex or thought or writing. We are however increasingly faced with the question of whether sex can rearrange us when it is transformed into an object, the measure of inclusion and exclusion. [...]

Following these considerations, I want to now turn to ways of putting the doubledness of sex and food to work: to use their enfolding as both analytic vectors and as sites of ethical becoming. From the various food-sex sites I have touched upon, it seems to me that those that work, those that send off new lines and beg new connections, are the ones motivated by what makes cooking, eating and sex all potent. [...] My wager is that through food we may begin to formulate an ethics of living that works against the logics of categorisation that now dominate much of the politics of identity. To return to my question of 'what's eating us', I want to be clear that food cannot simply supersede sex. Rather it is a way of retraining the ethical and political impulse that propelled much of queer theorisation: the wish to make connections between our sexualities and our lives; the imperative not to be subsumed within sex. Thus for me food offers a way of returning to questions about pleasure within restraint, sympathy understood as a means of respecting the situatedness of identity. It also returns our attention to the forces that regulate our everyday lives: in short to a very practical figuring of an everyday ethics of living. [...] To extend Deleuze and Guattari's point, this is to recognise that while alimentary and sexual regimes regulate the 'interminglings of bodies in a society', how we practise *le juste milieu*, alimentary or sexual, is what allows for more ethical arrangements of bodies.

Thinking of the limits and possibilities provoked by this, in conclusion I want to draw on [an example] of the sexual alimentary that flays food and sex into their composite dimensions, and then recombines them in suggestive ways. As many will remember, Dorothy Allison's wonderful short story 'A Lesbian Appetite' opens with an homage to biscuits, buttermilk, beans, pork fat, bacon and greens. With a scrumptious list of meals, she remembers her girlfriends by what they ate together. Later she will describe both the girls and the meals, but first she writes of the 'one lover who didn't want to eat at all. We didn't last long. The sex was good, but I couldn't think what to do with her when the sex was finished. We drank spring water together and fought a lot'.[37]

Reflecting on this experience, Allison refuses to conflate sex and food. Rather, she uses food to trace out one direction, which then intersects with the tracing provided by sex. Yet another line is clearly and distinctly drawn as she tells of her childhood worry and shame that they were not getting enough vitamin D. A teacher instructs her that 'the children of the poor have a lack of brain tissue simply because they don't get the necessary vitamins at the right age'. The child is horrified by the image 'of my cousins, big-headed, watery-eyed, and stupid': 'We will drink milk, steal it if we must'.[38] Like salt on an eggplant, with these images Allison draws out the meaning of food within poverty, and gives us a profound understanding of the connections between food, family, pride, shame and love.

In Allison's story, women are hungry for other women, for real Southern barbecue, coleslaw and hush puppies, for sex, for chocolate, for remembering.[39] While 'A Lesbian Appetite' strikes me as a great deal more erotic than some of the current food-porn, it is also a deeply pedagogic tale of the ethics, the modes of living that food and sex can forge. Her text strangely echoes or embodies Foucault's argument. If, as he argued, 'homosexuality … is an historic occasion to re-open affective and relational virtualities',[40] in Allison's tale affective and relational possibilities are embodied in the slow caress given to each detail, each ingredient, the sense of timing and movement so essential to eating, cooking, loving and being. Lest one think that this is only possible in an avowedly lesbian text, this exploration of timing and touch is also what makes the *Two Fat Ladies* so suggestive: food here is something to be felt, touched ('get those hands in there'), enquired after (who has grown it and can we go play with it on the hoof), cared for and ultimately eaten with appreciation. In short, food is the opportunity to explore the tangible links between what we eat, who we think we are, how and with whom we have sex, and what we are becoming. In short, what we have here are descriptions of the lines that can be wound between food, sex, bodies: an ethics of connection and disconnection between the various assemblages we inhabit.

To end, let me be clear that if I have argued that certain representations of food and sex belie the limits of sex as the sole optic through which to elaborate an ethics of existence, it should also be clear that I am not advocating the wholesale replacement of sex by food. On the contrary, what I have tried to suggest is that thinking *through* food to sex may make us 'infinitely more susceptible to pleasure'. Pleasure and ethics, sex and food are all about breaking up the strict moralities which constrain us. Just as 'food' must break open into production, preparation, exploitation, consumption, reading, writing, play and work, so too should sex fall apart. In articulating an alternative ethics of social connection between all those aspects that have been too summarily subsumed by sex, we need to proceed with respect for the inherent qualities of each element. Guided by the question of what is eating us, and the exigency of reflecting on our manners of living, this may also remind us of the necessity of enacting *le juste milieu*, a care for the self and for others guided by pleasure and restraint, in theory and in practice. It is an alimentary matter of common sense that delicacy and restraint make for good cooking; they are equally essential for an alternative ethics of existence.

16

Piercings

Marianna Torgovnick

THE VIDEO

Performance artist Monte Cazazza has made a video of his own genital piercing. There are no titles or credits. We go right to a close-up of a circumcised penis, totally flaccid, lying amid a tangle of pubic hair against a white thigh. Electronic music erupts, punctuated by the word 'surgeon', repeated over and over in a robotic, heavily synthesised voice. The music increases in sound level and pace, but ceases to be noticed about twenty seconds into the five-minute video.

A hand holding a metallic, needlelike device enters the frame, wielded by an unseen operator. The needle pierces the head of the penis, leaving behind a single, small gold stud, a rounded ball identical to those used to pierce ears in malls all over the United States. The head of the penis, now adorned by the ball, is displayed to the camera for perhaps five seconds, then the penis is flipped over and an identical procedure is performed two to three times more, at the head and along the shaft, still to the rhythmic chant 'surgeon'.

Then, in a sequence that prompts a collective gasp from the audience, a tweezerlike device descends upon the head of the penis, pulling it out like cotton candy further than anyone would have imagined the glans penis could be extended. The organ is pretty much a visual object by now, except that the perception of it as penis is what prompts the deep collective gasp.

Now a broader needle, almost a lance, enters the taffy-shaped, stretched and narrowed head of the penis; it makes a hole clear through, into which a metal bolt is inserted and secured at each end by a gleaming metal hemisphere. For reasons I can't explain there is no blood, even though the video is in a grainy-textured colour. The procedure completed, the penis is once again arranged on the thigh, as at the beginning of the video. For a few seconds, we are asked to admire the new adornments, the difference from the beginning. Then the camera pans up, to the performance artist's face. He is grinning and mouthing some words at us that are inaudible since the sound track consists only of music. But he seems to be saying 'It was great, man, Unbelievable'. I'm inclined to believe him, even as I feel a distinct sense of repulsion.

167

THE BACKGROUND

The video was shown at a conference at which I was one of the speakers, a conference organised by jewellery-makers and craftspeople at the University of the Arts in Philadelphia. It is part of a quasi-underground phenomenon known as 'piercing', which was on everybody's mind at this conference, whose subject was modern primitivism in the crafts, and especially in jewellery-making. Many of the participants, students and artists alike, had multiple ear or nose piercings and (I now suspect), sometimes more.

After my lecture, the night before, on primitivism and covert sadistic images in Man Ray's photographs, I was swamped by private questions. Perhaps thirty people came up after the public question period and waited their turn – an unusual post-lecture turnout. Several of the students at the university (both undergraduate and graduate) said my talk raised questions for them about piercing – a practice for which their amply decorated ears and (in some cases) noses testified at least a qualified support. One member of the audience later presented me with a special issue of *Re-Search*[1] called *Modern Primitives* and devoted to the contemporary arts of piercing and tattooing, especially on or around the genitals: a full regalia of penis and testicle piercing, labia and clitoris piercing, and nipple piercing for both sexes.

I answered the question of whether piercing was a form of primitivism with a qualified 'yes'. Yes, it alluded to certain practices in parts of Africa, the South Pacific and Indian Ocean regions, and the Americas. But it also had a heavy overlay of Western associations: with pirates and buccaneers, with motorcycle gangs, with gays and lesbians, and with adolescent 'gang' piercings of ears with needles, popular at girls' sleepovers. I pointed out as well that, so far as I knew, no African group pierced the genitals for decorative purposes, and relatively few groups elsewhere were known to have decorated them with tattoos, or scarification – subjects also treated in the *Modern Primitives* volume. That volume claims that both piercing and tattooing were common in the past and are still widespread among certain groups around the Indian Ocean. These claims appear to be at least partially true.

I have found, for example, passing references to genital tattooing of women in Malinowski's ethnographies, and selected scholarly references to piercing practices, especially in societies in the Indian ocean.[2] James Boon describes the exotic Balinese custom of inserting bells in the penis.[3] *The Blood of Kings* documents instances of ritual bloodletting from ancient Mayan culture that includes bloodletting from the penis. Anthropologists have studied Hindu rituals in Sri Lanka that entail various forms of bodily mutilation.[4] In archaic societies, initiation rituals frequently include bodily mutilation (sometimes of the genitals) that is intended (scholars say) to imitate death and confirm the mature being's awareness and acceptance of it.[5] These initiation rituals seem to me closest in spirit to postmodern piercing and I will return later to them.

The best-documented instances among the Maya, the Hindus, and archaic peoples function, however, in specific and organised religious systems that make them quite different from examples in contemporary primitivism.

It is difficult both to uncover and to assess information on a touchy subject like this one. The motivations of those who discuss these topics, and those who do not, are often suspect. The basic fact remains: in traditional societies, piercing for decorative or ritual purposes, or both, while common, is usually confined to ears and noses; scarification and tattooing are usually limited to faces, chests, backs, and (in some cases) navels. The current vogue for genital piercing is a postmodern phenomenon, with affinities to, but not completely traceable from, primitive peoples. Its motivations are often more narcissistic than religious and, even when religious, generally operate outside any traditional or organised religious systems.

I knew that the next speaker, Lonette Stinich, an editor, clothing designer, and artist, planned to speak critically about piercing in ways she anticipated that her student audience would not want to hear. Her lecture turned out to be more complicated than that brief description indicated. This woman, brilliant but highly eccentric, provided some startling insights into piercing as a phenomenon. Since I heard her talk, I have read several accounts of piercing in the popular press, where the phenomenon is usually sanitised (omitting, for example, genital piercing) or treated as an amusing fad.[6] Stinich's approach is both more unflinching and more profound than anything I have see subject in the popular press, and so I summarise it here.

STINICH'S LECTURE

Lonette Stinich, at the time an editor at *New Art Examiner*, supports herself mostly by her paintings, for which she has a waiting list of commissions. [...] Lonette has been into piercing, but in this talk (reaching back to her degrees in ethics from the University of Chicago and Harvard) she was interested in the question of when piercing ceases to be an acceptable private expression and becomes a troubling public phenomenon. She clearly feels that the line – which she is unable to draw absolutely – has been crossed.

My notes from her lecture turn up the following arresting words or phrases, which I give in the order she gave them, with more attempt to order them than she did:

- Piercing is a 'modern ritual acted out in seclusion from the modern world and yet conditioned by it'.
- 'Committed' piercers mean to represent the ugliness or decline of the modern world and are connected to surrealism, expressionism, and dada – earlier movements anchored in a protest against cultural decay.

- Piercing is a withdrawal into being 'a magical person' but also into a 'blank wall of subjectivity'.
- Piercing also represents a form of 'compulsive transgression' and 'alternative culture provincialism'.
- Piercing wants a return to mystery, to the body, and to sensations; it evokes initiatory moments.
- Piercing seeks a crossing of the mineral with the living.
- Piercing sanctifies blood and marks; the body is the 'woof' for such practices as scarification and piercing.
- Piercing contains the danger of morbidity or selfish isolation. Modern primitives turn the body into a boutique item.

THE ETHICS OF PIERCING

What would motivate a man in the United States today to pierce his penis? A woman her clitoris? Or either the highly sensitive tissue of the nipple? The impulse might be decorative, but the hidden location immediately suggests that something more, something deeper, is involved. The decorative value of the piercing could only be experienced in a setting (a beach or nudist gathering, or certain clubs) in which the chest or genitals could be freely displayed. It could also exist as a highly charged erotic moment at an initial undressing. But here the mind reels with further questions.

What is the ethics of lovemaking in a pierced relationship? Are the studs, rings, and bolts removed – like rings in adulterous lovemaking? Or would the removal defeat the point, the purpose, the motivation for the piercing? For pain is what the piercing evokes, although pain in no simple form. For the piercer the pain would be momentary, as fleeting as that involved in ear piercing, though perhaps more fraught with concerns of infection. Is the pain reactivated during sexual contact? Or is the sensation then transferred to the sexual partner, especially when it is the penis that has been pierced and adorned at the head with studs and bolts? Is heightened sensation for the partner the motivation – and if so, is it heightened pain or heightened pleasure? Or are pain and pleasure pretty much the same for everyone involved? I learned after writing this paragraph that the piercers in the *Modern Primitives* volume unequivocally attribute heightened sexual pleasure for the pierced person and lovers as a motivation for piercing.

Is the piercer motivated by hatred – self-hatred or hatred of the culture – as some people suggest? Or is love the motivation – self-love unto narcissism or love for minerals and metals unto love of the flesh or cosmos? Is the piercing a desire to test and transcend the flesh – as in the Native American rituals enacted by Modern Primitives that also form part of the piercing phenomenon: long hours without water in the sun, suspended by the chest tendons, as some Native Americans used to be for initiation? Is piercing related to Christian images of crucifixion or martyrdom: Saint Sebastian riddled by arrows, the Mexican Saint Julian crisscrossed by lances, Saint Theresa receiving the power of divinity, kneeling at the feet of Bernini's spear-bearing, leering angel? Are these parables of decay or of transcendence – counter-cultural, religious, or both?

What of the element of performance? Cazazza being pierced without the camera is different from Cazazza being pierced for the video. The video preserves the 'ing' in 'piercing': it repeats the moment of pain that would otherwise be lost once the wound is healed, the ring or bolt installed. The video solves what must be a common problem for the piercer: the desire to have the marks seen competes with taboos against genital display in our culture.

All these questions lead back to the ethics of piercing evoked in Stinich's often brilliant observations – with the term 'ethics' meaning for her and for me the principles (whether stated or not) that govern individual or group actions. The term 'ethics' is, admittedly, a term open to 'moral' considerations and standards of reaction and evaluation. Yet Stinich was not narrowly or prescriptively moralistic in her approach – and I would like to avoid being moralistic as well.

The first issue raised is precisely the decorative, display element of piercing, the disjunction between the private and the public. In modern American culture, piercing serves private needs. There is no imperative except within a few small subcultures – a point to which I will return – to pierce or be pierced. Indeed, the piercing marks a difference from the majority culture: one earring per ear – sure – or even one nose stud, plus earrings. Even two or three earrings per ear function within limits of what is considered normal. But five or six earrings, plus nose ring, make some statement of difference, mark some allegiance to what is now mostly a youthful or outsider experience. And when we suspect genital piercing, an important line has been crossed between decoration for private purposes and an action designed to make some kind of statement.

In its extreme, especially its public, forms, like Cazazza's video, piercing functions inevitably as ritual, by which I mean a stylised, repeatable action with a public dimension, an action designed to give order and meaning to the flux of experience. Cazazza's video and the testimony in the *Modern Primitives* volume make this point quite clear. The video repeats the word 'surgeon', but it sounds like 'searching', a word that immediately prompts the question 'searching for what?' Searching to be sure for the right spot for the piercing. But searching perhaps for the ritual itself, for the things that will get to the essential – the difference between living flesh and mineral or, perhaps, the alliance between both. These are rituals in a Dionysiac mode, not the routinised rituals of so many contemporary churches. Like certain art movements, they attract people who think of themselves as anti-bourgeois, as outsiders in contemporary culture.

Decay as art; the body as found object: one sees, immediately as Stinich says the words, the connection between piercing and surrealism and dada (including writers affiliated at times with the surrealists, such as Bataille) – though also a difference. The surrealists and dadaists mostly wrought upon canvas, or in print, or upon objects: they knew the difference between flesh and matter, and rarely asserted the body itself as art, although (as in Man Ray's photographs) the body could become art's constitutive formal elements. In related avant-garde movements, such as futurism, the reduction of bodies to inanimate matter or physical forces occurs in theory, but not in a fully realised way in the art.[7] In recent decades we have been more open to body art, more obsessed with the body. So perhaps, for performance artists, piercing was an inevitable next step – the logical conclusion of trends – under way at least since the sixties.

Naked Charlotte Moorman playing her cello in darkened spaces once sent me into spasms of uncontrollable laughter when a moose call pierced the concert hall along with the strokes of a strobe lamp. I have never been able to explain or forget that moment – very late sixties, very surreal. Something similar is involved in piercing when it becomes public display, but it is not the subconscious that is moved, nor is one affected in quite so inexplicable a way. We know that what is being touched is the alliance of pain and the erotic. We know that what is being evoked are rituals of pain that aim at the transcendent.

The term 'Modern Primitives' for advanced piercers is both unfortunate and apt. What is evoked in stringing people up by their chest tendons is Native American rituals. The actions are the same, whether performed by Native Americans, now or in the past, or by men who are not Indians. But there are, and must be, gaps between the meanings of such acts when performed in different contexts: the Plains in the early nineteenth century; a Native American reservation in the late twentieth century; a late twentieth-century white man's city apartment or wilderness campsite.

Practices of genital piercing are not as widely publicised in anthropological literature as the African rituals they evoke – specifically the village rituals of adolescent male circumcision and (for some groups) adolescent female clitorectomy. These practices have held a special fascination for Western ethnographers and have been well documented.[8]

In African villages, circumcision was usually a collective rite, at a specified point in a man's life, a form of bonding with his cohort and also a sign that he would be leaving the cohort to establish new alliances, in marriage for example. The same was true of female clitorectomy, a subject that I, as a female, find harder to contemplate since it limits sexual pleasure, as circumcision does not. Moreover, circumcision is common in our culture (though for infants, not youths), while clitorectomy is exceptional. What is being sought in contemporary piercing is a new form of community – based on holes and jewellery inserted in various parts of the body. We who are pierced are one. We are one as tribal villagers are one. We recognise each other and are recognised as different from the mass. We establish our difference from the norm – hint at it with the multiple pieces we wear in our ears and noses, confirm it with the pieces we wear in 'private' zones we have willed into public speech. Modern Primitive piercing privatises what was once communal in an attempt to regain the communal. It eroticises what was never simply erotic. And that eroticisation bespeaks one ethical dilemma raised by contemporary forms of piercing. So does the incommensurability between the public and approved quality traditional ritual (adults, after all, orchestrating the event and proud of their young passing into adulthood) and the furtive quality of current piercing (its arbitrary timing, its separation from adult and, almost certainly, parental approval).

'Compulsive transgression', Lonette Stinich said. It is the nature of the 'compulsion' that makes contemporary piercing ethically problematic. That, and the way a social form of entrance (such as African circumcision) is converted into a ritual of exit, 'transgression'. What does it say when one culture (our own) borrows so freely and loosely from others? What does it say when rituals affirming overall communal continuity become something else – the establishment of fringe communities? Does this promote decay or forestall it? Create meaning or deny it? Or is piercing all more trivial than that – is it merely what Stinich called 'alternative culture provincialism', a fad and a fashion similar to wearing Indian clothing or African jewellery?

Among people who teach the students practising piercing, one view commonly recurs, always to be dismissed a little uneasily: the extensive body piercing is like long hair and beards in the sixties; it's just the kids' way of protesting, of marking themselves as different. Often the people advancing the view then trail off into a sense that something *is* different – that the kids are filled with self-hatred, not self-love, that they shave their hair and wildly colour it and pierce their genitals in a rage of despair, over drugs, over their parents' divorces, over their lives. So the comforting argument that it's just the sixties all over again, but in different terms, does not work. It is not just kids' rebellion. Nor is it just peer pressure that makes people get pierced – though when peer pressure does operate, that is surely a factor making contemporary piercing ethically problematic. But peer pressure is not the major issue – it is a red herring.

Mineral and flesh. Life force or death force. The matter-of-fact acquaintance with death that is at stake in archaic initiation rituals. That is the real issue. Piercing gets to us because it gets to these issues, and we suspect that contemporary piercing favours the death force, something repressed and feared in our culture. It is not just kids, and, even if it were, the kids might not be all right, but they *would* be right in picking this way to get under *our* skin. [...]

PRINCE ALBERTS

In the month after the crafts conference, during which I began work on this essay, I found myself repeatedly telling people about what I had learned – a contemporary Ancient Mariner with a postmodern tale. My auditors did not disappoint. Like the wedding guest in Coleridge's poem, they were fascinated despite themselves. They had a universal interest and, sometimes, bits and pieces of information, often gleaned from troublesome teenagers or young adults. For my auditors as for me, and between them and their children, genital piercing was a taboo subject and a transgressive one – that was part of the conversations' zest.

In the *Modern Primitives* volume, published in 1989 as a collection of interviews with people heavily involved in tattooing and piercing practices, the subject plays out quite differently. Though only spotty information is available elsewhere, the volume claims a detailed history for these practices. It matter-of-factly provides names, facts, and distinctions: the Prince Albert is a small hoop on the underside of the head of a penis, named after Victoria's spouse, who reportedly had one; the horizontal penis bolt installed in Cazazza's video is an ampellang similar to those used in areas surrounding the Indian Ocean. A guiche is a ring through the perineum. Mayans, Hindus, French legionnaires, and Europeans during the Middle Ages all practised forms of genital piercing; which kinds and why they were used are discussed in a cool, historical tone in one section of the volume. This is a world with names, addresses, famous people, and idols. Each section of *Modern Primitives* provides an address for further information to which any reader is welcomed to write.

By the middle of the volume, I found myself, almost against my will, losing the distaste with which I had begun reading it. This effect comes from the reading experience itself; it does not mean that the pictures and text failed to shock me on later viewings. But after spending some time with *Modern Primitives*, I found myself actually admiring the work of tattooer Ed Hardy beyond that of the other tattooers, and believing contributors who described him as inspirational in their lives. I was entering a text where my usual tastes and judgments were temporarily suspended.

To my surprise, all the people represented in *Modern Primitives* have histories and philosophies that are fully coherent and intersect in complicated ways with philosophies in mainstream culture. Several have travelled extensively in New Guinea or Polynesia, living in villages and learning and studying much as ethnographers might. Many have done extensive research and claim ancient precedents for their practice: if these are fringe groups, they are not as nutty as they might at first appear.

Here, for example, is Wes Christensen (described as a painter scholar of Mayan history) on what piercing means to the male piercer: through genital piercing 'the Male expresses the desire to own the magically fertile menstrual flow by mimicking it, the symbol seems less important than its function of linking the opposing forces of mother/father, sky/earth in one ritual practitioner'.[9] Male piercer and performance artist Genesis P-Orridge invokes a similar mélange of Jung and contemporary desires for androgyny: 'my nipples were a dead zone before they got pierced. Then they became a whole new discovery. It was nice – like being female as well' (p. 176).

The idea of connection to or wilful separation from universal images or the images of a culture comes up frequently in these interviews. Tattooer Ed Hardy's interest in tattooing began at age twelve, when he was attracted to the way that tattooers 'were like the Keepers of Images. They'd have displayed the whole emotional gamut: love: hate and sex and death – all on codified designs that were bright and bold' (p. 52). He sees tattooing as a tribute to the universal and the individual, as 'an affirmation: that this body is yours to have and enjoy' (p. 53). Satanic cultist Anton Lavey agrees that control over the body is the point of such practices, though his accent is less upbeat than Hardy's, stressing separation, not connection, as the point of tattooing: 'if a person feels alienated ... [and] they didn't happen to be born looking freaky or strange, then activities like getting a tattoo [or piercing] are a way of stigmatising one's self' (p. 92).

Jewellery-maker Raelyn Gallina sees piercing as a way to move from the alienation stressed by Lavey to the affirmation stressed by Hardy: 'Piercing started at a time in my life when I was experiencing a lot of death, and grief, and transformation. For a lot of people it's a rite of transformation, when they go from one state to the next' (p. 101).[10] Gallina emphasises that the emotions surrounding the experience must be devoid of violence and filled with trust and support; when that happens, she says, 'A lot of times being cut is a very strengthening and powerful experience' (p. 101). Gallina's statement and others like it were important for me. If there had been no women involved in this phenomenon, or if there had been a sense of violence, especially violence towards women, I would have found it impossible to read the *Modern Primitives* volume at all sympathetically. [...]

ART AND LIFE

One could say that piercing and its performative aspect – so vividly expressed in the Cazazza video – test the limits of art and representation, especially what we have come to recognise as body and performance art, by pressing the boundaries of what can and cannot be displayed in museums or other cultural institutions.[11] Most saliently, piercing questions the difference between process and product, action and finished work, permanence, transience, and absence. It reveals how the finished work, the thing reproduced in textbooks and hung in museums – represents an action or process that has occurred in the past and remains a trace or residual element in the finished piece. The artistic process is 'the real thing'; but it can only achieve permanence when embodied in a formal object. The permanent art object memorialises the primary process of creation and thus inevitably announces its own secondariness. In this typically postmodern aesthetic, the objects we fetishise as art always represent but do not coincide with creative impulse, person, or act.[12]

In this sense, it is tempting to regard piercing as one of a series of postmodern practices that challenge traditional notions of creator and created object, art and thing, museum and memorial. Piercing is art *in* the body, remaining the same even as the body that surrounds it changes and ages. It has a biographical, life-history dimension, like a series of self-portraits from youth to middle age, but it is not separable from the artist's body in the way that Rembrandt's or Van Gogh's self-portraits were. The body becomes not just the subject for the art but its medium and condition; the 'art' or 'mark' travels with the body and is part of it. It dies when the artist dies; it cannot survive the artist except in photographs or narrative accounts. Money may change hands when a piercing or tattooing takes place, but no secondary markets for resale and purchase exist. Only a video or photograph of the piercing or tattooing can have a secondary market or be permanently 'hung' in a museum. Piercing and tattooing resist becoming part of the institutionalised world of high culture. They expose the processing of art as commodity that usually obtains in our culture.

Piercing presses and erodes the boundary between body and thing – an observation that returns us to the most disturbing of Stinich's remarks about the practice. Piercing explores the crossing between mineral and flesh, the contemplation of both on the same plane of being, with equal valuation. This crossing of mineral and flesh has long cultural histories that have always been fraught with double potentialities, some spirit- or life-affirming, some not: Buddhist enlightenment and Freudian death wish.

I find it tempting to assimilate piercing to at least some of these intellectual contexts about the relationship of art and life – tempting, but perhaps not quite right. For that intellectualisation evades certain distinctions and questions that I feel to be important – for example, the distinction between 'committed' piercers and faddists or hangers-on. Or the question of what it is legitimate to borrow from other cultures and transform through re-enactment. I also sense a 'can you top this?' mentality behind many of these practices that disturbs me and raises further questions. Would, for example, a video of a person's voluntary sterilisation be susceptible to analysis as performance art? How about a video of a person's embalming? These prospects return to the morbidity that I sense in these practices and that provoked initial repulsion.

A phenomenon like piercing may not belong in intellectual contexts: for other reasons as well. At the moment when piercing enters museums or classrooms, or even an essay like this one, something of its essential motivation is betrayed. We may not want this subject in the official portrait of our culture. But it may reject us more fully than we reject it. And so while I have posed the question of piercings as a question about representation – and represented it, deliberately, in a series of expanding circles – I do not see it as 'simply' or 'merely' about representation in the abstract. I feel it to be – and have wanted you to feel it as – a gut issue.

Summaries and Notes

1. TIFFANY ATKINSON, INTRODUCTION

1. The term comes from the French poststructuralist psychoanalyst Jacques Lacan. It denotes that which exists prior to the subject's entry into the symbolic (signifying) order. Language can be seen as that which has always already replaced the real: the real is thus by this very condition inaccessible to language and the speaking subject.
2. Gunther von Hagens, from *Fascination Beneath the Surface*, a guide to the exhibition.
3. See, for example, Susan Sontag's *Illness as Metaphor* (London, 1979), where, amongst other arguments, she attacks the notion of a 'cancer phenotype', whereby the cancer victim is typically characterised as someone fatally unresponsive to 'the irrational indulgence of desire' which informs advanced capitalist society: 'Cancer is described in images that sum up the negative behaviour of twentieth-century *homo economicus*: abnormal growth; repression of energy, that is, refusal to consume or spend' (p. 63).
4. Jonathan Sawday, *The Body Emblazoned: Dissection and the human body in Renaissance culture* (London and New York, 1995), p. 11. See also David le Breton, 'Dualism and Renaissance: Sources for a Modern Representation of the Body', *Diogenes* (1998), 47–69.
5. Michel Foucault, *Power/Knowledge: Selected Interviews and Other Writings 1972–1977*. Ed. Colin Gordon. Trans. Colin Gordon, Leo Marshall, John Mepham and Kate Soper (Brighton, 1980), p. 58.
6. Judith Butler, *Bodies That Matter: On the Discursive Limits of 'Sex'* (London and New York, 1993), p. 30.
7. Jacques Derrida, *Donner le Temps*, cited in Butler, *Bodies That Matter*, p. 1.
8. Caroline Bynum, 'Why All the Fuss about the Body? A Medievalist's Perspective', *Critical Inquiry*, (Autumn 1995), 1–33, p. 15.
9. Ibid., p. 21.
10. Ibid., p. 16.
11. See, for example, Caroline Bynum, *Jesus as Mother: Studies in the Spirituality of the High Middle Ages* (Berkeley, CA, 1982) and Sarah Beckwith, *Christ's Body: Identity, Culture, and Society in Late Medieval Writings* (London, 1993).
12. le Breton, 'Dualism and Renaissance', p. 49.
13. Sawday, *The Body Emblazoned*, p. 11.
14. Ibid.
15. Sawday, *The Body Emblazoned*, p. 86.
16. The neo-primitive aesthetic of modernist art, particularly that of Picasso and the Cubists, challenged traditional concepts of volume, perspective and proportion most strikingly in the redrawing of the human figure. As evidenced by Picasso's

178

celebrated *Les Demoiselles D'Avignon* (1907) the perceived bourgeois arrogance of perspectival realism is unsettled when the body is drawn from multiple perspectives, and the flatness of the picture plane foregrounded.

17. See pp. 28–9 this volume.
18. Francis Barker, *The Tremulous Private Body: Essays on Subjection* (Ann Arbor, MI, 1995), p. vi.
19. See Michel Foucault, *Discipline and Punish: The Birth of the Prison*. Trans. Alan Sheridan (Harmondsworth, 1977), *Madness and Civilization: A History of Insanity in the Age of Reason*. Trans. Richard Howard (London, 1965) and *The Birth of the Clinic: An Archaeology of Medical Perception*. Trans. A. M. Sheridan (London, 1973).
20. Foucault, *Discipline and Punish*, p. 187.
21. See his 1926 essay, 'The Question of Lay Analysis'.
22. Lieve Spaas, 'Surrealism and Anthropology: in search of the primitive', *Paragraph*, 18: 2 (1995), 164.
23. The Dianne Pretty case is a good example of the debate around euthanasia: see Zosia Kmietowicz, 'Woman fights for right to die with dignity', *British Medical Journal* (2001), 323: 416. With regard to assisted conception and the individual's rights over their body-parts and fluids, see Robert G. Lee and Derek Morgan, *Human Fertilization and Embryology: Regulating the Reproductive Revolution* (London, 2001), Justine Burley, *The Genetic Revolution and Human Rights* (Oxford, 1999), Sally Sheldon and Michael Thomas (eds), *Feminist Perspectives on Health Care Law* (London, 1998), and A. Bainham, S. D. Sclater and M. Richards (eds), *Body Lore and Laws* (Oxford, 2002).

DEPTHS

2. JONATHAN SAWDAY, 'THE RENAISSANCE BODY: FROM COLONISATION TO INVENTION'

(From *The Body Emblazoned: Dissection and the Human Body in Renaissance Culture* [London, 1995], pp. 16–32, abridged.)

Summary

The broad project of Jonathan Sawday's compelling book *The Body Emblazoned* is the study of the 'culture of dissection' in the English Renaissance, and the ways in which it informed intellectual discourse in Europe for nearly two hundred years. In the edited chapter reprinted here, Sawday details how the body-interior, newly visible in the early Renaissance anatomy theatre, posed a challenge to structures of understanding and representation not merely in the scientific community, but in culture at large: as he states in the introductory chapter, 'as the physical body is fragmented, so the body of understanding is held to be shaped and formed'. In this chapter Sawday explores how anatomy feeds into the metaphorical registers of John Donne and his contemporaries, outlining two distinctive discursive strands – those of colonisation and invention – which sought to make sense of the new body, liberated form theology by the scientific gaze.

Notes

1. Plato, *Phaedo* 80B–81C, in Plato, *Euthyphro, The Apology, Crito, Phaedo*. Trans. Hugh Tredennick (Harmondsworth, 1954), pp. 133–4.

2. Augustine, *De Civitate Dei*. Trans. Henry Bettenson (Harmondsworth, 1972), II, XIII, 16 (525). See also Augustine, Sermon 361 in *Augustine on Immortality*. Trans. J. Mourant (Villanova PA, 1969), p. 52; Augustine, *The Care to be Taken for the Dead* ('De cura pro mortuis gerenda') in Roy J. Defferati (ed.), *The Fathers of the Church*, vol. 15 (New York, 1955); Aquinas, *Summa Theologia*, Suppt. to Pt. III.Q.80.Art.1,Obj.2. For discussion of medieval debates on corporeality see Elizabeth A. R. Brown, 'Death and the Human Body in the Later Middle Ages: The Legislation of Boniface VIII on the Division of the Corpse', *Viator*, 12 (1981), 221–70; R. C. Finucane, 'Sacred Corpse, Profane Carrion: Social Ideas and Death Rituals in the Later Middle Ages' in Joachim Whalley (ed.), *Mirrors of Mortality: Studies in the Social History of Death* (New York, 1981), pp. 40–60.

3. St Athanasius, the fourth-century Patriarch of Alexandria, argued in his *De incarnatione* that, although the body was 'the medium of a person's concrete and physical presence', to think of the soul as 'entrapped' in some way within the body is to argue that Christ, considered as *Logos*, suffered such an entrapment. The idea that the body *contains* a soul, Athanasius reasoned, serves only to promote a dualism which places body and soul in a mutually antagonistic relationship to one another. An alternative conception is to try and see body and soul as complementary to one another – to understand the role each plays as components of a larger whole. 'True humanity', Athanasius claimed, 'is both corporeal and incorporeal.' See Alvyn Pettersen, *Athanasius and the Human Body* (Bristol, 1990), pp. 6–8, 21.

4. Thus Calvin: 'But anyone who knows how to distinguish between body and soul, between the present transitory life and the eternal life to come, will not find it difficult to understand that the spiritual kingdom of Christ and civil government are things far removed from one another.' Jean Calvin, *Institutio Christianae Religionis* (1536) IV.20 in Harro Höpfl (ed.), *Luther and Calvin on Secular Authority* (Cambridge, 1991), p. 48.

5. [Andreas Vesalius (1514–64): Belgian physician, anatomist and author of *De Humani Corporis Fabrica* (1543), a seven-volume treatise on the structure of the human body, illustrated with engravings based on his own drawings.]

6. John Donne, *Poetical Works*, ed. Sir Herbert Grierson (London, 1933). Unless otherwise specified, all references to Donne's poetry are to this edition.

7. [William Harvey (1578–1657): physician to Charles I, whose theories on the circulation of blood were published to great acclaim in his 1628 treatise, *Exercitatio Anatomica de Motu Cordis et Sanguinis in Animalibus (On the Motion of the Heart and Blood in Animals)*.]

8. George R. Potter and Evelyn M. Simpson (eds), *The Sermons of John Donne* (Berkeley and Los Angeles, 1953–62), III, 235. All references to Donne's sermons are to this edition.

9. It was passages such as these which prompted some commentators to conclude that Donne must have known of Harvey's work since the proof of circulation in *De Motu Cordis* rested in part on measurement of the rate of blood flow in relation to the cubic capacity of the heart. That possibility looks unlikely when it is recalled that, in his anatomical lectures of 1616, Harvey did not develop his ideas on circulation. *De Mortu Cordis* was not, of course, published until 1628 – long after the sermon under discussion.

10. François Rabelais, *Gargantua*. Trans. Sir Thomas Urquhart (1653), ed. D. B. Wyndham Lewis (London, 1949), I, 17.

11. See Mikhail Bakhtin, *Rabelais and his World*. Trans. Hélène Iswolsky (Cambridge, MA, 1968), particularly chs 5 and 6.

12. Peter Stallybrass and Allon White, *The Politics and Poetics of Transgression* (London, 1986), pp. 21, 23.
13. For a discussion of the literary use such 'touchstones' of interiority could be put to, see the reading of the significance of the handkerchief in *Othello* in Peter Stallybrass, 'Patriarchal Territories: The Body Enclosed' in Margaret Ferguson, Maureen Quilligan and Nancy J. Vickers (eds), *Rewriting the Renaissance: The Discourses of Sexual Difference in Early Modern Europe* (Chicago, 1986), pp. 137–9.
14. Burton's discussion of the soul in the *Anatomy* is a comprehensive digest of traditional and early seventeenth-century thought on a subject which he describes as 'pleasant but ... doubtful'. See Burton, *The Anatomy of Melancholy*, ed. Thomas C. Faulkner, Nicholas K. Kiessling, Rhonda L. Blair with a commentary by J. B. Bamborough and Martin Dodsworth (Oxford, 1992), 1.1.2.5–9. For a more recent study of the subject see Emma Ursula Harriet Seymour, 'Dangerous Conceits: Mind, Body and Metaphor 1590–1640' (University of Cambridge, PhD diss. 1993).
15. See Andrew Wear, 'Puritan Perceptions of Illness in Seventeenth-Century England' in Roy Porter (ed.), *Lay Perceptions of Medicine in Pre-Industrial Society* (Cambridge, 1985), pp. 56–7.
16. Andrew Marvell, *The Poems and Letters*, ed. H. M. Margoliouth (3rd edition, Oxford, 1971), I.22. All references to Marvell's poems are to this edition. For a discussion of the convention of body-soul debates in the seventeenth century see Rosalie Osmond, 'Body and Soul Dialogues in the Seventeenth Century', *English Literary Renaissance*, 4 (1974), 364–403.
17. [Gr. *Logos*, 'word': within Christian discourse, the Word of God incarnate.]
18. [Pre-Cartesian: prior to prevalence of the mind/body dualism attributed to philosopher Réné Descartes (1596–1650): see Chapter 3 of this volume.]
19. Michel Foucault, *The Order of Things* (1966, trans. London, 1970), p. 55. The literature exploring ideas of correspondence in the Renaissance, ideas which are rooted as much in St Paul as in the writings of pre-Socratic philosophers, is vast. A selection would include: C. P. Conger, *Theories of Microcosm and Macrocosm in the History of Philosophy* (New York, 1922); Arthur A. Lovejoy, *The Great Chain of Being* (Cambridge, MA, 1936); Rudolph Allers, 'Microcosmos from Anaximandros to Paracelsus', *Traditio*, 2 (1944), 319–407; J. B. Bamborough, *The Little World of Man* (London, 1952); Joseph Mazzeo, 'Metaphysical Poetics and the Poetry of Correspondence', *Journal of the History of Ideas*, 14 (1953), 221–34; C. A. Patrides, 'The Microcosm of Man: Some References to a Commonplace', *Notes and Queries* (1960), 54–6; Leonard Barkan, *Nature's Work of Art: The Human Body as Image of the World* (New Haven, CT, 1975); Don Parry Norford, 'Microcosm and Macrocosm in Seventeenth-Century Literature', *Journal of the History of Ideas*, 38 (1977), 408–29.
20. On the creation of the hero-figure in scientific investigation, see John M. Steadman, 'Beyond Hercules: Bacon and the Scientist as Hero', *Studies in the Literary Imagination*, 4 (1971), 3–47.
21. Browne, *Selected Writings*, ed. Sir Geoffrey Keynes (London, 1968) p. 44.
22. Michel de Montaigne, *Essays*. Trans. J. M. Cohen (Harmondsworth, 1958), p. 117.
23. Thus, in 1663, Henry Power was able to write: 'The process of art is indefinite,and who can set a *non-ultra* to her endeavours'. See Henry Power, *Experimental Philosophy in Three Books* (London, 1663), sig. C3.
24. John Donne, *Selected Prose*, ed. Neil Rhodes (Harmondsworth, 1987), pp. 198–9.

25. [Cogito: the individual rational mind, from Descartes's famous maxim '*cogito, ergo sum*' ('I think, therefore I am').]
26. [Galen (130–c.200): Greek physician and surgeon whose physiological system, inherited virtually unchanged by Vesalius and his counterparts, divided the body into 'similar' and 'dissimilar' parts, and 'noble' and 'inferior' organs.]
27. Christopher Columbus, 'Letter on his First Voyage' (February 1493) in J. M. Cohen (ed.), *The Four Voyages of Christopher Columbus* (Harmondsworth, 1969), p. 122.
28. Margarita Zamora has written of Columbian narratives of discovery, that the very term 'Indies' came to function as 'a feminised and ultimately eroticised sign ... inscribed into Western culture figurally, as a feminine value, intended for consumption in a cultural economy where femininity is synonymous with exploitability'. See Margarita Zamora, 'Abreast of Columbus: Gender and Discovery', *Cultural Critique*, 17 (1990–1), 127–49 (149).
29. See Thomas Healy, *New Latitudes: Theory and English Renaissance Literature* (London, 1992), pp. 145–6.
30. Joseph Glanvill, *The Vanity of Dogmatizing* (London: 1661), 42.
31. Abraham Cowley, *The Advancement of Experimental Philosophy* (London, 1661), sig. A5.
32. Walter Charleton, *Enquiries into Human Nature in VI Anatomic Praelectiones* (London, 1680), sig. E.
33. René Descartes, *Discourse on the Method of Properly Conducting One's Reason and of Seeking the Truth in the Sciences* (1637). Trans. F. E. Sutcliffe (Harmondsworth, 1968), p. 73.
34. For a critical discussion of the biological implications of mechanism, see Owesi Temkin, *The Double Face of Janus and Other Essays in the History of Medicine* (London and Baltimore, 1977). Temkin makes the point that the body and the machine are strictly incomparable since the body does not conform to the 1st Law of Thermodynamics: that a *perpetuum mobile* cannot be constructed (p. 279). Seventeenth-century mechanism has been scrutinised in E. J. Dijksterhuis, *The Mechanization of the World Picture*. Trans. C. Dikshoorn (Oxford, 1961). On the scientific implications of the 'mechanical philosophy' see Michael Hunter, *Science and Society in Restoration England* (Cambridge, 1981), pp. 173–4.
35. Though Harvey did not, as was once thought, develop his mechanical analogy as early as 1616, it has certainly been argued that it was the example of hydraulic engineers which enabled him to address the dynamics of the circulatory system. For a discussion of this topic see Charles Webster, 'William Harvey and the Crisis of Medicine in Jacobean England' in Webster (ed.), *William Harvey and his Age: The Professional and Social Context for the Discovery of Circulation*, The Henry E. Sigerist Supplements to *The Bulletin of the History of Medicine*, ns 2 (Baltimore and London, 1979), 21–2.
36. Harvey, *The Movement of the Heart and Blood*, p. 3.
37. William Harvey, *De Motu Cordis* (London, 1653), sig. 2.
38. For a discussion of the political implications of the changes in Harvey's text between 1628 and 1653 see the exchange which took place between Christopher Hill and Gweneth Whitteridge in *Past and Present* (April 1964 to July 1965). The exchange is reprinted in Charles Webster (ed.), *The Intellectual Revolution of the Seventeenth Century* (London, 1974), pp. 160–96. Recently, the debate between Hill and Whitteridge has been revisited in I. Bernard Cohen, 'Harrington and Harvey: A Theory of the State Based on the New Physiology', *Journal of the History of Ideas*, 55 (1994), 187–210.
39. C. H. Wilkinson (ed.), *The Poems of Richard Lovelace* (Oxford, 1930), p. 155.

40. Francis Bacon, *Works*, ed. J. Spedding, R. L. Ellis, and D. D. Heath, 7 vols (London, 1858–61), I.202–3.
41. 'Thou hast ordered all things in measure, and number, and weight' (*Wisdom*, 11.21). The English anatomist Walter Charleton was to echo the scriptural text when he wrote that the anatomist, when opening the body, should 'chiefly consider number, weight, and measure, i.e. the MECHANISM'. See Walter Charleton, *Three Anatomic Lectures* (London, 1683), 3.
42. Thomas Willis, 'Of Musculary Motion' in *The Remaining Medical Works*. Trans. Samuel Pordage (London, 1681), p. 35.
43. Henry Power, *Experimental Philosophy in Three Books* (London, 1664), sigs. C2r-v.
44. On Harvey's use of measurement see F. G. Kilgour, 'Harvey's use of Quantitative Method', *Yale Journal of Biology and Medicine*, 26 (1954), 410–21.

3. RENÉ DESCARTES, 'SECOND MEDITATION: OF THE NATURE OF THE HUMAN MIND; AND THAT IT IS EASIER TO KNOW THAN THE BODY' (1644)

(From *Discourse on Method, and The Meditations*. Trans. F. E. Sutcliffe [Harmondsworth, 1968], pp. 102–12.)

Summary

The Meditations of René Descartes, who is often considered the 'father' of modern philosophy, marked a decisive break with the Aristotelian and Scholastic philosophical traditions of the Medieval period, and sought instead to integrate philosophy within the new sciences. The foundation of his methodology, detailed throughout the Discourse on Method and the Meditations, is a radical and hyperbolic scepticism, whereby all that can be doubted must be rejected in pursuit of an indubitable truth. Descartes opens his second Meditation, reprinted here, by describing the extent of this doubt, especially with regard to the dubious 'knowledge' acquired through the bodily senses. By ruthless process of elimination, Descartes can ultimately state only that he cannot doubt that he doubts, and that this thereby proves a mental existence, thinking substance or *cogito* which functions independently of physical substance, and which, indeed, precedes and makes possible all knowledge of the material world. The first-person, almost *autobiographical* narrative style of Descartes's writing is not incidental to his intellectual project, replicating textually the newly appointed centrality of individual consciousness in ontological and epistemelogical enquiry.

Notes

1. [In the *First Meditation: About the Things We May Doubt*, Descartes establishes the foundations of his rationalist philosophy, which is an exaggerated and systematic doubt. He resolves to reject all which can be doubted, including the evidence of his senses; yet he cannot doubt that he himself, even as he doubts, exists. The thinking mind is therefore distinct from the body, and indeed, from all that it comprehends in the external world.]
2. [Archimedes (287–212 BC): Greek inventor and engineer who defined the principle of the lever, allegedly announcing 'give me a fulcrum and a firm point, and I alone can move the earth.' The analogy is that Descartes's one indubitable truth – the principle that '*I am, I exist*' – provides the 'firm point' upon which a true philosophical system can turn.]
3. [*A fortiori*: with stronger reason, all the more.]

4.   SIGMUND FREUD, 'A CASE OF HYSTERIA: FRÄULEIN ELISABETH VON R.' (1895)

(From the Pelican Freud Library Volume 3, *Studies on Hysteria*. Trans. James and Alix Strachey [Harmondsworth, 1980], pp. 202–35, abridged.)

Summary

Hysteria owns a long and complex medical pedigree. From Hippocrates through to French neurologist Jean-Martin Charcot (one of Sigmund Freud's own teachers), it designated a gender-specific pathology whereby nervous disorders were invariably, often ingeniously, linked to the 'unruly' behaviour of the female reproductive organs, and 'treated' accordingly. Following Charcot's experimentation with hypnosis, Freud and Breuer's *Studies on Hysteria* marked a decisive shift in emphasis. In maintaining that hysteria was a psychosomatic (cultural) disorder rather than a physiological (natural) one, their work technically uncoupled hysteria from biological determinism; inscribing its physical symptoms instead with the deep psychological significance of repressed Oedipal conflict, a condition to which both men and women might be susceptible. The externalising, through speech, of this inner psychic distress, as prompted and interpreted by the analyst (described by one of Breuer's own patients, 'Anna O.' as the 'talking cure') became the core methodology of the new psychoanalytic project. This often richly metaphorical case-study illustrates the analytic process of uncovering, and to a large extent *authorising* the latent meaning of the hysteric's inarticulate 'body language'. The implicit coding of probing analytic discourse as masculine, knowing and civilised, and the symptomatic, penetrable body as feminine, unknowing or primitive, is not, of course, without its own problematic sexual and cultural politics.

Notes

1. [A phrase attributed by Freud to Jean Martin Charcot (1825–1893), a French physician who pioneered work on female hysterical disorders at his Paris clinic, La Salpêtrière.]
2. [Hyperalgesia: heightened sensitivity to pain.]
3. A hypochondriac or a person affected with anxiety neurosis.
4. [Affect: instinctual or emotional energy, either positive or negative.]
5. [This is also a term regularly used by Charcot.]
6. 'Her mask reveals a hidden sense.' Adapted from Goethe's *Faust*, Part I (Scene 16.) – Nevertheless, it will be seen later that I was mistaken in this.
7. [The 'young man' was the orphaned son of friends, who professed admiration both for Fraulein R.'s father and the women of the family. Encouraged by her acquaintances' hints, she had come to anticipate a marriage proposal from him as soon as he was better able to support himself financially.]

5.   MICHEL FOUCAULT, 'THE INCITEMENT TO DISCOURSE' (1976)

(From *The History of Sexuality*, Volume One. Trans. Robert Hurley [Harmondsworth, 1978], pp. 17–35, abridged.)

Summary

Broadly speaking, Michel Foucault's characteristically wide-ranging genealogies examine how the human subject constructs itself (and its others) sociohistorically and discursively, often emphasising the complex and mutually sustaining relationships which pertain between knowledge and power. The three volumes of *The History of Sexuality* explore how sex and sexual behaviours are not natural and given, but produced in, and to some extent productive of, the discursive and ethical structures of a historical moment. In the extract reprinted here from Volume One, Foucault counterintuitively maintains that European culture between the sixteenth and nineteenth centuries did not so much repress sexuality (as the commonplace would have it) as encourage and manage its expression by myriad discursive and disciplinary means. Central to these is the notion of confession, whose imperative is the ongoing and minute translation of fleshly desire into discourse. The description of sexual activities in the confessional effectively put sex into the public domain, where agencies of power could better classify and manage them, notably in the embryonic 'social sciences', pedagogy and psychiatry.

Notes

1. [Discourse in the Foucauldian sense implies more than a specialist mode of utterance. Foucault is concerned with how language actively *produces* knowledges and identities in different social contexts, practices and institutions. Within any discursive field (e.g., medicine, or the family), competing discourses describe and produce relations of power between truth and untruth, centre and margin, normative and deviant, etc. Knowledge and power own an intimate connection. While individuals are defined by these discourses, discursive constructions are historically specific and, as a consequence, open to contestation.]
2. [Council of Trent: the 19th ecumenical council of the Roman Catholic church, held at Trent in northern Italy between 1545 and 1563. Its re-affirmation and strengthening of Catholic dogma marked a major turning point in the efforts of the Catholic church to respond to the challenge of the Protestant Reformation, and it thus formed a key part of the Counter-Reformation.]
3. Paolo Segneri, *L'Instruction du pénitent* (French trans. 1695), p. 301.
4. Alfonso de' Liguori, *Pratique des confesseurs* (French trans. 1854), p. 140.
5. Segneri, *L'Instruction du pénitent*, pp. 301–2.
6. The reformed pastoral also laid down rules, albeit in a more discreet way, for putting sex into discourse. This notion [is] developed in the next volume, *The Body and the Flesh*.
7. Alfonso de' Liguori, *Précepts sur le sexième commandement* (French trans. 1835), p. 5.
8. Donatien-Alphonse de Sade, *The 120 Days of Sodom*. Trans. Austryn Wainhouse and Richard Seaver (New York, 1966), p. 271.
9. Anonymous, *My Secret Life* (New York, 1966).
10. Condorcet, cited by Jean-Louis Flandrin, *Familles: parenté, maison, sexualité dans l'ancienne société* (Paris, 1976).
11. Auguste Tardieu, *Étude médico-légale sur les attentats aux moeurs* (1857), p. 114.
12. Johann von Justi, *Éléments Généraux de police* (French trans. 1769), p. 20.
13. The French Revolution of 1789–1815.
14. [Sigmund Freud's *Three Essays on the Theory of Sexuality* (1905), which trace the development of the human sexual instinct from infancy to maturity. 'Little Hans' was Freud's first case-study in infantile sexuality, published in 1909 as 'Analysis of a Phobia in a Five-Year-Old Boy'.]

15. *Réglement de police pour les lycées* (1809), art. 67: 'There shall always be, during class and study hours, an instructor watching the exterior, so as to prevent students who have gone out to relieve themselves from stopping and congregating.':

    art. 68: 'After the evening prayer, the students will be conducted back to the dormitory, where the schoolmasters will put them back to bed at once.'
    art. 69: 'The masters will not retire except after having made certain that every student is in bed.'
    art. 70: 'The beds shall be separated by partitions two meters in height. The dormitories shall be illuminated during the night.'

16. H. Bonnet and J. Bulard, *Rapport médico-légal sur l'état mental de Ch.-J. Jouy*, January 4, 1968.

17. Jouy sound like the past participle of *jouir*, the French verb meaning to enjoy, to delight in (something), but also to have an orgasm, to come. (Translator's note.)

18. Erethism: unusual excitement or physical stimulation.

DIFFERENCE

6. CATHERINE CLÉMENT, 'SEDUCTION AND GUILT' (1975)

(From *The Newly Born Woman*, trans. Betsy Wing [Minneapolis, 1986], pp. 41–57 abridged.)

Summary

The Newly Born Woman (*La jeune née*), co-authored by Catherine Clément and Hélène Cixous, is considered a pivotal text in the French feminist theoretical movement, especially insofar as it considers the possibilities of *écriture féminine* (or 'feminine writing'), the rhetorical matrix within which woman might adequately 'write herself', her sexuality and her experience beyond phallogocentric logic. The latter, Cixous and Clément maintain, has systematically excluded women from its cultural narratives, be these classical myths or the more contemporary legends of psychoanalysis. *The Newly Born Woman* is structured as a dialogue between the authors over the signifying agency of the excluded feminine.

The hysterogenic body, with its ancient historical pedigree, is a key figure in this deliberation: questions as to whether the hysteric's cryptic body language renders her a victim or a heroine for feminist theory, or whether her 'sickness' signifies complicity with, or dissent from, patriarchal society oscillate throughout the book. Broadly speaking, the two theorists approach different conclusions on this point; Cixous tending to emphasise the radical potential of non-linear hysterical language, while Clément, in the extract reprinted here, reminds the reader of the hysteric's troubling association with the stigmatic, the witch and the heretic. Moreover, Clément unpicks the Freudian narrative whereby the infant's bonding with the mother's body (so crucial a premise of *écriture féminine*) is inscribed with seduction, guilt and repression; the cornerstones of the Oedipally-structured bourgeois family, and ultimately (via analysis), the means of bringing hysterical discourse back under the rubric of the patriarchal family narrative.

Notes

1. [Fräulein Elisabeth Von R.: see Chapter 4 of this volume.]
2. [Melanie Klein (1882–1960): a pioneer of child analysis and research into depressive and schizoid states. Kleinian theory is less an instinct theory, like Freud's, than an object theory. Ego-development is regarded more as a process of continual introjection and projection of objects (especially regarding the infant's ambivalence toward the 'mother' and the 'breast'), rather than a progress of the self through various stages.]

7.   SANDER L. GILMAN, ' "WHO KILLS WHORES?" "I DO" ', SAYS JACK: RACE AND GENDER IN VICTORIAN LONDON

(From *Death and Representation*, ed. Sarah Webster Goodwin and Elizabeth Bronfen [Baltimore and London, 1993], pp. 263–84, abridged.)

Summary

In examining Victorian speculations about the Jack the Ripper murders in the East End of London, Sander L. Gilman reveals how the body of the murdered prostitute, together with the unsolved enigma of Jack's identity, together enacted a powerful confluence of bourgeois anxieties about sexuality, race, revolutionary politics and class. In these anxious discourses, the contaminating sexuality of the prostitute, and the perversity of the prostitute's murderer (or seducer), activate a closed symbolic circuit held in place both by viral and economic metaphors: as Gilman points out, the Jew and the prostitute are linked in the Victorian imagination by their association with sexual disease, and their 'sexualised' relation to capital – a moral pathology supposedly inscribed on the skins and genitals of both. As symbolic counterparts, the bodies of the Jew and the prostitute defined a complex otherness against which the social body defended its own sexual, political and economic health: a cultural narrative which found an opportune crystallisation in the (ongoing) mystery of the Whitechapel murders.

Notes

1. Michael Parry (ed.), *Jack the Knife: Tales of Jack the Ripper* (London, 1975), p. 12.
2. Dorothy Nelkin and Sander L. Gilman, 'Placing the Blame for Devastating Disease', *Social Research*, 55 (1988), 361–78.
3. Lynda Nead, 'Seduction, Prostitution, Suicide: *On the Brink* by Alfred Elmore', *Art History*, 5 (1982), 309–22; Judith R. Walkowitz, *Prostitution and Victorian Society: Women, Class and the State* (Cambridge, 1980).
4. W. R. Greg, 'Prostitution', *Westminster Review*, 53 (1850), 456.
5. *The Language of Flowers* (London, 1849), pp. 19, 22.
6. Nead, 'Seduction, Prostitution, Suicide', p. 316.
7. William M. Sanger, *The History of Prostitution: Its Extent, Causes and Effects Throughout the World* (New York, 1927), p. 322.
8. William Tait, *Magdalenism: An Inquiry into the Extent, Causes and Consequences of Prostitution in Edinburgh* (Edinburgh, 1840), p. 96.

9. William Tait, *Magdalenism: An Inquiry into the Extent, Causes and Consequences of Prostitution in Edinburgh* (Edinburgh, 1840), p. 96.
10. Thomas Hood, *The Complete Poetical Works of Thomas Hood*, 4 vols (New York, 1869), 1: 27.
11. The image of the dead woman is a basic trope within the art and literature of the nineteenth century; see Elisabeth Bronfen, *Over Her Dead Body: Death, Femininity and the Aesthetic* (New York, 1992). On the general background of the fascination with and representation of death in the West see Philippe Ariès, *The Hour of Our Death*. Trans. Helen Weaver (New York, 1981), as well as Mario Parz, *The Romantic Agony*. Trans. Angus Davidson (Cleveland, 1956), John McManners, *Death and the Enlightenment: Changing Attitudes to Death among Christians and Unbelievers in Eighteenth-Century France* (Oxford, 1981) and Bram Dijkstra, *Idols of Perversity: Fantasies of Feminine Evil in Fin-d-Siècle Culture* (New York, 1986).
12. Sigmund Freud, 'Notes on the Medusa's Head' 1940, *The Standard Edition of the Complete Psychological Works (SE)*. Trans. James Strachey, 24 vols (London, 1986), 18: 273–4.
13. Gottfried Benn, *Sämtliche Werke* (Stuttgart, 1986), 1: 22. My translation (S.L.G.).
14. Cited in Parry, *Jack the Knife*, p. 14.
15. Christopher Frayling, 'The House that Jack Built: Some Stereotypes of the Rapist in the History of Popular Culture', *Rape*, ed. Sylvana Tomaselli and Roy Porter (Oxford, 1986), p. 183.
16. Ibid., p. 187.
17. Robert Anderson, 'The Lighter Side of My Official Life', *Blackwood's Magazine*, 187 (1910), 356-67.
18. Alexander Kelley and Colin Wilson, *Jack the Ripper: A Bibliography and Review of the Literature* (London, 1973), p. 14.
19. Frank Wedekind, *Five Tragedies of Sex*. Trans. Frances Fawcett and Stephen Spender (New York, n.d.), p. 298.
20. Cesare Lambroso and Guglielmo Ferrero, *La donna deliquente: La prostituta a la donna normale* (Turin, 1893).
21. Alexander Lacassagne, *L'Homme criminal comparé à l'homme primitif* (Lyons, 1882); *Vacher l'eventreur et les cromes sadiques* (Lyons, 1889).
22. Peter Pulzer, *The Rise of Political Anti-Semitism in Germany and Austria* (London, 1988), p. 6.
23. Tom Brown, *Amusements Serious and Comical and Other Works*, ed. Arthur L. Hayward (London, 1927), p. 200.
24. Ibid.
25. Ibid., p. 199.
26. Gray Joliffe and Peter Mayle, *Man's Best Friend* (London, 1984).
27. Joseph Banister, *England under the Jews* (London, 1901), p. 61.
28. Adolph Hitler, *Mein Kampf*. Trans. Ralph Manheim (Boston, 1943), p. 247.
29. Ibid., p. 57
30. Marcel Proust, *Remembrance of Things Past*. Trans. C. K. Scott Moncrieff and Terence Kilmartin. 3 vols (Harmondsworth, 1986), 2: 639.
31. Ibid., 2: 1086.
32. Ibid., 1: 326.
33. Joseph Jacobs, *Studies in Jewish Statistics, Social, Vital, and Anthropometric* (London, 1891), p. xl.
34. Banister, *England under the Jews*, p. 61.
35. Jacobs, *Studies in Jewish Statistics*, pp. xxxii–xxxiii.

36. Frank J. Sulloway, *Freud: Biologist of the Mind* (New York, 1979), pp. 147–58.
37. Francisco Lopez de Villalobos, *El somario de la medicina con un tratado sobre las pestiferas bubas*, ed. Maria Teresa Herrera (Salamanca, 1973), pp. 159–61.
38. Houston Stewart Chamberlain, *Foundations of the Nineteenth Century*. Trans. John Lees, 2 vols (London, 1910), 1: 388–9.
39. Nathan Birnbaum, 'Über Houston Steward Chamberlain' *Ausgewähle Schriften zur jüdischen Frage*, 2 vols (Czernowitz, 1910), 2: 201.
40. Adam G. Gurowski, *America and Europe* (New York, 1857), p. 177.
41. Karl Marx, *The Letters of Karl Marx*, ed. and trans. Saul R. Padover (Eaglewood Cliffs, NJ, 1979), p. 459.
42. Otto Weininger, *Geschlecht und Charakter* (Vienna, 1903).

8.   MAURIZIA BOSCAGLI, 'NIETZSCHEANISM AND THE NOVELTY OF THE SUPERMAN'

(From *Eye on the Flesh: Fashions of Masculinity in the Early Twentieth Century* [Oxford, 1996], pp. 77–91.)

Summary

Eye on the Flesh examines changes in the representation of the male body in European culture between 1880 and 1930, as models of 'unassuming' bourgeois masculinity ceded to a modern ideal of virile musculature which found its keenest expression in fascist statuary. The spectacular, warrior-like male body, signifier of 'phallic plenitude', was, Maurizia Boscagli observes, coincident with the rise of early mass consumer culture, and was thus inserted alongside the female body in the circuitry of commodity culture, conformity and display. Boscagli reads in this phenomenon a complex masculine anxiety about gender roles, authority, sexuality and national identity. In the extract reprinted here, she explores how the Nietzschean ideal of the superman provided a structuring trope for the re-imaging of the male body: a transformation whose effects may still be discernible in the physical culture of today.

Notes

1. [Much of Friedrich Nietzsche's philosophy was a polemic against Christianity and what he regarded as a slavish Christian morality. In its place he resurrected the pagan morality of the ancient Greeks, the morality of 'the will-to-power' (*Will zum Macht*), and put forward the idea of the 'superman' (*Übermensch*) as one who lives beyond the conventions of good and evil. In placing in opposition two philosophies, the Apollonian and the Dionysian (after the Greek gods Apollo and Dionysius), which represented respectively the rational and the sensual, Nietzsche rejected the Apollonian values as stultifying and a fetter to the life force, and embraced the Dionysian values of impulsiveness and immediacy.]
2. Stephen Ascheim, *The Nietzsche Legacy in Germany 1890–1990* (Berkeley, CA, 1992), p. 75.
3. Emile Zola, *La bête humaine* (Harmondsworth, 1977). Further references to the novel are given in parentheses in the text.
4. Friederich Nietzsche, *On the Genealogy of Morals*, ed. and trans. Walter Kaufmann (New York, 1969); *Twilight of Idols*, in *The Portable Nietzsche*, trans.

and ed. Walter Kaufmann (Harmondsworth, 1983); and *Thus Spoke Zarathustra*, ed. and trans. R. J. Hollingdale (Harmondsworth, 1986).

5. Nietzsche, *Twilight of Idols*, p. 549.
6. Nietzsche, *On the Genealogy of Morals*, p. 40.
7. Ibid.
8. Heterotopia: from Greek *hetero-* 'other, different' + *topos*, 'place': literally, displacement of an organ of the body, but also used by Michel Foucault (*Des Espace Autres*, 1967) to designate the opposite of a utopia; a space of incommensurable difference which nonetheless does take place. Foucault gives examples such as brothels, churches, hotel rooms, libraries, prisons, asylums, Roman baths, the Turkish hammam, and the Scandinavian sauna.
9. Nietzsche, *Thus Spoke Zarathustra*, p. 62.
10. Ibid.
11. As Stephen Ascheim points out, 'About 150,000 copies of a specially durable wartime *Zarathustra* were distributed to the troops. Even Christian commentators were struck that *Zarathustra* had taken its place alongside the Bible in the field. Indeed, this very combination was a key way for the interpreters to integrate the notorious author of the *Antichrist* into respectability.' See Ascheim, *The Nietzsche Legacy*, pp. 135–6.
12. Nietzsche, *Twilight of Idols*, p. 511.
13. Oscar Wilde, *The Picture of Dorian Gray* (Harmondsworth, 1983), p. 18.
14. 'Just look at those superfluous people! They acquire wealth and make themselves poorer with it. They desire power and especially the lever of power, plenty of money. These impotent people! ... Leave the idolatry of the superfluous! A free life still remains for great souls. Truly, he who possesses little is so much the less possessed; praised be a moderate poverty! Only then, when the state ceases, does the man who is not superfluous begin; does the song of the necessary man, the unique and irreplaceable melody begin. ... Do you not see it: the rainbow and the bridge to the Superman?' Nietzsche, *Thus Spoke Zarathustra*, pp. 77–8.
15. For the relation between movement, speed, and physical efficiency in the early twentieth century see Stephen Kern, *The Culture of Time and Space 1880–1918* (Cambridge, MA, 1983).
16. John Hoberman, *Sport and Political Ideology* (Austin, TX, 1984), p. 130.
17. Quoted in Hoberman, *Sport and Political Ideology*, p. 77. In *The Political Training of the Body* (1937), Baumler anthropomorphises the state into a giant athlete representing the 'collective body' of the *Volk*. Thus society is seen as an organised and trained body.
18. Walter Lacquer, *Young Germany: A History of the German Youth Movement* (London and New Brunswick, 1962), p. 18.
19. Carl Boesch, 'Vom deutschen Mannsideal', *DerVortrupp*, 2, 1 (1 January 1913), p. 3; quoted in George L. Mosse, *Nationalism and Sexuality: Middle Class Morality and Sexual Norms in Modern Europe* (Madison, WI, 1985), p. 46.
20. Lord Robert Baden-Powell, *Rovering to Success: A Book of Life Sport for Young Men* (London, 1920), pp. 11–28.
21. Cesare Lombroso, *The Delinquent Woman* (Colorado, 1909: 1980); *Havelock Ellis, Studies in the Psychologgy of Sex* (Philadelphia, 1904), vol. 1.
22. Mosse, *Nationalism and Sexuality*, p. 32.
23. Otto Weininger, *Sex and Character* (London and New York, 1907).
24. Baden-Powell, *Rovering to Success*, p. 206.
25. [(T.S.) Eliot's typist: from *The Waste Land*, III: 'The Fire Sermon', in *Selected Poems* (London, 1976).]

9. KLAUS THEWELEIT, 'MALE BODIES AND THE WHITE TERROR' (1977)

(From *Male Fantasies Volume 2: Male Bodies: Psychoanalyzing the White Terror.* Trans. Chris Turner and Erica Carter [Cambridge, 1989], pp. 143–64, abridged.)

Summary

Klaus Theweleit's two-volume study, *Male Fantasies* (*Männerphantasien*), might be described as a psycho-sexual history of fascist male desire in Germany from its inception in the aftermath of World War 1. Theweleit seems especially informed by the psychoanalytic paradigms of Gilles Deleuze and Félix Guattari, insofar as their work, like Theweleit's, consistently emphasises the productive force of fantasy or the unconscious in relation to the material world and its sociopolitical formations. Stylistically, *Male Fantasies* is made up of textual fragments – diaries, memoirs, letters, works of fiction, visual art – which, although historically and culturally specific, are not presented in a stable or overarching historical, narrative or theoretical framework. Instead, Theweleit's text suggests affinities or connotations between symbolic and bodily practices, material production and fantasy, which are not limited to a given historical moment, but which, arguably, maintain both resonance and relevance today.

According to Theweleit it is through the body, and the discourses of the body, that fascist desires (and anxieties) take their sociopolitical formations and effects. The threat to the soldier male of bodily dissolution and collapse is played out, or in psychoanalytic terms, *projected* onto the bodies of its others – notably those of women, Jews, communists, the proletariat, homosexuals, and other marginalised groups, who can thus be subjected and annihilated in fantasy – if not in reality. The extracts reprinted here illustrate the brutalising symbolic practices and fantasies by which the soldier male's 'armoured' body is structured and impelled to action.

Notes

1. Elias Canetti, *Crowds and Power*. Trans. Carol Stewart (Harmondsworth, 1973).
2. E. Von Salomon, *Die Kadetten* (Berlin, 1933), p. 44. The following references are taken from the first part of the book, which described how Salomon settles into the academy.
3. For an account of how from the eighteenth century onward the construction of prisons came to serve as the model for types of social supervision, see Michel Foucault, *Discipline and Punish: The Birth of the Prison*, trans. Alan Sheridan (Harmondsworth, 1977), pp. 195ff., particularly plates 3 and 4: panopticon and discipline.
4. Salomon, *Die Kadetten*, p. 44.
5. Ibid., p. 48.
6. Freud, *Analysis Terminable and Interminable*, SE, vol. XXIII, 226. See also *Introductory Lectures on Psychoanalysis*, SE, vol. XVI, 312.
7. Freud, *An Outline of Psycho-Analysis*, SE, vol. XXIII, 155; see also *Psycho-Analytic Notes on an Autobiographical Account of a Case of Paranoia*, SE, vol. XII, 60–1.
8. As elsewhere, Freud calls such an urge: *Psycho-Analytic Notes*, SE, vol. XII, 63. On the puberty of German boys of the time, see Erikson, 'The Legend of Hitler's Childhood', in *Childhood and Society*, 2nd edn, revised and enlarged (New York, 1963). pp. 307ff.

9. Salomon, *Die Kadetten*, p. 42.
10. Ibid., p. 68.
11. Ibid., p. 49.
12. Ibid., pp. 55–6.
13. Ibid., p. 56.
14. Ibid., p. 57.
15. Ibid., p. 58.
16. Ibid., p. 61.
17. Ibid., pp. 62–3.
18. The term refers to the custom of throwing a sailor into the ocean the first time he crosses the equator. [Translator's note.]
19. Ibid., pp. 63–4.
20. Ibid., p. 64.
21. Ibid., p. 69.
22. Ibid., p. 65.
23. 'Walls ... in the end become part of him,' Canetti emphasized (*Crowds and Power*, p. 362). By contrast, his account of the command is very precise (pp. 349–50).
24. Salomom, *Die Kadetten*, p. 114.
25. Hartmut Plaas, 'Das Kapp-Unternehmen', in Ernst Jünger, *Der Kampf um das Reich* (Essen, 1929), p. 178.
26. Ibid., p. 178. In Volck, *Rebellen um Ehre* (Gütersloh, 1932) we find the 'troop with a soul of steel' (p. 66).
27. Salomon, *Die Kadetten*, p. 115.
28. Ernst Jünger, *Feuer und Blut* (Berlin, 1929) pp. 84–5
29. Foucault, *Discipline and Punish*, p. 169, describes how from the eighteenth century onward the human body was disciplined in relation to the construction of social institutions, which were meant to serve as models for the body. His description pays less attention to the body's actual physical changes.
30. Ernst Jünger, *Kampf als inneres Erlebnis* (Berlin, 1922), pp. 32–3; see also p. 55.
31. 'The German is "Der neue Mensch" which could also be translated "the new human being" since Theweleit's point is however precisely that species being created is *masculine*, "men" has been used here as a general term for human beings' [Translator's note.]
32. Ibid., p. 74.
33. Manfred Nagl's *Science Fiction in Deutschland* (Tübingen, 1972), a survey based on extremely interesting material, shows that the attempt to create a superman in the image of the machine, by excluding women in favour of machines, is not an invention of the futurists. It is a core element of 'pre-fascist' nineteenth century literature, which, to a large extent, has been dismissed as 'trivial' by literary history (see e.g., pp. 125ff.).
34. Freud, *The Ego and the Id*, SE, vol. XIX, pp. 25–6.

10.　FRANTZ FANON, 'THE FACT OF BLACKNESS' (1952)

(From *Black Skin, White Masks*. Trans. Charles Lam Markmann, 1967 [London, 1993], pp. 109–40, abridged.)

Summary

If the core psychological imperative of Frantz Fanon's *Black Skin, White Masks* is to understand how black consciousness, both individual and social, has been shaped by the (colonial) forces of history, its political aim is to consider how black identity might be (re)claimed on a different set of terms. Central to Fanon's work is the premise that *racism objectifies*: a contention which can be (and indeed is, by Fanon himself and his many commentators) variously interpreted in grammatical, political, psychological, philosophical, anthropological and economic aspects. In 'The Fact of Blackness', however, it is the corporeal sense of racist objectification which is most powerfully emphasised. The fact of blackness as Otherness is detailed autobiographically here at the level of the bodily schema, the first ground of objectification. For Fanon, the black body is a barrier in the humanist dialectic between self and world, since it is always already defined from without by white power. In Fanonian terms, the black has 'no ontological resistance' in the eyes of the white. Even the Negritude movement, which sought to articulate and celebrate blackness in and on its own terms, proves for Fanon a false ally, insofar as its discourses retain traces of a western racist ethnology which always positions blackness as 'primitive'. Fanon's dialogic style is distinctively powerful in its yoking of intimate physicality to a sweeping range of conceptual, philosophical and psychological thinking.

Notes

1. [Georg Wilhelm Friedrich Hegel (1770–1831): German idealist philosopher, whose later work was especially concerned with theories of self-determining *and* social subjectivity. Here Fanon is referring to Hegel's dialectical logic, which posits that any term in a dualism requires and ultimately sublates its opposite. Individuals therefore depend on 'others' for their identity, ideally in an act of mutual dependence and definition. Fanon clearly finds this theory inadequate for the lived experience of race relations.]
2. Jean Lhermitte, *L'Image de notre corps* (Paris, 1939), p. 17.
3. [Albert Lebrun (1871–1950): allegedly uncharismatic President of the Third French Republic 1932–40, who came from a peasant family in eastern France.]
4. Jean-Paul Sartre, *Anti-Semite and Jew* (New York, 1960), pp. 112–13.
5. Ibid., p. 115.
6. John Alfred Mjoen, 'Harmonic and Disharmonic Race-Crossings', The Second International Congress of Eugenics (1921), *Eugenics in Race and State*, vol. II, p. 60.
7. In the English in the original. [Translator's note.]
8. [Ankylosis: the fusion of bones or skeletal parts.]
9. 'Ce que l'homme noir apporte', in Claude Nordey, *L'Homme de couleur* (Paris, 1939), pp. 309–10.
10. Aimé Césaire, *Cahier d'un retour au pays natal* (Paris, 1956), pp. 77–8.
11. My italics – F.F.
12. My italics – F.F.
13. Léopold Senghor, 'Ce que l'homme noir apporte', in Nordey, *L'Homme de couleur*, p. 205.
14. Jean-Paul Sartre, *Orphée Noir*, preface to *Anthologie de la nouvelle poésie nègre et malgache* (Paris, 1948), pp. xl ff.
15. Though Sartre's speculations on the existence of The Other may be correct (to the extent, we must remember, to which *Being and Nothingness* describes an alienated consciousness), their application to a black consciousness proves fallacious. That is because the white man is not only The Other but also the master, whether real or imaginary.

16. In the sense in which the word is used by Jean Wahl in *Existence humaine et transcendence* (Neuchâtel, 1994).
17. Jean-Paul Sartre, *The Respectful Prostitute*, in *Three Plays* (New York, 1949), pp. 189. Originally, *La Putain respecteuse* (Paris, 1947). See also *Home of the Brave*, a film by Mark Robson.
18. By Chester Himes (Garden City, NY, 1945).
19. *Home of the Brave*.

DECONSTRUCTIONS

11. JOAN RIVIERE, 'WOMANLINESS AS A MASQUERADE' (1929)

(From *Formations of Fantasy*, ed. Victor Burgin, James Donald and Cora Kaplan [London and New York, 1993], pp. 35–44, abridged.)

Summary

This best-known of Joan Riviere's writings holds a key place in discussion of female sexuality in psychoanalysis, and the masquerade has become an important and nuanced theoretical aspect of femininity and its representation. Insofar as Riviere wrote this extraordinary essay in 1929, it is hard not to infer some symmetry between Riviere's own situation and her patient's struggle to understand what it means to be a woman and an intellectual in a patriarchal world.

In psychoanalytic terms, the patient's academic performance is the assumption of a masculine role, or castrating in order to possess the phallus. Her exaggerated display of femininity following a professional presentation is a means of averting the retribution of men: by presenting herself as a sexual object she placates rivals by flaunting her own castration or lack, thus disguising herself as *only a woman*. The theory thus far is relatively straightforward. The knotty bit arises later, when Riviere is obliged to make a distinction between authentic womanliness and its masquerade, wherepon she concludes that heterosexual femininity admits no such distinction; it is only ever a dissimulation with no organic integrity. Femininity, in other words, is *essentially superficial*. This tantalising oxymoron still seems very germane to discussions of female bodily culture and recent debates around cosmetic surgery, for example.

Notes

1. This article was first published in *The International Journal of Psychoanalysis (IJPA)*, 10 (1929).
2. [Ernest Jones (1879–1958): British follower, correspondent and biographer of Freud.]
3. E. Jones, 'The early development of female sexuality', *IJPA*, 8 (1927).
4. S. Ferenczi, 'The nosology of male homosexuality', in *Contributions to Psychoanalysis*, 1916.
5. [Riviere follows Kleinian practice of spelling 'phantasy' thus.]

12. ABIGAIL BRAY, 'THE ANOREXIC BODY: READING DISORDERS'

(From *Cultural Studies*, 10.3 [1996], 413–29, abridged.)

Summary

This essay examines a popular and 'commonsense' feminist interpretation of anorexia nervosa: that it is a pathology brought about by women's excessive consumption of media images of thin femininity. The anorexic body, so the theory goes, hyperbolises the general alienation of female corporeality from phallocentric representation.

Abigail Bray takes to task this negative view of women's uncritical 'consumption' of media texts and connects it with nineteenth-century discussions of the causes of hysteria, revealing a similar pathologisation of women's reading practices. In so doing, she complicates notions of a causal, coercive or 'toxic' relationship between the cultural representation of bodies and lived corporeality. Instead, invoking the paradigms of Michel Foucault and Judith Butler (see chapters 5 and 13 of this collection, respectively) she emphasises the sheer volume of discourses which continue to be inscribed on the anorexic body, and which it persistently evades and subverts. Bray herself resists a totalising approach to anorexic identity, preferring to open the idea of the 'metabolic' body as a means of discussing the historical specificity of contemporary anorexia in relation to an ongoing negotiation between production and consumption.

Notes

1. Paula A. Treichler, 'AIDS, homophobia and biomedical discourse: an epidemic of signification', *Cultural Studies*, 1(3) (1987), 263–305.
2. Elizabeth Grosz, *Volatile Bodies: Toward a Corporeal Feminism* (Sydney, 1994), p. 40.
3. Kim Chernin, *Womansize: The Tyranny of Slenderness* (London, 1989).
4. Naomi Wolf, *The Beauty Myth* (London, 1990).
5. Louise J. Kaplan, *Female Perversions: The Temptations of Madame Bovary*, (Harmondsworth, 1991), pp. 453–84.
6. Robert Romanyshyn, *Technology as Symptom and Dream* (London, 1989), pp. 133–751.
7. Gilles Deleuze and Félix Guattari, *A Thousand Plateaus: Capitalism and Schizophrenia*. Trans. Brian Massumi (Minneapolis, 1987), p. 151.
8. Susie Orbach, *Fat is a Feminist Issue* (London, 1984).
9. Matra Robertson, *Starving in the Silences: An Exploration of Anorexia Nervosa* (Sydney, 1992).
10. This information comes from *The International Journal of Eating Disorders*. L. K. George Hsu, Arthur H. Crisp and John S. Callender, 'Recovery in anorexia nervosa – the patient's perspective', 11(4) (1992), 341–50 relate the case histories of six recovered anorexic women. Case 5 'got out of family and leucotomy' reports that after the operation on her brain she lacked the will-power to diet. The authors conclude that 'the leucotomy seemed to have broken the obsessional habit of counting calories and having only a certain amount of food to eat each time'. After acknowledging the positive effects of surgical intervention they also suggest that clomipramine and fluoxetine should be 'given a fair trial' (p. 346). In James Ferguson, 'The use of electroconvulsive therapy in patients with intractable anorexia nervosa', 13(2) (1993), 195–201, it is reported that Ms C., 'a 23-year old single woman' who was raped when she was fourteen, was subjected to

'16 bilateral ECT treatments after she attempted suicide and became anorexic. Due to treatment related cognitive defects, ECT was abandoned' (p. 199). And yet Ferguson concludes by affirming that 'it is possible that anorexia nervosa may respond to ECT by virtue of the same well-documented effects on brain cate-cholamine systems that have been proposed to underlie the anti-depressant effect of ECT' (p. 200). It seems that while these authors speculate on the effects of various treatments, they all agree that brain damage in the form of leucotomies and ECT abuse seems to 'cure' anorexia.

11. M. Boskind-White, 'Cinderella's stepsisters: a feminist perspective on anorexia nervosa and bulimia', *Signs*, 2 (1970), 342–56.
12. Linda Brown, 'Women, weight and power: feminist theoretical and therapeutic issues', *Women and Therapy*, 1 (1985), 61–71.
13. Bryan S. Turner, *The Body and Society: Explorations in Social Theory* (Oxford, 1984), p. 196.
14. Chernin, *Womansize*.
15. O. Wayne Wooley and Susan Wooley, 'The Beverly Hills eating disorder: the mass marketing of anorexia nervosa', *International Journal of Eating Disorders*, 1(3) (1982), 57–69.
16. Robertson, *Starving in the Silences*.
17. Philippa Rothfield, 'A conversation between bodies', *Melbourne Journal of Politics*, 22 (1994), 30–44.
18. Susie Orbach, *Hunger Strike: The Anorectic's Struggle as a Metaphor for our Age* (London, 1986), p. 90.
19. Maud Ellmann, *The Hunger Artists: Eating, Writing and Imprisonment* (Cambridge, MA, 1993).
20. Gilles Deleuze and Claire Parnet, *Dialogues*. Trans. Hugh Tomlinson (New York, 1987).
21. [Marshall McLuhan (1911–80): Canadian communications theorist who studied the impact of electronic media on the circulation and reception of information, perhaps most famously in *The Medium is the Message: An Inventory of Effects* (1967).]
22. Ellmann, *The Hunger Artists*, p. 24.
23. [Freud, in a famously imperialist trope, described femininity as a 'dark continent' in *The Ego and The Id* (1923) *SE* Vol. 2.]
24. Robertson, *Starving in the Silences*, p. 70.
25. Treichler, 'AIDS, homophobia and biomedical discourse', p. 265.
26. Janice A. Radway, 'Reading is not eating: mass-produced literature and the theoretical, methodological, and political consequences of a metaphor', *Book Research Quarterly*, 2(3) (1986), 7–29.
27. Bernard Rosenberg, 'Mass culture in America', in Bernard Rosenberg and David Manning White (eds), *Mass Culture: The Popular Arts in America* (Glencoe, IL, 1957), pp. 9–10; Radway, 'Reading is not eating', p. 10.
28. Allison Lynn, 'Skin and bone', *Who Weekly*, 19 July 1993, p. 15.
29. Abigail Bray, 'The edible woman: reading/eating disorders and femininity', *Media Information Australia*, 27 (May 1994), 4–10.
30. Robertson, *Starving in the Silences*, p. 74.
31. Moira Gatens, 'Corporeal representations in/and the body politic', in Rosalyn Diprose and Robyn Ferrell (eds), *Cartographies: Poststructuralism and the Mapping of Bodies and Spaces* (Sydney, 1991).
32. Rosalyn Diprose, *The Bodies of Women: Ethics, Embodiment and Sexual Difference* (New York, 1994).

33. Boskind-White, 'Cinderella's stepsisters', p. 438.
34. Robertson, *Starving in the Silences*, p. 52.
35. Grosz, *Volatile Bodies*.
36. Rothfield, 'A conversation between bodies'.
37. Grosz, *Volatile Bodies*, p. 72.
38. Orbach, *Fat is a Feminist Issue*.
39. Brown, 'Women, weight and power', p. 63.
40. Wolf, *The Beauty Myth*, pp. 171, 164.
41. Chernin, *Womansize*, pp. 135–44.
42. Kate Flint, *The Woman Reader: 1837–1914* (Oxford, 1993), p. 53.
43. Orbach, *Hunger Strike*, pp. 97–118.
44. Ibid., p. 36.
45. Hilde Bruch, *The Golden Cage: The Enigma of Anorexia Nervosa* (Cambridge, MA, 1978).
46. Ibid., p. viii.
47. Hilde Bruch, *Conversations with Anorectics*, Danita Czyzewski and Melanie A. Suhr (eds) (New York, 1988), p. 4.
48. Ellmann, *The Hunger Artists*, p. 24. My emphasis.
49. Susan Bordo, 'Anorexia nervosa: psychopathology as the crystallization of culture', in Deane W. Curtin and Lisa M. Heldke (eds), *Cooking, Eating, Thinking: Transformative Philosophies of Food* (Bloomington, IN, 1992).
50. Ibid., p. 47.
51. Susan Bordo, 'How television teaches women to hate their hungers', *Mirror Images* (Newsletter of Anorexia/Bulimia Support, Syracuse, New York), 41(1) (1986), 8–9.
52. Elspeth Probyn, 'The anorexic body', in Arthur and M. Kroker (eds), *Body Invaders: Sexuality and the Postmodern Condition* (New York, 1987), p. 203. My emphasis.
53. Helen Irving, 'Little elves and mind control: advertising and its critics', *Continuum: An Australian Journal of the Media*, 4(2) (1991), 98–111, p. 10.
54. Karl Popper, 'Knowledge: subjective versus objective', in David Miller (ed.), *A Pocket Popper* (London, 1983), p. 58.
55. Irving, 'Little elves and mind control', p. 99.
56. Rita Felski, *The Gender of Modernity* (Cambridge, MA, 1995), p. 88.
57. Patrice Petro, 'Mass culture and the feminine: the "place" of television in film studies', *Cinema Journal*, 25(3) (1986), 5–21, p. 14.
58. Robertson, *Starving in the Silences*, p. 53.
59. Probyn, 'The anorexic body', p. 210.
60. Elspeth Probyn, *Sexing the Self: Gendered Positions in Cultural Studies* (New York, 1993), p. 12.
61. Eva Szekely, 'Reflections on the body in the anorexia discourse', *New Feminist Research*, 17(4) (1988), 8–11, p. 10.
62. Arthur W. Frank, 'Bringing bodies back in: a decade in review', *Theory, Culture and Society*, 7 (1990), 131–62, pp. 148–9.
63. Judith Butler, *Gender Trouble: Feminism and the Subversion of Identity* (New York, 1990), p. 147.
64. Ibid., p. 146.
65. Ibid., p. 145.
66. Charlotte Perkins Gilman (1892), 'The yellow wallpaper', in Catherine Golden (ed.), *The Captive Imagination: A Casebook on 'The Yellow Wallpaper'* (New York, 1992).
67. Bray, 'The edible woman'.

68. Fiona Place, *Cardboard* (Sydney, 1989).
69. Ludwig Binswanger, 'The case of Ellen West'. Trans. Werner M. Mendal and Joseph Lyons, in Rollo May, Ernst Angel and Henri F. Ellenberger (eds), *Existence: A New Dimension in Psychiatry and Psychology* (New York, 1958), p. 254.
70. Joan Jacobs Brumberg, *Fasting Girls: The Emergence of Anorexia as a Modern Disease* (Cambridge, MA, 1988), p. 270.
71. Michel Foucault, *The Uses of Pleasure*. Trans. Robert Hurley (Harmondsworth, 1992), p. 101.
72. Ibid., p. 102.
73. Ibid., pp. 103–4.
74. Liz Brody, 'Burn fat faster', *She* (June 1994), 98–100, p. 98.
75. Brumberg, *Fasting Girls*, pp. 232–8.
76. Ibid., p. 237.
77. Ibid., p. 241.
78. Ibid., p. 243.
79. Jan Wienpahl, 'Fourteen days in the High Sierra ... excerpts from a diary', in Leslea Newman (ed.), *Eating Our Hearts Out: Personal Accounts of Women's Relationship to Food* (Freedom, CA, 1993), p. 160.
80. Paul Virilio, *The Aesthetics of Disappearance*. Trans. Philip Beitchman (New York, 1991), p. 43.

13.   JUDITH BUTLER, '*BODIES THAT MATTER*'

(From *Bodies That Matter: On the Discursive Limits of 'Sex'* [London and New York, 1993], pp. 1–16.)

Summary

With the publication of *Gender Trouble* in 1990, Judith Butler spearheaded a movement in feminist theory which has become known as 'radical constructivism'. Taking its departures from psychoanalytic and poststructuralist theory, and also informed by speech-act theory, *Gender Trouble* contends (albeit with sophistication and nuance infinitely greater than this) that gender is not an internal essence, but one produced 'in anticipation' by a repeated and naturalised set of acts, behaviours and stylings. Gender and sexual categories are held in place by the restrictive norms of heterosexuality, but these can be revealed as artificial by their very citability – as demonstrated *in extremis* by, for example, drag and camp performance.

In *Bodies That Matter* (1993) Butler extends and complicates the theories put forward in *Gender Trouble* to contend that not only gender, but the materiality of the body itself, is discursively and performatively produced. We cannot, therefore, speak of a natural, prelinguistic, 'given' body, because what we think we know about bodies is an effect rather than a cause of signification. As with *Gender Trouble*, this is not to say that bodies are entirely, unchangingly *determined* by language, but a recognition that, in Butler's words, there can be 'no reference to a pure body which is not at the same time a further formation of that body' (1993, p. 10). Referring to a body is thus, in quite a strict linguistic sense, always almost performative or constitutive, and governed largely (though not entirely) by habitual understandings and norms (such as heterosexism). Again, the citation and iterability of the norms that subjects are expected 'naturally' to embody belies their instability in a classic deconstructive manoeuvre: the natural or intelligible body shores itself up against, and thereby defines or summons the appearance of the deviant or unintelligible (just as the legitimate summons the illegitimate, the authentic the false, the proper the improper, and so forth). The 'performance' of alternative sexualities and gender identities both denaturalises normative suppositions, and pushes for the articulation of new bodily possibilities.

In the introductory chapter reprinted here, Butler outlines her theory of how bodies are produced, or materialised, in discourse, and clarifies the oft-cited notion of performativity in its twinned senses of speech-act and theatrical agency. The textual style in this instance is relatively straightforward by Butler's standards: her work is renowned for what can seem like a wilfully opaque syntax. This, however, is central to her critique, which is shot through with a relentless critical suspicion of the 'common sense' of linguistic transparency.

Notes

1. Clearly, sex is not the only such norm by which bodies become materialised, and it is unclear whether 'sex' can operate as a norm apart from other normative requirements on bodies. This will become clear in later sections of this text.

2. Abjection (in latin, *ab-jicere*) literally means to cast off, away, or out and, hence, presupposes and produces a domain of agency from which it is differentiated. Here the casting away resonates with the psychoanalytic notion of *Verwerfung*, implying a foreclosure which founds the subject and which, accordingly, establishes that foundation as tenuous. Whereas the psychoanalytic notion of *Verwerfung*, translated as 'foreclosure', produces sociality through a repudiation of a primary signifier which produces an unconscious or, in Lacan's theory, the register of the real, the notion of *abjection* designates a degraded or cast out status within the terms of sociality. Indeed, what is foreclosed or repudiated *within* psychoanalytic terms is precisely what may not re-enter the field of the social without threatening psychosis, that is, the dissolution of the subject itself. I want to propose that certain abject zones within sociality also deliver this threat, constituting zones of uninhabitability which a subject fantasises as threatening its own integrity with the prospect of a psychotic dissolution ('I would rather die than do or be that!'). See the entry under 'Forclusion' in Jean Laplanche and J.-B. Pontalis, *Vocabulaire de la psychanalyse* (Paris, 1967), pp. 163–7.

3. See Sherry Ortner, 'Is Female to Male as Nature is to Culture?', in *Woman, Culture, and Society*, ed. Michele Rosaldo and Louise Lamphere (Stanford, CA, 1974), pp. 67–88.

4. For different but related approaches to this problematic of exclusion, abjection, and the creation of 'the human', see Julia Kristeva, *Powers of Horror: An Essay on Abjection*, trans. Leon Roudiez (New York, 1982); John Fletcher and Andrew Benjamin (eds), *Abjection, Melancholia and Love: The work of Julia Kristeva* (New York and London, 1990); Jean-François Lyotard, *The Inhuman: Reflections on Time*, trans. Geoffrey Bennington and Rachel Bowlby (Stanford, CA, 1991).

5. For a very provocative reading which shows how the problem of linguistic referentiality is linked with the specific problem of referring to bodies, and what might be meant by 'reference' in such a case, see Cathy Caruth, 'The Claims of Reference', *The Yale Journal of Criticism*, 4, no. 1 (Fall 1990), pp. 193–206.

6. Although Foucault distinguishes between juridical and productive models of power in *The History of Sexuality, Volume One*, trans. Robert Hurley (New York, 1978), I have argued that the two models presuppose each other. The production of a subject – its subjection (*assujetissement*) – is one means of its regulation. See my

'Sexual Inversions', in Domna Stanton (ed.), *Discourses of Sexuality* (Ann Arbour, MI, 1992), pp. 344–61.

7. It is not simply a matter of construing performativity as a repetition of acts, as if 'acts' remain intact and self-identical as they are repeated in time, and where 'time' is understood as external to the 'acts' themselves. On the contrary, an act is itself a repetition, a sedimentation, and congealment of the past which is precisely foreclosed in its act-like status. In this sense an 'act' is always a provisional failure of memory. In what follows, I make use of the Lacanian notion that every act is to be construed as a repetition, the repetition of what cannot be recollected, of the irrecoverable, and is thus the haunting spectre of the subject's deconstitution. The Derridean notion of iterability, formulated in response to the theorisation of speech acts by John Searle and J.L. Austin, also implies that every act is itself a recitation, the citing of a prior chain of acts which are implied in a present act and which perpetually drain any 'present' act of its presentness. See note 9 below for the difference between a repetition in the service of the fantasy of mastery (i.e., a repetition of acts which build the subject, and which are said to be the constructive or constituting acts of a subject) and a notion of repetition-compulsion, taken from Freud, which breaks apart that fantasy of mastery and sets its limits.

8. The notion of temporality ought not to be construed as a simple succession of distinct 'moments', all of which are equally distant from one another. Such a spatialised mapping of time substitutes a certain mathematical model for the kind of duration which resists such spatialising metaphors. Efforts to describe or name this temporal span tend to engage spatial mapping, as philosophers from Bergson through Heidegger have argued. Hence, it is important to underscore the effect of *sedimentation* that the temporality of construction implies. Here what are called 'moments' are not distinct and equivalent units of time, for the 'past' will be the accumulation and congealing of such 'moments' to the point of their indistinguishability. But it will also consist of that which is refused from construction, the domains of the repressed, forgotten, and the irrecoverably foreclosed. That which is not included – exteriorised by boundary – as a phenomenal constituent of the sedimented effect called 'construction' will be as crucial to its definition as that which is included; this exteriority is not distinguishable as a 'moment'. Indeed, the notion of the 'moment' may well be nothing other than a retrospective fantasy of mathematical mastery imposed upon the interrupted durations of the past.

To argue that construction is fundamentally a matter of iteration is to make the temporal modality of 'Construction' into a priority. To the extent that such a theory requires a spatialisation of time through the postulation of discrete and bounded moments, this temporal account of construction presupposes a spatialisation of temporality itself, what one might, following Heidegger, understand as the reduction of temporality to time.

The Foucaultian emphasis on *convergent* relations of power (which might in a tentative way be contrasted with the Derridean emphasis on iterability) implies a mapping of power relations that in the course of a genealogical process form a constructed effect. The notion of convergence presupposes both motion and space; as a result, it appears to elude the paradox noted above in which the very account of temporality requires the spatialisation of the 'moment'. On the other hand, Foucault's account of convergence does not fully theorise what is at work in the 'movement' by which power and discourse are said to converge. In a sense, the 'mapping' of power does not fully theorise temporality.

Significantly, the Derridean analysis of iterability is to be distinguished from simple repetition in which the distances between temporal 'moments' are treated as uniform in their spatial extension. The 'betweenness' that differentiates 'moments' of time is not one that can, within Derridean terms, be spatialised or bounded as an identifiable object. It is the nonthematisable différance which erodes and contests any and all claims to discrete identity, including the discrete identity of the 'moment'. What differentiates moments is not a spatially extended duration, for if it were, it would also count as a 'moment', and so fail to account for what falls between moments. This 'entre', that which is at once 'between' and 'outside', is something like non-thematisable space and non-thematisable time as they converge.

Foucault's language of construction includes terms like 'augmentation', 'proliferation', and 'convergence', all of which presume a temporal domain not explicitly theorised. Part of the problem here is that whereas Foucault appears to want his account of genealogical effects to be historically specific, he would favour an account of genealogy over a philosophical account of temporality. In 'The Subject and Power' (Hubert Dreyfus and Paul Rabinow (eds), *Michel Foucault: Beyond Structuralism and Hermeneutics* [Chicago, 1983]), Foucault refers to 'the diversity of ... logical sequence' that characterises power relations. He would doubtless reject the apparent linearity implied by models of iterability which link them with the linearity of older models of historical sequence. And yet, we do not receive a specification of 'sequence': Is it the very notion of 'sequence' that varies historically, or are there configurations of sequence that vary, with sequence itself remaining invariant? The specific social formation and figuration of temporality is in some ways unattended by both positions. Here one might consult the work of Pierre Bourdieu to understand the temporality of social construction.

9. See J.L. Austin, *How to Do Things With Words*, ed. J.O. Urmson and Marina Sbisà (Cambridge, MA, 1955), and *Philosophical Papers* (Oxford, 1961), especially pp. 233–52; Shoshana Felman, *The Literary Speech-Act: Don Juan with J.L. Austin, or Seduction in Two Languages*, trans. Catherine Porter (Ithaca, NY, 1983); Barbara Johnson, 'Poetry and Performative Language: Mallarmé and Austin', in *The Critical Difference: Essays in the Contemporary Rhetoric of Reading* (Baltimore, 1980), pp. 52–66; Mary Louise Pratt, *A Speech Act Theory of Literary Discourse* (Bloomington, 1977); and Ludwig Wittgenstein, *Philosophical Investigations*, trans. G.E.M. Anscombe (New York, 1958), part 1.

10. Jacques Derrida, 'Signature, Event, Context', in *Limited, Inc.*, ed. Gerald Graff; trans. Samuel Weber and Jeffrey Mehlman (Evanston, IL, 1988), p. 18.

11. See Michel Borch-Jacobsen, The *Freudian Subject*, trans. Catherine Porter (Stanford, CA, 1988). Whereas Borch-Jacobsen offers an interesting theory of how identification precedes and forms the ego, he tends to assert the priority of identification to any libidinal experience, where I would insist that identification is itself a passionate or libidinal assimilation. See also the useful distinction between an imitative model and a mimetic model of identification in Ruth Leys, 'The Real Miss Beauchamp: Gender and the Subject of Imitation', in Judith Butler and Joan Scott (eds), *Feminists Theorize the Political* (New York, 1992), pp. 167–214; Kaja Silverman, *Male Subjectivity at the Margins* (New York, 1992), pp. 262–70; Mary Ann Doane, 'Misrecognition and Identity', in Ron Burnett (ed.), *Explorations in Film Theory: Selected Essays from Ciné-Tracts* (Bloomington, 1991), pp. 15–25; and Diana Fuss, 'Freud's Fallen Women: Identification, Desire, and "A Case of Homosexuality in a Woman" ', in *The Yale Journal of Criticism*, 6, no. 1 (1993) pp. 1–23.

12. Sigmund Freud, *The Ego and the Id*, ed. James Strachey; trans. Joan Riviere (New York, 1960), p. 16.

13. Nietzsche argues that the ideal of God was produced '[i]n the same measure' as a
    human sense of failure and wretchedness, and that the production of God was,
    indeed, the idealisation which instituted and re-enforced that wretchedness; see
    Friedrich Nietzsche, *On the Genealogy of Morals*, trans. Walter Kaufmann
    (New York, 1969), section 20. That the symbolic law in Lacan produces 'failure' to
    approximate the sexed ideals embodied and enforced by the law, is usually
    understood as a promising sign that the law is not fully efficacious, that it does not
    exhaustively constitute the psyche of any given subject. And yet, to what extent
    does this conception of the law produce the very failure that it seeks to order, and
    maintain an ontological distance between the laws and its failed approximations
    such that the deviant approximations have no power to alter the workings of the
    law itself?
14. [*Paris is Burning* (1991): film directed by Jennie Livingston, which documents the
    subculture of 'voguing' and the Harlem drag balls: discussed in detail by Butler in
    Chapter 4 of *Bodies That Matter*.]

14. ELIZABETH GROSZ, 'INTENSITIES AND FLOWS'

(From *Volatile Bodies: Toward a Corporeal Feminism* [Bloomington and Indianapolis,
1994], pp. 160–80, abridged.)

Summary

As a key figure in the development of 'corporeal feminism', Elizabeth Grosz, like
Judith Butler, negotiates between traditional philosophy and postmodern feminism
from the premise that the body has no natural status or origin outside culture and signification. Moreover, corporeality has, historically, been theorised in a patriarchal culture which posits a masculine norm and fails to account adequately for female
corporeal experience. In *Volatile Bodies*, Grosz's 'wager' is that subjectivity can be
rethought through the matrix of the body (rather than through sovereign consciousness as with Descartes, or the unconscious as with Freud, for example); but in order
for this rethinking to move beyond the conventional hierarchical dualisms of western
metaphysics, the body itself must be retheorised, through paradigms which allow the
disruption of binaries and a new configuration of the relation between inside and outside, surface and depth, body and psyche. Such paradigms of the body are those emer-
gent largely (though not exclusively) in feminist thought, and tend to refigure
conventional depth-models of body and subject with an emphasis on discontinuous
relations of surfaces, flows, organs, energies and libidinal intensities.

In the argument reprinted here however, Grosz recovers the usefulness of a 'masculine' theory (Deleuze and Guattari's notions of rhizomatics, 'becoming woman' and
the 'Body without Organs') as concepts which, though problematic to feminism in
some respects, can 'clear the ground of metaphysical oppositions' for a fresh theoris-
ing of the body, desire and subjectivity.

Notes

1. Gilles Deleuze and Félix Guattari, *A Thousand Plateaus*: *Capitalism and
   Schizophrenia*. Trans. Brian Massumi (Minneapolis, 1987).
2. [Phallocentric: the 'malecentredness' of language and culture, predicated on a mistaken identification of masculinity with the phallus, and of femininity with lack.]

3. Of those feminists with whom I am familiar, there are certainly a number who have written on Gilles Deleuze and Félix Guattari's work – but this is far from the capturing of feminist imagination that has occurred with the writings of other French theorists, such as Lacan, Foucault, and Derrida. I have in mind here such diverse feminist writers as Rosi Braidotti, Judith Butler, Dianne Chisholm, Marie Curnick, Karin Emerton, Anna Gibbs, Alice Jardine, Meaghan Morris, and Dorothea Olkowski.

4. [Invagination: a term used (not unproblematically) to describe the structural ambiguity of skin's ability to 'fold back' on itself, to be at once both toucher and touched. See also Didier Anzieu, *The Skin Ego* (London, 1989) and Maurice Merleau-Ponty, *The Phenomenology of Perception*. Trans. Colin Smith (London, 1962).]

5. Alice Jardine, *Gynesis: Configuration of Woman and Modernity* (Ithaca, NY, 1985).

6. See also Luce Irigaray, *This Sex Which Is Not One*. Trans. Gillian Gill (Ithaca, NY, 1985), pp 140–1, and Rosi Braidotti, *Patterns of Dissonance* (Oxford, 1991), pp. 120–1.

7. [Rhizomatics: from the botanical sense of an underground tuber that ramifies and diversifies in unforeseeable directions; a network of relations which is non-hierarchical, proliferating, hybrid, contrary to conceptualisation and identity.]

8. This is, more broadly, Arthur Kroker's claim in *The Possessed Individual* (New York, 1991), pp. 113–17.

9. Gilles Deleuze and Felix Guattari, *Anti-Oedipus: Capitalism and Schizophrenia*. Trans. Robert Hurley, Mark Seem and H.R. Lane (Minneapolis, 1983).

10. Deleuze and Guattari, *A Thousand Plateaus*, p. 74.

11. E.g., Dominique Grisoni, 'The Onomatopoeia of Desire'. In Peter Botsman (ed.), *Theoretical Strategies* (Sydney, 1982), pp. 162–89.

12. Deleuze and Guattari point out that unlike the tree, the rhizome is not the object of reproduction: neither external reproduction as image-root nor internal reproduction as tree-structure. The rhizome is an antigenealogy. It is a short-term memory or antimemory. The rhizome operates by variation, expansion, conquest, capture, offshoots ... the rhizome is an acentred, non-hierarchical, nonsignifying system without a General and without an organising memory or central automaton, defined solely by a circulation of states. *A Thousand Plateaus*, p. 21. [subsequent references indicated by page numbers in the text.]

13. Colin Gordon provides a plausible explanation of the notion of multiplicity which relates it closely to the concept of assemblage and machine; the notion of a multiplicity is based on developments in non-Euclidian geometry: 'Multiplicities ... This concept, due originally to Reimann's non-Euclidian geometries description of certain kinds of "assemblages" as "flat" ... By "flatness" Deleuze and Guattari mean a situation ... where condition and conditioned inhabit the same space, with no extra dimension for an overview "in depth". The fact that there is no resemblance or analogy of condition and conditioned is what gives its point to their concept of "assemblage" ' (Gordon, 'The Subtracting Machine', *IC*, no. 8 (Spring 1981), 35–6).

14. Gilles Deleuze and Claire Parnet, *Dialogues*. Trans. Hugh Tomlinson (New York, 1987).

15. Spinoza and Spinozism clearly remain an abiding interest for Deleuze throughout his intellectual career; see Deleuze, *Expressionism in Philosophy: Spinoza*. Trans. Martin Joughin (New York, 1990) and *Spinoza: Practical Philosophy*. Trans. Robert Hurley (San Francisco, 1988).

16. Deleuze's understanding of masochism seems to have developed considerably in the period between *Masochism: Coldness and Cruelty*. Trans. Jean McNeil (New York, 1989) and *A Thousand Plateaus*. In the latter, he discusses masochism not as a devious detour of pleasure through or around pain (the psychoanalytic view, which reduces masochism to the counterpart of sadism through the restructuring provided by Oedipalisation), but as the production of intricate machinic connections which distribute intensities across bodies and objects, experimenting with the plane of consistency of desire itself: Take the [psychoanalytic] interpretation of masochism: when the ridiculous death instinct is not invoked, it is claimed that the masochist, like everybody else, is after pleasure but can only get it through pain and phantasied humiliations whose function is to allay or ward off deep anxiety. This is inaccurate; the masochist suffering is the price he must pay, not to achieve pleasure but to untie some pseudobond between desire and pleasure as an extrinsic measure. Pleasure is in no way something that can be attained only by a detour through suffering; it is something that must be delayed as long as possible because it interrupts the continuous process of positive desire ... In short, the masochist uses suffering as a way of constituting a body without organs and bringing forth a plane of consistency of desire. That there are other ways, other procedures, and certainly better ones is beside the point. It is enough that some find this procedure suitable for them. (*A Thousand Plateaus*, p. 155) The masochist engages in the conversion of body parts, partial objects, libidinal investments, pleasures, and desires into machinic components, the transformation of organs into sites and rituals, the becoming or partial becoming of a BwO.

17. William Burroughs, *The Naked Lunch*, quoted in *A Thousand Plateaus*, pp. 153–4.

15.   ELSPETH PROBYN, 'BEYOND FOOD/SEX: EATING AND AN ETHICS OF EXISTENCE'

(From *Theory, Culture and Society*, 16.2 [1999], 215–28, abridged.)

Summary

In this provocative and often playful essay, Elspeth Probyn performs a twist on Foucault's 'repressive hypothesis' (see Chapter 4 of this volume), by suggesting that eroticised alimentary discourses have usurped the banally sexual in the popular circulation and management of pleasure and identity formation. The text also makes a movement away from abstract theorisations of the body to, quite literally, the level of the guts – for food is considered here not as a metaphor, but a material and social concern imbricated in economics, desire, gender, sexuality, history, ethnicity and class, and a rich means of studying the workings of power.

Notes

1. Etienne Balibar, *Spinoza and Ethics*. Trans. Peter Snowdon (London, 1998), p. 82.
2. [Former US president Bill Clinton who, under oath, denied having had a 'sexual relationship' with White House Intern Monica Lewinsky – and was subsequently threatened with impeachment.]
3. Michel Foucault, 'What is Enlightenment?', in *Michel Foucault: Ethics, Subjectivity and Truth*, ed. Paul Rabinow (New York, 1997), p. 303.

4. Paul Rabinow (ed.), 'Introduction: The History of Systems of Thought', in *Michel Foucault: Ethics, Subjectivity and Truth* (New York, 1997), p. xviii.
5. Gilles Deleuze, *Foucault* (Paris, 1986), p. 102.
6. Georg Simmel, 'The Sociology of the Meal'. Trans. M. Symons, *Food and Foodways*, 5(4) (1994), 345–50, p. 346.
7. Ibid.
8. Ibid.
9. Michael Symons, 'Simmel's Gastronomic Sociology: An Overlooked Essay', *Food and Foodways*, 5(4) (1994), 333–51, p. 339.
10. Arjun Appadurai, 'Gastro-Politics in Hindu South Asia', *American Ethnologist*, 8 (1981), 494–511, p. 509.
11. Ibid., p. 507.
12. Roland Barthes, 'Toward a Psychosociology of Contemporary Food Consumption', in R. Forster and O. Ranum (eds), *Food and Drink in Historical Selections from Annales*, vol. 5 (Baltimore, MD, 1979; orig. 1961), p. 171.
13. Ibid.
14. Rabinow, *Michel Foucault*, p. xxvii.
15. Ibid., p. xxxi.
16. Antoine Laurent, *Cuisine Novella* (London, 1989), p. 24.
17. *Two Fat Ladies: A Gastronomical Adventure* (1997). An Optomen Production for the BBC.
18. Jennifer Paterson and Clarissa Dickson Wright, *Two Fat Ladies Full Throttle* (London, 1998), p. 7.
19. Wendy Harmer, 'Rock 'n' Rollingpins', *HQ Magazine* (March/April 1998), 26–9, p. 29.
20. In Barbara Karpinski, 'Top Tart: Cream Queen Christine Manfield is Sydney's Mistress of the Kitchen', *Blue* (Feb. 1998), 84–8, p. 88.
21. Gilles Deleuze and Félix Guattari, *A Thousand Plateaus*. Trans. Brian Massumi (Minneapolis, 1991), p. 90.
22. Michel Foucault, *The Uses of Pleasure: The History of Sexuality*, vol. 2. Trans. Robert Hurley (New York, 1986), p. 97.
23. Ibid., p. 98.
24. Peter Hulme, 'Introduction: The Cannibal Scene', in Francis Barker, Peter Hulme and Margaret Iverson (eds), *Cannibalism and the Colonial World* (Cambridge, 1988). For a fascinating discussion of the range of uses of the cannibal, see this anthology.
25. Jacques Derrida, ' "Eating Well", or the Calculation of the Subject: An Interview with Jacques Derrida', by Jean-Luc Nancy, in Eduardo Cadava, Peter Connor and Jean-Luc Nancy (eds), *Who Comes After the Subject* (London and New York, 1991).
26. bell hooks, 'Eating the Other: Desire and Resistance', in *Black Looks: Race and Representation* (Boston, 1993).
27. Derrida, 'Eating Well', p. 114. Elsewhere I take up Derrida's argument more fully in the context of the concept of citizenship, and Balibar's (Etienne Balibar, 'The Subject Citizen', in Cadava, Connor and Nancy [eds], *Who Comes After the Subject*) compelling analysis of equality (Elspeth Probyn, *Visceral: Sex, Eating and Ethics* [London, forthcoming]).
28. Angela Carter, 'Speculative Finale: The Function of Flesh' in *The Sadeian Women: An Exercise in Cultural History* (London, 1979), p. 137.
29. Ibid., p. 138.
30. Ibid., pp. 144, 145.

31. Ibid., p. 146.
32. [Sheila Jeffreys: contemporary feminist theorist, whose work regularly critiques the male supremacist ideology which she perceives to underpin the sex industry in all its manifestations.]
33. Linda Jaivin, *Eat Me* (Melbourne, 1995), pp. 1–7.
34. Carole Adams, *The Sexual Politics of Meat: A Feminist Vegetarian Critical Theory* (New York, 1990), p. 187.
35. Ibid., pp. 187, 189.
36. Of course, Adams is hardly representative of the more developed arguments on 'ethical eating'. As David Bell and Gill Valentine put it, 'Being a citizen of the world also means, for some people, eating only your share, and eating only what is ethical.' The push to 'green cuisine' is 'an important countercultural response to being in the world' (Bell and Valentine, *Consuming Geographies: We Are Where We Eat* [London and New York, 1997], p. 188). In Lisa Heldke's argument, this entails thinking of our relations with food as 'participatory', that 'acting in the world is a communal, relational activity – that we are in correspondence with, and are also responsive and responsible to, others in the world' (Lisa M. Heldke, 'Food Politics, Political Food', in Deane W. Curtin and Heldke [eds], *Cooking, Eating, Thinking: Transformative Philosophies of Food* [Bloomington, IN, 1992], p. 310). However, the confusion over sex and food reappears in Wendall Barry's summation that, 'Like industrial sex, industrial eating has become a degraded, poor and paltry thing.' It follows for him that the contemporary eater is 'passive and uncritical – in short, a victim' (Wendall Barry, 'The Pleasures of Eating', in Curtin and Heldke, *Cooking, Eating, Thinking*, p. 375).
37. Dorothy Allison, 'A Lesbian Appetite', in *Trash* (Ithaca, NY, 1988), pp. 151–2.
38. Ibid., p. 156.
39. Ibid., p. 163.
40. Michel Foucault, 'Friendship as a Way of Life'. Trans. John Johnston, in Sylvère Lotringer (ed.), *Foucault Live* (New York, 1984), p. 207.

16.   MARIANNA TORGOVNICK, 'PIERCINGS'

(From *Late Imperial Culture*, ed. Román de la Campa et al. [London and New York, 1995], pp. 197–210.)

Summary

In this candid and often speculative essay, Marianna Torgovnick considers how best to theorise the contemporary phenomenon of 'modern primitivism', the multiple piercings, tattoos and scarification which have recently emerged from subculture into the mainstream. Torgovnick is troubled by these bodies' ability to confuse familiar binary systems of categorisation, such as primitive/postmodern, adornment/ mutilation, rebellion/conformity, life-force/death-force, pleasure/pain, and so forth. Arguably such bodies push the limits of cultural intelligibility, and pose a timely challenge to prevailing modes of understanding embodiment. Indeed, this concluding text seems emblematic of the necessary collision between theory and lived corporeality which is part of the ongoing business of cultural criticism. (Parenthetically, it is interesting that in the penultimate paragraph, Torgovnick cynically anticipates the contemporary work of German anatomist Gunther von Hagens – see the Introduction to this volume).

Notes

1. [*Re-Search:* an alternative cultures journal published in the US.]
2. See Bronislaw Malinowski, *The Sexual Life of Savages* (1929; reprinted Boston, 1988), p. 257. For more extensive bibliographic information, see Donald E. Brown, James W. Edwards, and Ruth P. Moore, *The Penis Inserts of Southeast Asia: An Annotated Bibliography with an Overview and Comparative Perspectives*, Occasional Paper Series no. 15 (Berkeley, CA, 1988).
3. James Boon, *Affinities and Extremes: Crisscrossing the Bittersweet Ethnology of East Indies History, Hindu-Balinese Culture, and Indo-European Allure* (Chicago, 1990).
4. Linda Schele and Mary Ellen Miller, *The Blood of Kings: Dynasty and Ritual in Maya Art* (New York, 1986). A sequel to this volume, *The Forest of Kings*, was a Quality Paperback Book Club first-choice selection in March 1991, testifying to the widespread appeal of the topic. On Hindu ritual in Sri Lanka, see Gananath Obeyeskere, *Medusa's Hair: An Essay on Personal Symbols and Religious Experience* (Chicago, 1981).
5. See, for example, Mircea Eliade, *Myths, Dreams, and Mysteries: Between Contemporary Faith and Archaic Realities*, trans. by Philip Mairet (New York, 1975); originally published in French in 1957. Eliade sees terror and death imagery as typical of initiations; he reports the flaying of the penis in one group. Although Eliade's structuralist, religious-studies approach to archaic societies overstates similarities and reduces archaic cultures to a single model, I nevertheless find portions of his work locally useful.
6. For a fully sanitised account, see 'Piercing Fad is Turning Convention on its Ear', *New York Times*, 19 May 1991, Y15. For an account that suppresses ethical issues, see Stanley Miess, 'The Cutting Edge', *Newsday*, 21 August 1991, pp. 50–1, 70.
7. See, for example, Tommaso Filippo Marinetti, 'The Founding and Manifesto of Futurism', reprinted in *Marinetti: Selected Writings*, ed. R. W. Flint and Arthur A. Coppotelli (New York, 1971).
8. See, for example, Michel Leiris with Jacqueline Delange, *African Art*, trans. Michael Ross, Arts of Mankind series (1967; reprinted London, 1968).
9. V. Vale and Andrea Juno (eds), *Modern Primitives*, special issue of *Re-Search* (San Francisco, 1989), p. 88; hereafter cited parenthetically in the text by page number.
10. The stories of the Hindu mystics in *Medusa's Hair* often reveal a point of personal crisis (a parent's death or a marital crisis) as the point of initiation into trance experiences and body piercing.
11. Piercing resembles the phenomena discussed by Henri Sayre in *The Object of Performance* (Chicago, 1989). The terms in which I discuss it in this section are indebted to his book. Sayre writes about performance arts such as modern dance, landscape art, and (for him, conceptually, the parent of them all) photography. See also Hal Foster (ed.), *The Anti-Aesthetic: Essays on Postmodern Culture* (Port Townsend, Washington, 1983).
12. This typically postmodern aesthetic underscores problems and paradoxes that have always resided in art objects and their acquisition of status, value, and the right to permanent display. But these problems and paradoxes have now acquired conscious, conceptual interest.

Suggestions for
Further Reading

DEPTHS/ HISTORIES AND PHILOSOPHIES OF THE BODY

Bakhtin, Mikhail, *Rabelais and his World*, trans. Hélène Iswolsky (Bloomington, IN, 1984).

Barker, Francis, *The Tremulous Private Body: Essays on Subjection* (Ann Arbor, MI, 1995).

Beizer, Janet, *Ventriloquized Bodies: Narratives of Hysteria in Nineteenth Century France* (Ithaca, NY, 1994).

Bell, Rudolph M., *Holy Anorexia* (Chicago, 1985).

Berman, Morris, *Coming to Our Senses: Body and Spirit in the Hidden History of the West* (New York, 1989).

Bermudez, Jose Luis, Anthony Marcel, and Naomi Eilan (eds), *The Body and the Self* (Cambridge, MA and London, 1995).

Bernheimer, Charles, and Claire Kahane (eds), *In Dora's Case: Freud–Hysteria–Feminism* (London, 1985).

Bottomley, F., *Attitudes to the Body in Western Christendom* (London, 1979).

Bourdieu, Pierre, *Outline of a Theory of Practice*, trans. Richard Nice (Cambridge, MA, 1989).

Brooks, Peter, *Body Work: Objects of Desire in Modern Narrative* (London and Massachusetts, 1993).

Brown, Peter, *The Body and Society: Men, Women and Sexual Renunciation in Early Christianity*. Lectures on the History of Religions, no. 13 (New York, 1988).

Bynum, Caroline Walker, *Holy Feast and Holy Fast: The Religious Significance of Food to Medieval Women* (Berkeley, CA, 1989).

——, *Fragmentation and Redemption: Essays on Gender and the Human Body in Medieval Religion* (New York, 1991).

Carella, Michael Jerome, *Matter, Morals, and Medicine: Ancient Greek Origins of Science, Ethics, and the Medical Profession* (New York, 1991).

Carter, Richard B., *Descartes' Medical Philosophy: The Organic Solution to the Mind–Body Problem* (Baltimore, MD, 1983).

Churchland, Paul M., *Matter and Consciousness: A Contemporary Introduction to the Philosophy of the Mind*. Revised edn (Cambridge, MA, 1988).

Csordas, Thomas (ed.), *Embodiment and Experience. The Existential Ground of Culture and Self* (Cambridge Studies in Medical Anthropology: Cambridge, 1994).

Davies, Catherine Glyn, *Conscience as Consciousness: The Idea of Self-Awareness in French Philosophical Writing from Descartes to Diderot* (Oxford, 1990).

Dixon, Laurinda S., *Perilous Chastity: Women and Illness in Pre-Enlightenment Art and Medicine* (Ithaca, NY, 1995).

Douglas, Mary, *Natural Symbols: Explorations in Cosmology* (New York, 1973).

Eagleton, Terry, *The Ideology of the Aesthetic* (Oxford, 1990).

Elliott, Dyan, *Fallen Bodies. Pollution, Sexuality, and Demonology in the Middle Ages* (Philadelphia, 1998).

Epstein, Julia, *Altered Conditions: Disease, Medicine, and Story Telling* (New York and London, 1995).

Featherstone, Mike, Mike Hepworth, and Bryan S. Turner (eds), *The Body: Social Process and Cultural Theory* (London, 1991).

Michel Foucault, *Discipline and Punish: The Birth of the Prison*, trans. Alan Sheridan (Harmondsworth, 1979).

——, *The Uses of Pleasure: The History of Sexuality*, 3 vols , trans. Robert Hurley (New York, 1986).

Gallagher, Catherine, and Thomas W. Laqueur (eds), *The Making of the Modern Body: Sexuality and Society in the Nineteenth Century* (Berkeley, CA, 1987).

Garland, Robert, *The Eye of the Beholder: Deformity and Disability in the Greco-Roman World* (Ithaca, NY, 1995).

Gent, Lucy and Nigel Llewellyn (eds), *Renaissance Bodies: The Human Figure in Renaissance Culture 1540–1660* (London, 1990).

Gliserman, Martin, *Psychoanalysis, Language, and the Body of the Text* (Gainesville, FL, 1996).

Hagstrum, J., *The Romantic Body: Love and Sexuality in Keats, Wordsworth, and Blake* (Knoxville, TN, 1985).

Hillman, David and Carla Mazzio (eds), *The Body in Parts: Fantasies of Corporeality in Early Modern Europe* (London, 1999).

Hunt, Lynn (ed.), *Eroticism and the Body Politic* (Baltimore, MD, 1990).

Jaquart, Danielle and Claude Thomasset, *Sexuality and Medicine in the Middle Ages* (Princeton, NJ, 1988).

Jay, Martin, 'Scopic Regimes of Modernity', in *Vision and Visuality*, ed. Hal Foster (Seattle, 1998), pp. 3–23.

Johnson, Mark, *The Body in the Mind: The Bodily Basis of Meaning, Imagination, and Reason* (Chicago, 1987).

Kay, Sarah and Miri Rubin (eds), *Framing Medieval Bodies* (Manchester and New York, 1994).

King, Helen, *Hippocrates' Women. Reading the Female Body in Ancient Greece* (New York and London, 1998).

Kunzle, David, *Fashion and Fetishism. A Social History of the Corset, Tight-Lacing and Other Forms of Body-sculpture* (Totowa, NJ, 1982).

Laqueur, Thomas W., *Making Sex: Body and Gender from The Greeks to Freud* (Cambridge, MA and London, 1990).

Le Breton, David, 'Dualism and Renaissance: Sources for a Modern Representation of the Body', *Diogenes*, 142 (1988), 47–69.

Leder, Drew, *The Absent Body* (Chicago, 1990).

Lupton, Deborah, *Medicine as Culture: Illness, Disease and the Body in Western Societies* (London, 1994).

Marshall, Tim, *Murdering to Dissect: Grave-robbing, 'Frankenstein' and the anatomy literature* (Manchester, 1995).

Merleau-Ponty, Maurice, *The Primacy of Perception and other Essays on Phenomenological Psychology, the Philosophy of Art, History and Politics*, trans. James M. Edie et al. (Evanston, IL, 1964).

Micale, Mark S., *Approaching Hysteria: Disease and its Interpretations* (Princeton, NJ, 1995).

Minois, Georges, *History of Old Age, from Antiquity to the Renaissance* (Chicago, 1989).

Outram, Dorinda, *The Body and the French Revolution: Sex, Class, and Political Culture* (New Haven, CT, 1989).

Petroff, Elizabeth, *Body and Soul: Essays on Medieval Women and Mysticism* (Oxford, 1994).

Pfeffer, Naomi, *The Stork and the Syringe: A Political History of Reproductive Medicine* (Oxford, 1993).

Polhemus, Ted, *The Body Reader: Social Aspects of the Human Body* (New York, 1978).

Pouchelle, Marie-Christine, *The Body and Surgery in the Middle Ages* (New Jersey, 1990).

Rieber, R. (ed.), *Body and Mind: Past, Present, Future* (New York, 1980).

Rozemond, Marleen, *Descartes's Dualism* (Cambridge, MA and London, 1998).

Richardson, Ruth, *Death, Dissection and the Destitute* (London, 1989).

Rousseau, G. (ed.), *Languages of Psyche: Mind and Body in Enlightenment Thought* (Berkeley, CA, 1990).

Sawday, Jonathan, *The Body Emblazoned: Dissection and the Human Body in Renaissance Culture* (London and New York, 1995).

Scholz, Suzanne, *Body Narratives: Writing the Nation and Fashioning the Subject in Early Modern England* (Basingstoke, 2000).

Sennett, Richard, *Flesh and Stone: The Body and the City in Western Civilization* (New York, 1994).

Shorter, Edward, *A History of Women's Bodies* (Harmondsworth, 1983).

Showalter, Elaine, *The Female Malady: Women, Madness and English Culture, 1830–1980* (London, 1987).

——, *Hystories: Hysterical Epidemics and Modern Culture* (London, 1997).

Spooner, Catherine, *Fashioning Gothic Bodies* (Manchester, 2004).

Stafford, Barbara Maria, *Body Criticism: Imaging the Unseen in Enlightenment Art and Medicine* (Cambridge, MA, 1991).

Stallybrass, Peter and Allon White, *The Politics and Poetics of Transgression* (Ithaca, NY, 1986).

Steele, Valerie, *Fashion and Eroticism. Ideals of Feminine Beauty from the Victorian Era to the Jazz Age* (Oxford, 1985).

Taylor, C., *Sources of the Self: The Making of the Modern Identity* (Cambridge, MA, 1989).

DIFFERENCE/ CONSTRUCTIONS OF OTHERNESS

Apter, Emily and William Pietz (eds), *Fetishism as Cultural Discourse* (Ithaca, NY, 1993).

Bordo, Susan, *Unbearable Weight: Feminism, Western Culture, and the Body* (Berkeley, CA, 1993).

Boscagli, Maurizia, *Eye on the Flesh: Fashions of Masculinity in the Early Twentieth Century* (Oxford, 1996).

Brumberg, Joan Jacobs, *The Body Project: An Intimate History of American Girls* (New York, 1997).

Caplan, Jane (ed.), *Written on the Body: The Tattoo in European and American History* (Princeton, NJ, 2000).

Carter, Angela, *The Sadeian Woman and the Ideology of Pornography* (New York, 1978).

Conboy, Katie, Nadia Medina, and Sarah Stanbury (eds), *Writing on the Body; Female Embodiment and Feminist Theory* (New York, 1997).

Delaney, Janice, *The Curse: A Cultural History of Menstruation* (Illinois, 1988).

Dickerson, Vanessa D., *Recovering the Black Female Body: Self-Representations by African-American Women* (New Brunswick, NJ, 2000).

Douglas, Mary, *Purity and Danger: An Analysis of the Concepts of Pollution and Taboo* (London, 1966).

Dreger, Alice Domurat, *Hermaphrodites and the Medical Invention of Sex* (Cambridge, MA, 1998).

Ellmann, Maud, *The Hunger Artists: Starving, Writing and Imprisonment* (London, 1993).

Epstein, Julia, 'Either/Or–Neither/Both: Sexual Ambiguity and the Ideology of Gender', *Genders*, 7 (1990), 99–130.

Fanon, Frantz, *Black Skin, White Masks*, trans. Charles Lamm Markmann (London, 1986).

Foster, Hal, *Compulsive Beauty* (Massachusetts, 1993).

Gilman, Sander L., *Disease and Representation: Images of Illness, Madness to AIDS* (Ithaca, NY, 1988).

——, *Sexuality: An Illustrated History: Representing the Sexual Machine and Culture from the Middle Ages to the Age of AIDS* (New York, 1989).

——, *The Jew's Body* (New York and London, 1991).

——, *Health and Illness: Images of Difference* (London, 1995).

Gordon, Lewis R., T. Denean Sharpley-Whiting and Renée T. White (eds), *Fanon: A Critical Reader* (Oxford and Cambridge, MA, 1996).

Hyam, Ronald, *Empire and Sexuality: The British Experience* (Manchester, 1990).

Irigaray, Luce, *Speculum of the Other Woman*, trans. Gillian C. Gill (Ithaca, NY, 1985).

Jordan, Glenn and Chris Weedon, *Cultural Politics: Class, Gender, Race and the Postmodern World* (Oxford, 1995).

Katz, Jonathan, *The Invention of Heterosexuality* (London, 1995).

Klein, Alan, *Little Big Men: Bodybuilding Subculture and Gender Construction* (Albany, NY, 1993).

Kristeva, Julia, *Powers of Horror: An Essay on Abjection*, trans. Leon S. Roudiez (New York, 1982).

Levy, Anita, *Other Women: The Writing of Class, Race, and Gender, 1832–1898* (Princeton, NJ, 1991).

Lyotard, Jean-François, 'Can Thought go on without a Body?', in *The Inhuman: Reflections on Time*, trans. Geoffrey Bennington and Rachel Bowlby (Cambridge, 1991), pp. 8–23.

MacSween, Morag, *Anorexic Bodies: A Feminist and Sociological Perspective on Anorexia Nervosa* (London, 1993).

Malossi, Giannino (ed.), *Material Man: Masculinity, Sexuality, Style* (New York, 2000).

Malson, Helen, *The Thin Woman: Feminism, Post-structuralism and the Social Psychology of Anorexia Nervosa* (London, 1998).

Miles, Robert, *Racism* (London and New York, 1989).

Moore, Henrietta L., *A Passion for Difference: Essays in Anthropology and Gender* (Cambridge, 1994).

Morrison, Toni, *Playing in the Dark: Whiteness and the Literary Imagination* (New York, 1992).

Plasa, Carl, 'Reading "The Geography of Hunger" in Tsitsi Dangarembga's *Nervous Conditions*: From Frantz Fanon to Charlotte Brontë', in *Journal of Commonwealth Literature*, 33.1 (1998), 35–45.

Porter, Roy (ed.), *The Anatomy of Madness: Essays in the History of Psychiatry* (London, 1985).

Price, Janet and Margrit Shildrick (eds), *Feminist Theory and the Body: A Reader* (London and New York, 1999).

Russett, Cynthia Eagle, *Sexual Science: The Victorian Construction of Womanhood* (Cambridge, MA, 1989).

Sabo, Donald and David Frederick Gordon (eds), *Men's Health and Illness: Gender, Power and the Body* (Thousand Oaks, CA, 1995).

Sanday, Peggy Reeves, *Female Power and Male Dominance: On the Origins of Sexual Inequality* (Cambridge, 1981).

Scarry, Elaine, *The Body in Pain: The Making and Unmaking of the World* (Oxford and New York, 1985).

Sontag, Susna, *Illness as a Metaphor* (London, 1979).

——, *AIDS as a Metaphor* (London, 1989).

Spaas, Lieve, 'Surrealism and Anthropology: in search of the primitive', *Paragraph*, 18.2 (1995), 163–73.

Stoller, Robert J., *Sex and Gender: the Development of Masculinity and Femininity* (London, 2000).

Suleiman, Susan Rubin (ed.), *The Female Body in Western Culture: Contemporary Perspectives* (Massachusetts, 1985).

Theweleit, Klaus, *Male Fantasies, Volume One: Women, floods, bodies, history*, trans. Stephen Carter (Minneapolis, 1987).

——, *Male Fantasies, Volume Two: Male Bodies: Psychoanalyzing the White Terror*, trans. Erica Carter and Chris Turner (Minneapolis, 1989).

Torgovnick, Marianna, *Gone Primitive: Savage Intellects, Modern Lives* (Chicago, 1991).

——, *Primitive Passions: Men, Women and the Quest for Ecstasy* (Chicago, 1998).

Ussher, Jane M. (ed.), *Body Talk: The Material and Discursive Regulation of Sexuality, Madness and Reproduction* (London and New York, 1997).

Vila, Anne C., *Enlightenment and Pathology* (Baltimore and New York, 1988).

Wendell, Susan, *The Rejected Body: Feminist Philosophical Reflections on Disability* (New York and London, 1996).

Yegenoglu, Meyda, *Colonial Fantasies: Towards a Feminist Reading of Orientalism* (Cambridge, 1998).

DECONSTRUCTIONS/ FUTURE DIRECTIONS

Ahmed, S. and J. Stacey (eds), *Thinking Through Skin* (London and New York, 2001).

Balsamo, Anne, 'Forms of Technological Embodiment: Reading the Body in Contemporary Culture', *Body and Society*, 1 (1995), 215–37.

Bataille, Georges, *Eroticism: Death and Sensuality*, trans. Mary Dalwood (San Francisco, 1986).

——, *Visions of Excess: Selected Writings, 1927–1939*, trans. and ed. Allan Stoekl (Minneapolis, 1985).

Baudrillard, Jean, *America*, trans. Chris Turner (London, 1988).

——, *Symbolic Exchange and Death*, trans. Iain Hamilton Grant (London, 1993).

Botting, Fred, *Sex, Machines and Navels: Fiction, Fantasy and History in the Future Present* (Manchester, 2003).

Braidotti, Rosi, *Nomadic Subjects: Embodiment and Sexual Difference in Contemporary Feminist Theory* (New York, 1994).

Butler, Judith, *Gender Trouble: Feminism and the Subversion of Identity* (New York and London, 1990).

——, *Bodies That Matter: On the Discursive Limits of 'Sex'* (New York and London, 1993).

Connor, Steven, 'Fascination, skin and the screen', *Critical Quarterly*, 40.1 (1998), 9–24.

——, *The Book of Skin* (London, 2003).

Davis, Kathy, *Reshaping the Female Body: The Dilemma of Cosmetic Surgery* (London and New York, 1995).

—— (ed.), *Embodied Practices: Feminist Perspectives on the Body* (London, Thousand Oaks and New Delhi, 1997).

Featherstone, Mike and Roger Burrows, 'Cultures of Technological Embodiment: An Introduction', *Body and Society*, 1 (1995), 1–19.

Fraiberg, Alison, 'Of AIDS, cyborgs and other indiscretions: resurfacing the body in the postmodern', in *Essays in Postmodern Culture*, ed. Eyal Amirna and John Unsworth (New York and Oxford, 1993), pp. 37–55.

Gil, José, *Metamorphoses of the Body: Theory out of Bounds*, trans. Stephen Meucke (Minneapolis, 1998).

Grosz, Elizabeth, *Volatile Bodies: Toward a Corporeal Feminism* (Bloomington, IN, 1994).

Grosz, Elizabeth and Elspeth Probyn (eds), *Sexy Bodies: The Strange Carnalities of Feminism* (London, 1995).

Halberstam, Judith, *Posthuman Bodies (Unnatural Acts)* (Indianapolis, 1995).

Haraway, Donna, *Simians, Cyborgs and Women: The Reinvention of Nature* (London, 1991).

Heath, Steven, *The Sexual Fix* (London, 1982).

Horner, Avril and Angela Keene (eds), *Body Matters: Feminism, Textuality, Corporeality* (Manchester, 2003).

Krary, Jonathan and Sanford Kwinter (eds), *Incorporations* (New York, 1992).

Lingis, Alphonso, *Foreign Bodies* (New York, 1994).

Lowe, Donald M., *The Body in late Capitalist USA* (Durham and London, 1995).

Lyotard, Jean-François, *Libidinal Economy*, trans. Iain Hamilton Grant (London, 1993).

Murphy, Julien S., *The Constructed Body: AIDS, Reproductive Technology, and Ethics* (Albany, NY, 1995).

Probyn, Elspeth, *Carnal Appetites: Food–Sex–Identities* (London and New York, 2000).

Samuel, Geoffrey, *Mind, Body and Culture. Anthropology and the Biological Interface* (Cambridge, 1990).

Shildrick, Margrit, *Leaky Bodies and Boundaries: Feminism, Postmodernism and (Bio)ethics* (London and New York, 1997).

Springer, Claudia, 'The pleasure of the interface', *Screen*, 32.3 (1991), 303–23.

——, *Electronic Eros: Bodies and Desire in the Postindustrial Age* (Texas and London, 1996).

Steinberg, Deborah Lynn, *Bodies in Glass: Genetics, Eugenics, Embryo Ethics* (Manchester, 2003).

Wolf, Susan M. (ed.), *Feminism and Bioethics: Beyond Reproduction* (Oxford, 1996).

Notes on Contributors

Maurizia Boscagli is an Associate Professor in the Department of English at the University of California at Santa Barbara. She specialises in feminist cultural critique, gender studies, British and European modernism, *fin-de-siècle* literature, the body, theories of mass culture, and Marxist critical theory. She has published widely on masculinity, Walter Benjamin and James Joyce, and is author of *Eye on the Flesh: Fashions of Masculinity in the Early Twentieth Century* (1996).

Abigail Bray teaches at Murdoch University, Australia. She has published widely on media representations of eating disorders and corporeal feminism.

Judith Butler is Maxine Elliot Professor in Rhetoric and Comparative Literature at the University of California, Berkeley. Among her publications are *Gender Trouble: Feminism and the Subversion of Identity* (1990), *Bodies That Matter: On the Discursive Limits of 'Sex'* (1993), *The Psychic Life of Power: Theories of Subjection* (1997), *Excitable Speech* (1997), as well as numerous articles and contributions on philosophy, feminist and queer theory. Her recent project is a critique of ethical violence and an effort to formulate a theory of responsibility for an opaque subject that works with Kafka, Freud, Foucault and Nietzsche.

Catherine Clément is a novelist, essayist, diplomat and cultural critic, and has been editor of the Paris newspaper *Le Matin*. She writes on structuralism, psychoanalysis and Marxism, and her books in English translation include (with Hélène Cixous) *The Newly Born Woman* (1986), *Syncope: The Philosophy of Rapture* (1994), and *Opera: The Undoing of Women* (1999).

René Descartes (1596–1650), was born in La Haye near Tours, and educated at the Jesuit college at La Flèche. Like many of his generation he contested the value of an education based on Aristotelian logic and, after leaving college, he attempted to resolve the sceptical crisis of his age by inventing a method of reasoning based on mathematics. After serving as a soldier in Holland, Bohemia and Hungary, he left the army in 1621 and devoted himself to science and philosophy. In 1629 he retired to Holland where he lived and worked in great seclusion for twenty years, publishing, perhaps most famously, *Principia Philosophiae* and the *Meditations* in 1644. His doctrines involved him in some bitter arguments with Dutch theologians, and in 1648 he accepted an invitation from Queen Christina of Sweden to instruct her in philosophy. He lived in Stockholm until his death.

Frantz Fanon (1925–1961), was born in Martinique, and through his contributions to philosophy, psychiatry, social science and revolutionary action, became a key figure in colonial and postcolonial theory and twentieth-century revolutionary thought. He fought for the Allied forces against Germany in North Africa and Europe, before becoming head of the Blida-Joinville hospital in Algiers. Throughout this

214

time Fanon supported the increasingly popular Algerian liberation forces (FLN), training revolutionaries in emergency medicine and psychological techniques for resisting torture. Through his books, including (in English translation) *Black Skin, White Masks* (1952), *A Dying Colonialism, or Year Five of the Algerian Revolution* (1959), and *The Wretched of the Earth* (1961), he became one of the chief theoreticians of the Algerian struggle, earning him the lifelong enmity of the French government. He died in exile in America.

Michel Foucault (1926–1984), social scientist and historian of ideas, was Professor of History and Systems of Thought at the Collège de France. Among his most important publications in English translation are *Madness and Civilization* (1961), *The Order of Things* (1966) and the unfinished *The History of Sexuality* (1976–1984).

Sigmund Freud (1856–1939) is popularly credited as the inventor of psychoanalysis. Following his clinical training in Vienna, Freud practised neurology until he found it to be inadequate for the treatment of neurosis. He turned briefly to hypnotherapy before his experimental work with colleague Joseph Breuer on the 'cathartic' treatment or 'talking cure' of hysterical disorders between 1893 and 1895 – the foundation of his psychotherapeutic technique. The growth of his ideas was first formalised in *The Interpretation of Dreams* (1900). In 1902 he was made Professor Extraordinarius at the University of Vienna, and attracted a group of followers which was to become the Vienna Psychoanalytical Society in 1908. He developed psychoanalysis as a theory, a form of treatment and a movement for the rest of his highly prolific life. He died in London, an exile from the Nazi *Anschluss*.

Sander L. Gilman is a distinguished Professor of the Liberal Arts and Medicine at the University of Illinois in Chicago and the director of the Humanities Laboratory. A cultural and literary historian, he is the author or editor of over sixty books. Both his most recent monograph, *The Fortunes of the Humanities: Teaching the Humanities in the New Millennium* and his most recent edited book, *A New Germany in the New Europe* (with Todd Herzog) appeared in 2000. For 25 years he was a member of the humanities and medical faculties at Cornell University where he held the Goldwin Smith Professorship of Humane Studies and for 6 years he held the Henry R. Luce Distinguished Service Professorship of the Liberal Arts in Human Biology at the University of Chicago. He was the first non-historian to be awarded the Mertes Prize of the German Historical Institute (1997) and the first non-German-born Germanist to be awarded the Alexander von Humboldt Research Prize (1998) of the Humboldt Foundation.

Elizabeth Grosz is Director for the Institute of Critical and Cultural Studies, Monash University. She has been a Visiting Professor at University of California, Santa Cruz, University of California, Davis, Johns Hopkins University, the University of Richmond, George Washington University and the University of California, Irvine. Among her most recent publications are *Sexual Subversions: Three French Feminists* (1989), *Jacques Lacan: A Feminist Introduction* (1990), *Volatile Bodies: Toward a Corporeal Feminism* (1994) and *Space, Time and Perversion: Essays on the Politics of Bodies* (1995).

Elspeth Probyn is Associate Professor and Head of the Department of Gender Studies at the University of Sydney. Her research covers the body, space and sexuality, queer theory and theories of social subjectivity. Recent publications include *Sexing the Self: Gendered Positions in Cultural Studies* (1993), *Sexy Bodies: The Strange Carnalities of Feminism* (co-edited with Elizabeth Grosz, 1995) and *Carnal Appetites: Food–Sex–Identities* (2000).

Joan Riviere (1883–1962) Riviere's interest in psychoanalysis arose through her association with Cambridge intellectual circles, the Bloomsbury Group and the Society for Psychical Research, where she first encountered the work of Freud and Ernest Jones. She entered into analysis with Jones in 1916–1920, and by 1919 was treating patients of her own. In 1919 she also began translating Freud's work, and thereafter became translating editor for the *International Journal of Psychoanalysis* while undergoing analysis with Freud himself. She later changed allegiances and became a key figure in the reception of Melanie Klein's (then controversial) ideas about child analysis, taking an active role in psychoanalytic debate for the rest of her life.

Jonathan Sawday is Head of the Department of English Studies at the University of Strathclyde. His research is focused on the intersection between science, technology, and literature, particularly in the early-modern or Renaissance period. He has also written and published on the visual arts from sixteenth-century French funerary sculpture to contemporary body art. His major publications include (with Thomas Healy) *Literature and the English Civil War* (1990); *The Body Emblazoned: Dissection and the Human Body in Renaissance Culture* (1995), and (with Neil Rhodes) *The Renaissance Computer: Knowledge Technology in the First Age of Print* (2000). A book on the imaginative impact of machinery and technology in Europe is currently in preparation.

Klaus Theweleit teaches in the Institute for Sociology at the University of Freiburg, and is Professor of Art and Theory at the National Academy of the Performing Arts in Karlsrühe. His research interests include fascism theory, psychoanalysis, media and popular culture, gender studies, science fiction and colonialism. His books in English translation include *Male Fantasies*, Volumes 1 and 2 (1989) and *Object-Choice: All You Need Is Love* (1992).

Marianna Torgovnick is Professor of English at Duke University. Her research focuses on novel and novel theory, postcolonialism, modernism, twentieth-century British and American literature and culture. Her publications include *Closure in the Novel* (1981), *The Visual Arts, Pictorialism and the Novel: James, Lawrence, and Woolf* (1985), *Gone Primitive: Savage Intellects, Modern Lives* (1994), and *Primitive Passions: Men, Women and the Quest for Ecstasy* (1997).

Index